Disappearing Girl

Katherine Uher is a regular contributor to Huffington Post. Her first book *The Gifts of Autism* became an Amazon Bestseller. She also works as a psychotherapist and in her spare time gives talks and training sessions to parents and to professionals who care for children with ASD, as well as many local talks, she speaks annually At the UK Autism Show.

Visit her website at www.TheSensitivitySpectrum.com

DISAPPEARING GIRL

Katherine Uher

WSP

WHOLE SELF PUBLISHING

ISBN-13:978-1-9997413-0-3
*[Whole Self Publishing, Newcastle upon Tyne, England.]**

For Mrs. R.S.

CONTENTS

Connections, Boundaries & Social Gaps

"Do you know, I always thought unicorns were fabulous monsters, too? I never saw one alive before!" "Well, now that we have seen each other," said the unicorn, "if you'll believe in me, I'll believe in you."

Lewis Carroll, *Alice's Adventures in Wonderland & Through the Looking-Glass*

Chapter 0

MY OWN COCKTAIL OF CHEMICALS AND EXPERIENCES

The summer I turned nine I was sent to California to visit my great-grandmother Ada. She was a tiny woman who wore knitted caps over her short, frizzy red hair. Ada was a well-established china painter: she had pieces in museums; magazines did articles on her work; and young students came to learn from her. She lived alone in a 1920s two-storey house just outside Los Angeles; she had a workshop with a kiln in her back garden, which was also home to avocado and nectarine trees. Her house, furnished with Depression-era antiques, was very esoteric.

Every room was full of china, books on painting and tools for painting, and I took it all in with the eager curiosity of a child surrounded by paints and paintbrushes. It took only the tiniest bit of prompting for Ada to lead me to her shop for a lesson. To be clear, there was no free play with these paints and brushes: I sat with her in the shop trying to master the brush stroke to create the perfect petal. Her long bony fingers, which hinted at the decades spent mastering her craft, gripped firmly to my clumsy childish hands, which still hadn't mastered legible writing. She was loud and unforgiving, and at some point I finally asked if I could stop and go back to the house.

What I noticed more than anything else was how un-grandmotherly she was. On one occasion I tried to hug her and she pulled away so quickly that she almost fell backwards, and then yelled at me for the offence.

As a child, I heard things like, “Ada talks too much.” “She can't stand it when anyone else tries to interject.” Or, “She doesn't consider anyone else’s feelings.” I feel certain Ada had Asperger's, as well as her son (my mother's father) and, of course, my mother, but I didn't recognize Ada's rigidity or intense focus as anything abnormal. She and my mother were both part of my constant frame of reference for how people should behave and think.

We were rigidly opinionated and unforgivingly direct; we were also hard-working, stubborn and passionate. I had to admit that none of us seemed to make friends or have smooth relationships, but that was supposed to be because we were intellectually superior, and in theory it was the less intelligent people that possessed the best social skills. In theory.

In the last ten years many television shows have popped up that illustrate this idea, shows in which the lead characters tend to have poor social skills but exhibit superior intellect in other areas, such as crime-solving or medicine – shows such as *The Big Bang Theory, House, Elementary, Touch*, and others. My favourite to date is *The Bridge*. Inline with this theory Hans Asperger went so far as to write:

"It seems that for success in science or art, a dash of autism is essential. For success the necessary ingredients may be an ability to turn away from the everyday world, from the simple practical, an ability to rethink a subject with originality so as to create in new untrodden ways, with all abilities canalised into

the one speciality."

So, yes, it can work like that. Bad with people, great with special area of interest. And we love those flawed but focused characters. Focused. They are always focused. That's Asperger's, it's like looking at life through a close-up camera lenses, creating what I call a narrow *circumference of awareness*.

There is a mission, a goal, a mystery to solve and that's all that matters. Social niceties, like many things, are usually part of the unseen surroundings. Like a cat after a moth, Venetian Blinds be damned. And, it is shows such as I've listed, and media portrayals, that make Asperger's the "it" diagnosis right now.

But even with its popularity and geek-chic status, this idea that the intellectually superior need to be antisocial is regularly challenged in everyday life. Even in my childhood I was aware of better, more astute students, who, unlike me, had a well-tuned social radar, who made good grades *and* had friends. I wanted so much to be one of them, but I wasn't.

These students seemed to be calmer in general, better at paying attention to the other person, at seeing the chain of causality: the effect one thing has on another, the effect their words and actions would have on others at different times in different situations. They didn't seem to struggle with the kinds of issues that would interfere with me and my family's ability to have steady relationships.

Bad tempers ran through my family. There was a constant fluctuation between anxiety and anger. My mother and her father were not on speaking terms for the last years of his life. It was the same with her and my great-grandmother. It is difficult to be honest about this, but this isn't simply a consequence of being intelligent or quirky, it's a consequence of having poor social skills, emotional regulation, self-control and boundaries. It's just that great intellect seems to co-exist with all the other traits and therein lies the quirkiness.

For me, and many others, there has been no doubt that autism is a genetic condition. However, some people don't see the link. Some people blame vaccines. Some people swear that a gluten-free diet works wonders. We start to accept that there are many different types of autism and many different severities. But there is a link between all types. People on the autistic spectrum have irregular GABA (short for gamma-aminobutyric acid) function.

In 2015, a Harvard research team lead by Caroline Roberts established a clear link between the GABA neurotransmitter and autism. "This is the first time, in humans, that a neurotransmitter in the brain has been linked to autistic behaviour — full stop," Robertson said. Neurotransmitters act like automated bar tenders in our brain, giving us the right amount of what we need. Some neurotransmitters focus on giving and others holding back; they mix our cocktail and send it down the pipeline. Everyone's cocktail has the same ingredients, just different measures.

All the chemicals are meant to serve a function. Adrenaline, the fight or flight hormone, help us react to a threat. Melatonin helps us get to sleep. Sometimes the functions are primal and then the hormones are difficult to handle in our modern world. The endorphins one gets from hits of sugar might have given the hunter gather a much-needed spike of energy, but can be damaging in today's world where pastries and other sweet treats are too easily available.

When there is a problem with the bartender, sometimes the cocktail is too strong. Like with adrenaline, a big issue for me and my children. A crowded grocery store often triggers an over-abundance of that hormone. The instinct is to run, but if that's not possible then we start exhibiting signs of aggression. My gait becomes rigid, I start walking faster; I stop talking to my husband. My son starts talking to himself and gnashing his teeth. Then, if there is any other problem, like an argument about the music on the way home, there is a meltdown.

Dis-regulation of GABA has long been known to cause problems with anxiety, depression and ADHD, to name a few. Many people find great effectiveness in taking supplements to support GABA function, although in theory they shouldn't help. Supplements should be too big to pass through the blood brain barrier (a membrane that separates blood from the nervous system and brain). However, in many cases these supplements do seem effective.

The reason for this is that many people with irregular GABA levels have an underlying condition, a permeable blood brain barrier, making us vulnerable to heavy metals, gluten, dairy (but not always these things – which is why gluten-free diets work on some and not others.) and thus leading to irregular GABA levels. AKA poor emotional regulation.

My first sense of belonging to a group outside my family, of finding others whose chemical cocktails were uneven in the ways that mine was uneven, was in the eighth grade, and it did not happen with the "good" students. Or indeed the "bad". It happened with the students that often went unseen and uncounted in the mainstream school. This was the one year there seemed to be a lull in the bullying. I started working as a student volunteer at a special needs class within my school.

The students in this class varied considerably; some seemed to have extreme hyperactivity, and others had cerebral palsy, and some had autism. Some of the students labelled with autism were nonverbal, with the exception of some noises such as squeals or moans to express their emotions. Unaware of the varying degrees of ASD (unaware of my own heritage within this spectrum), *this* was my first impression of what autism looked like – and there wouldn't be much else for the next two decades.

There were two classrooms, one for the students who were more extreme and another for those who were relatively mild. I worked mainly with the more mild students. But amongst all the students there was a general lack of inhibition and lack of awareness of a need for it. And this was what I recognized within myself. I had a sense of belonging with these students, even though that wasn't how I wanted to feel. Forgive me for my honesty here, but what I wanted was to be caring and helpful and nothing like them. Instead what I felt was that I was very much like them.

Like me, these students had a fluctuating awareness of how others found them. I could see their hurt and confusion when the mainstream children mocked them as they crossed paths in the hallway. I've been accused of being too attuned to the feelings and intentions of others to have Asperger's. But even children with more profound autism pick up on the intentions of others.

It was the others, the neurotypicals, who lacked the awareness, the mainstream students who teased, not understanding how devastating their words and actions could be. Even the grown-ups could be oblivious. One day, when I was in the back room washing out paint pots, two male adult aids brought in this young post-pubescent girl about my age, placed her on the table and started changing her nappy.

They hadn't asked me to leave or made any effort to give her privacy. Certainly if I had required this service I would have wanted as much privacy as I could have gotten. Especially when it came to student volunteers (like myself): I was her peer and still in the room. Did anyone even consider that being changed by men might be traumatizing for her? I could see the girl had turned her head and was trying to dissociate herself from what was happening. I could feel her discomfort and humiliation. It was horrible. How could they not understand or care?

I felt more connected to these students than I had to anyone, because instinctively I knew I was like them. *It was only a matter of degree.* I soon felt guilty for my desire to separate myself from them, to not want to be seen as being like them. Even my twelve-year-old self could recognize that they had a kindness and innocence that others didn't have. So I made a conscious decision not to worry about being liked by the mainstream children. For that time I was able to let another feeling take over me – it was one of belonging.

Last summer I took my children to a science museum where we looked at a chart of eye colours. There were several rows of irises. According to the chart there were nine ways a blue iris could be blue, a brown iris brown, a green iris green, and so on. Every fleck made each eye a little different.

As I stared at this I began to wonder at all the ways in which a person can be unique. I thought about my brain, about autism, about how the autistic spectrum disorder looks different on my daughter and son than it does on me, and how they each exhibit the traits differently from one another. Then I thought about how my childhood shaped who I became.

I only received my diagnosis of Autistic Spectrum Disorder when I was thirty-three, shortly after my six-year-old son, Michael, was diagnosed. I tend to refer to my condition as Asperger's syndrome, a label which, as of May 2013, has been removed from the *Diagnostic and Statistical Manual of Mental Disorders* (the DSM) – used in North America to diagnose neurological and psychiatric disorders. In its place, autistic spectrum disorder (ASD) is used.

Before the removal, the terms "Asperger's syndrome" and "high-functioning autism" were used interchangeably; however, in some places, government and educational support were reserved only for people with a diagnosis of "autism", which is likely why the label

Asperger's has been removed. The term still continues to be used, however, in non-clinical settings, as it implies a certain set of traits: an average to high intellect and vocabulary, rigidity, obsessiveness and social awkwardness – which is more like what I live with.

Autism is an umbrella term, a description of outward traits, covering *many* different genetic mutations which cause people to have a different than expected perception of the world. And thus they exhibit certain key personality traits that we call autism. It works the same for ADD/ADHD, bi-Polar Disorder and other chemical imbalances. The distinguishing mark-ers can be very pronounced or they can blend into each other. Have you ever debated with someone over a colour? Is it blue or is it green? Is it pink or is it lilac? It's a spectrum.

Like colour, our brain chemistry exists on a spectrum. There is a scale called the Pantone Scale in which every shade of every colour has an identifying number. These colours make up the *visible* spectrum. I italicise "visible" because colour is really only a reflection of light bouncing off of objects: In the way that our behaviours, thoughts and feelings are a reflection of our brain chemistry responding to life. Geneticist are trying to chart the "autistic genes" but at the moment there is no way to take a blood or urine test and apply a label. What clinicians do is look at the behaviour we present.

I have read an article titled "ADHD Not a Real Disease" (Well I would never have called it a disease but more to the point... Is it real?) Well, to some degree it's not, if there is a physical way to test it we haven't found it. ADHD, Bi-polar disorder, ASD are all labels the way "red" is a label for 032X on the Pantone Scale. But if we didn't know the number for red wouldn't we still know what it looked like? Red is simply a commonly agreed upon term to express a colour that most of us recognize.

It's helpful to have these terms so we know what we're talking about. Recognizing that autism is a name for the traits, and not a name for one singular disorder, helps us to stop expecting we might find a one-size-fits-all answer. The truth is labels brings us a sense of containment. Being able to name something is calming. It's like have the right container to store all your bits and pieces in.

At the moment the core features that are supposed to present in order for someone to be classed as autistic are rigidity and a difficulty with social communication. There are many sub-features, but some of the more known include emotional sensitivity, reactivity, and sensitivity to over stimulation. These sub-features may earn the carrier of such traits a co-diagnosis (or missed diagnosis) of exclusively ADHD and or bi-polar disorder: two labels which, in my life, I have been given. I call this a missed diagnosis (rather than a misdiagnosis) because possibly some bi-polar and or ADHD traits were present. It's just that autism was also appropriate but was missed.

Some doctors will say that multiple labels can coexist. Other doctors will argue that a person can't have more than one. They want to see a dominant label and give only that. With the understanding that these labels are descriptions of traits, designed for the purpose of simplistic communication why not use both, to identify a person with autistic traits but also with a hyperactive or manic response to over-stimulation? It's a greenish blue. The point is to communicate our needs with each other so that we can be understood.

Then, like a light bulb that got too big a surge of electricity, my brain burns out. I'm staring again at the chart of irises with my kids. I find it all hugely interesting but also hugely overwhelming. Too fluid and unclear at the moment.

To give myself a more simple way to think of it I like to imagine all the variables that affect us are like coloured disks being stacked. (Genes, home environment, school, our own nature) To be sure there is a unique hue that shines through the autism glass, but by the time they are all in place we can't help but have created a new colour entirely. This is why we are all unique. This is why Dr. Stephan Shore famously said,

"If you've met one person with autism, you've met one person with autism".

Chapter 1

A MASS OBSERVATION EXPERIMENT WITH ME AS THE TEST SUBJECT

"So what do you hope to get from our work together?"

"Before we start I need to say I've been seeing psychologists, psychiatrists, therapists and every other kind of mental health professional on and off through out my life. I wouldn't be seeing you if it wasn't a course requirement. But, since I have to, I can tell you I don't want a passive therapist. I don't like those *and-how-does-that-make-you-feel* people."

"What is it like for you to experience that?"

"It's uncomfortable. It's patronizing and

insincere."

"I can hear it's really difficult for you to let someone be caring of you."

"That's what I want to work on. I want to be calm. I'm scared. I'm scared of rejection, scared that I'll be the odd one out in class, I'm scared that working as a therapist will just be one more job I can't hold."

In my handbag I have a list of over thirty jobs that I've had and lost in my life. Choosing to train as a counsellor, to pay more money towards an education when I never earned anything from my first degree, had been a huge leap of faith. I honestly felt I would make a good therapist, but I also really liked the idea that if I worked for myself no one could fire me. Still, there was fear. " I want to stop being so scared of everything all the time."

"Okay. Shall we contract to work on that then?"

School life was over-stimulating for me, and as my energy climbed I would alternate between acting out and zoning out, both of which made me an easy target for predators. On one occasion, in early primary school, when the teacher had left the room, another student got up and dumped a big box of crayons on the floor.

When the teacher returned everyone in the class said it was me. I was recognized, usually by the whole class, as a scapegoat. I could not say who had actually dumped the crayons on the floor or what the child looked like or where they had been sitting, because I had been off in Kate Land when it happened.

I lost my playtime that day. Things like this happened repeatedly and every time they reinforced my desire to be gone in my own mind, because if the world wasn't being over-stimulating, it was being unfair. The world wouldn't leave me alone but it wouldn't take care of me either.

Summers, when most American children get a three-month break from school, might have offered a welcome reprieve from being forced into the world. It could have been a season of peaceful solitude, but my mother was working on her master's degree in education, and even though she had summers off from teaching she still needed to be at university. This meant that I needed to be in day care, a noisy, busy environment which smelled of juice and tinned produce.

As an adult I can get very irritable when I'm in a place I don't like for too long a period of time, as I struggle between a desire to leave and a sense of obligation to stay, which will eventually induce resentment and aggression. As a child I often didn't have a choice, which made it all the more simple: I would simply disappear back inside myself.

At my summer day care there was a games table which was always empty, I used to go to it and busy myself with dominoes. I would arrange them in intricate patterns, perfecting my system of twists and turns so that each domino would collapse perfectly onto the next, ready for the moment when I deemed my design to be finished and I could tip the first one over.

Almost always, before I completed the design some other child would see me there, run over and start them off, then run away again. I would just sit there and start all over from the beginning, rebuilding for the next half hour or so until another child or the same one – I was never sure – came and knocked them down again. I never complained, because that would mean getting up, and I would never get up until I had completed a project from beginning to end.

There is a very distressing feeling that goes with being unable to finish something, whether it's a sentence, a social exchange, or a project. I will be like a record that has skipped. I *must* experience completion in order to move on. This has been a virtue in my life, as I tend to finish what I start, although sometimes the need for completion can be too rigid and drive people I care about out of my life. It can make them hate me, or it can make them scared of me.

If I'm talking and I get interrupted, I'll usually start over from the very beginning. If I'm fighting with someone, a situation ripe for interruptions, I will start over and over and over with the point I wanted to make until the other person has heard it all from start to finish without interruption.

I was quite good in my high school debate class, where I was allotted a few minutes of uninterrupted time in which to make my argument. Boyfriends, on the other hand, found my need to speak in this way punishing and controlling. If they walked away before I was done I would go crazy.

If someone does something kind, like handing me a drink, I will respond by saying, "Thank you." I understand that their response is supposed to be, "You're welcome." But sometimes people don't say that, sometimes they just nod, or don't respond at all, and so I will repeat myself, “Thank you,” over and over again until I get my, “You're welcome.”

At some point the children at my nursery started asking, “Are you retarded?” Whether the question was serious or insulting, and I suspect it was the latter, I didn't feel a deep sense of shame over it. I desperately wanted more patience from everyone, I wanted fewer tutors and therapists; I wanted a rest.

I started to think that if the answer was “Yes”, it would help people understand and accept me, rather than blame me for being so different, so I started to say yes. Soon after my mother heard of this, she started taking me to a child psychologist to be evaluated.

The evaluation involved a brief introduction in which it was explained that I was there to play and that the adults would be in the next room over, behind the mirror, watching. I was then left alone in a room with: anatomically correct dolls, a slab of wood with nails tapped lightly into place, and a variety of soft and hard toys all jumbled together.

I separated and organized the toys, as it seemed like it needed doing, then I pounded all the nails thoroughly into the wood for the same reason. Completion. I went back for many weeks and most visits were similar. In a way the space to play how I wanted was now being given to me – albeit with clinicians on the other side of the glass watching and taking notes, but still.

I understood in theory that the world was a big place and there were people all over it, but being in this room made real a feeling I had been having all my life. I could see that others shared, amongst themselves, a level of understanding that I didn't feel part of. I would play separately from everyone else and I didn't think much of them, but after a while I began to feel like most people – my classmates and teachers – shared a common regard for me.

Whatever this regard was – that I was weird, or vulnerable, or naughty – there was always this sense that everyone shared the same view. They had opinions about who I was, how I felt and why I did the things I did. They could talk with each other and share these opinions and confirm and agree, but I had very little understanding of them. Like the clinicians on the other side of the glass, there was only one of me but a whole group of them. And they could see me but I could not see them.

After a few visits to this room I started to wonder if my entire existence was a mass observation or experiment with me as the test subject. I felt alien. Being in that room was the physical manifestation of this feeling I had always had; but now my life as a six-year-old was tinted with this Orwellian fantasy.

I thought that when I was ready they would let me in on the secret. One day I would finally get to know all the many things that others seemed to know and understand. The window that divided them from me would be opened and I'd be one of them too. Like an initiation. I kept waiting. Waiting to see and understand the world (the full picture) the way everyone else did.

The doctors were kind; nothing I did or said ever seemed to be wrong to them, and I started to feel more comfortable interacting with them than I did with my peers. Maybe I didn't mind being studied, I thought. When the evaluations came to an end, the lead psychologist gave the report to my mother.

It was suggested that I had Asperger's Syndrome, a type of high functioning autism. My mother thought such a label implied a lack of intellect. She refused this diagnosis and I was taken to another psychologist and given a diagnosis of ADHD (attention deficit and hyperkinetic disorder). Following this diagnosis, I began taking Ritalin.

Most ADHD medications such as Ritalin

are stimulants designed to prevent the attention from being shifted from one thing to another. For some people this effectively grounds them in the moment. For people on the autistic spectrum, who *already* have a tenancy towards intense focus (fine circumference of awareness) such medications can lead to a more heightened autistic traits such as: rigidity, circular thinking, sensory awareness, anxiety, and emotional outbursts.

There are many different genetic mutations associated with autism, and many ways it presents in those who have it. For this reason it can be hard to predict how a person will respond to a given medication.

My personal philosophy is that parents and physicians should always seek to medicate with the minimal dosage that's effective, doing what can be done with environment and using alternative coping strategies to support the positive effects of the medication.

What I've noticed in my life – and my mother would agree – is that, without medication, when I was doing something I liked I was incredibly focused for long stretches of time. For hours and hours, when I had a day that was not very stimulating, my behaviour was calm and balanced. But I was hyper-sensitive to my environment, and my behaviour mirrored the chaos I experienced in the world.

Every year for the next three years following my diagnosis, I was taken to a psychologist and given the Wechsler Intelligence test, known more commonly as an IQ test. My scores were always found to be in the "superior" range. This was despite the fact that I was on the lower end of average at verbal reasoning, and my handwriting and spelling were poor (although my vocabulary seemed to help bring my scores up in that section).

All my invigilators commented on how well I did with creating block patterns meant to measure my perceptual reasoning. I could look at an image and recreate it almost instantly. Even with a large, complex image I could easily see the single blocks as separate units. I could isolate each unit and recreate the whole picture in a matter of seconds. On a few occasions the examiner turned the diagram towards herself (making it upside down for me) so that she could flick through the pages to find something more challenging; once she settled on a new picture, I was finished with recreating it before she could turn it around for me to look at it right side up. Adding in the extra step of mentally rotating each unit didn't affect my time. This is an area where a fine circumference of awareness is a gift. At nine I was told I exhibited the perceptual reasoning of a university student. This is an example of the intellectual imbalance that often exists within Aspergians. As Lorna Wing writes:

> "Typically, in autistic spectrum disorders, there are marked differences in the level of ability on psychological tests of different kinds of skills. Most often, visuo-spatial skills that do not involve language, like completing jigsaw puzzles, matching shapes and so on, are performed better than skills that do need language." (1996)

What this intellectual imbalance means is that the IQ, being an average of all sections tested, will not necessarily give a complete picture of a person's cognitive abilities. Looking at a single number means that areas of struggle may not be taken into account as much as they should be and areas of strength can also go under-appreciated. The fact that my scores were so high was a testament to my great visual reasoning and said little about my struggles in other areas such as literacy. Nevertheless, at a minimum, I had to acknowledge that I wasn't “retarded”, and I wasn't allowed to say that anymore.

The fantasy about my life being part of some mass observation experiment was dispelled during a trip to the ballet, the year I turned ten. I was listening to the muted padding of my black shoes on the red carpet as we walked to our seats. It was then that my mother pulled me out of my thoughts to tell me about a faux pas I had committed a few minutes earlier. She told me that addressing someone as “Lady” – as in, “Lady, could you please move?” – sounded rude. I couldn't understand why this was offensive, as being a lady was a good thing, and I had said “please”.

How to phrase things more delicately was one of those things I would have to learn over the course of a lifetime. I once told a teacher to “look at me when I'm talking to you”. I was shocked at her offence to this: adults had said this exact same thing to me more than once. But my mother's correction, on this day at the ballet, stands out for me because she made two statements that changed my life. They were: “Kate, other people have feelings just like you.”

And: “They're human too.” Did she know I had secretly been wondering about that?

Chapter 2

WHEN THE FACE CAME OUT OF THE WATER

I have had very few friends in my life. When I say this I often get people (who don't have Asperger's) saying that they haven't had many close friends in their lives either. (They usually insert the word "close" or "real" or "true") Having only a few friends isn't so uncommon, they argue. But when I say I haven't had many friends, what I mean is that I don't ever gel on a casual level with people. The thing that others call an "awkward silence" is a frequent visitor in my life.

I spent most of my compulsory education sitting alone at lunch, getting picked last for teams, and if ever there is an exception to that rule – like if the person next to me in class asks how I'm doing or someone does invite me to sit with them at lunch – I start referring to that person as “one of my friends” because other people are always referring to their friends and it makes me feel more normal to do the same.

But the truth is, when I'm referring to “my friend from class” I am not actually talking about someone whose phone number I have, whom I text with, whom I meet for coffee. We just say “hi” and “how are you?” once a week. So the other week my “friend” from class and I were talking about exactly all of this, and she said, “Well, I've also only had a few good friends in my life.” (Notice how she added the word “good”.) “But I mean I've always had mates too.” She had just made a great distinction for me. I've only had a few friends in my life. I've never had “mates”.

I find trying to navigate my way along the shores of shallow connections hugely tiresome. There are too many dangers lurking in the shallow end, too many ways to get something wrong. Sharp coral. Jagged rocks. These waters may be more appealing to people with better social skills. And because I worry so much about the mistakes I might make with new people, I rarely make new friends.

In his book *The Complete Guide to Asperger's Syndrome*, Tony Attwood uses the metaphor of a 5,000-piece jigsaw puzzle to explain how people develop socially:

> "Typical people have the picture on the box of the completed puzzle, the innate ability to know how to relate or connect to fellow humans. The social puzzle is completed in childhood relatively easily. The picture on the box, or intuition, can generally be relied on to solve a social problem. The child with Asperger's syndrome does not have the picture, and tries to identify the connections and patterns from experiences and, one would hope, some guidance. Eventually, some pieces of the puzzle fit together in small groups of disconnected 'islands', and after three or four decades, a pattern is recognized and the completion of the puzzle accelerates. Some people with Asperger's syndrome are eventually able to socialize reasonably well, with typical people unaware of the mental energy, support, understanding and education that is required to achieve such success."

Because of my narrow circumference of awareness, I could never see the big picture which Attwood speaks of in his book. I spent my life, focused in, trying too hard to connect the details, the "puzzle islands", to learn the rules of social engagement. In lieu of that I live in the deep end, where honesty and over-sharing, are the customary means of communication.

Many of my friends were people I met through work or school or some organized task that brought us together, that allowed bonding to happen through tasks rather than small talk. It relieved my anxiety when I could have a clearly defined reason for being with someone, a trivial activity that didn't have to mean trivial conversation.

It was a relief when we both had a role to play and we knew where our transactions would take us. To this day I still feel very strongly about people who have well-defined roles in my life. The guy at the video store who knows exactly what I'll want to see; my hairdresser; my son's doctor. Those people who have their place to be, and are kind to me when I go see them. These are the people who feed my social hungers and make the world feel safe to me.

Besides well-defined roles, I would find in

life that the people I had the best luck with as friends were people with whom there was somehow a naturally occurring social gap. For example, when I was a child an adult and I had an age gap, and there was a gender gap between boys and girls, which became more distinguished after puberty; another would be some form of cultural gap. In-line with this theory is the fact that my husband is a German man, seventeen years my senior.

At university I would meet a foreign exchange student who I would become great friends with. If they had "mates", which they often did, then I had a group to hang out with. The danger here was if I fell out with my friend, which I sometimes did, I would find myself abandoned by all of them. These house-of-cards style of social groups sometimes led to emotionally devastating ends for me and my self-esteem.

But as a young child, before the strong divide between boys and girls and before meeting foreign exchange students, I was most able to identify adults as being allies. When I was little I would make conversation with a grown woman in the bathroom at a restaurant, or a new teacher at my school, or indeed any random adult who would listen.

Because I lived in the deep end, I often told them personal details about what was really on my mind and I found that adults were more likely to be kind about this than children. Occasionally the grown-ups encouraged me to play with children my own age and I would explain the difficulty I had. I was usually told that things were more normal for me than I realized. And I was hearing so many people express this same sentiment, I started to accept that it was true. Was I just experiencing some hysteria over a reality that was bigger than I felt I could understand?

Sometimes a child might come by my house wanting to play and my mother would try to convince me to play with them. But I usually didn't want to play with the children from my neighbourhood. When I tried, I felt bored with them and overwhelmed at the same time, and would often end up playing by myself.

One problem I had was the frequency with which most children would switch activities. We might decide we were going to play reporters and walk around the neighbourhood gathering stories, for example. I would be prepared to do this for hours, whereas they would get bored and want to do something else after a short time. I found being expected to change quickly deeply frustrating, and yet no one else seemed to understand. I might scream and demand that they honour our plans, but they would look at me like I was being weird and/or I would get in trouble for shouting at my "friends".

Accepting what had been said to me, that my own life experiences and perceptions were the same as everyone else's, and that what I felt when I was with others was what everyone felt, I finally started making a few self-motivated attempts to be social.

On occasion at school I would see girls braiding each other's hair. I never knew how this got started – they seemed to have a mutual agreement about the activity, but I never witnessed how that agreement was reached or how their familiarity with each other had developed. This was the sort of thing I felt outside of.

Maybe, I reasoned, as I had been told, everyone was feeling this way; maybe there was no right way to initiate this or any other social activity. So one day at recess I sat down next to a girl and picked up her hair in order to braid it. She screamed at me for touching her. Others stared; I felt exposed and criminal. Like I was supposed to have known that wasn't how it was done.

This was not unlike the way in which I tried to get my first boyfriend. Again I had no idea how it was done. Neil had chestnut brown eyes and perfect skin; the first time I saw him he smiled at me. He was wearing hi-top trainers, pastel block-print jam shorts and a pristine white T-shirt.

At eleven I had decided I wanted Neil to be my first boyfriend. For me, most people were simply part of the over-stimulating background, but if someone caught my attention, actually connected with me, it was intense. To me, a smile from someone was an indication of the extreme love that I knew myself to feel.

People on the autistic spectrum often have an irregular endorphin production. Endorphins, the pleasure, calming, pain-killing hormones, are regulated by the GABA neurotransmitter. When the GABA is not functioning properly the hormones it controls will not function properly. It is like our bar tender grabs too much or not enough of what is needed. Not enough calming, pain-killing endorphins leads to meltdowns. Overproduction of this pleasure hormone can hijack the brain and lead to compulsive behaviour.

Neil was beautiful, so my new project was

following him around asking if he'd go out with me. His answers were, "I've got a girlfriend." and "No." and "No." and "No". I liked asking Neil out. The question in itself was exciting and gave me a surge of pleasure. I didn't necessarily connect the pleasure of the question to the pain of the answer. Plus, the rejection wasn't painful as it might have been to someone with a sense of how other people thought.

For me, the answer "no" didn't indicate how Neil saw me, it was just a lack of reward. Like pulling a lever on a slot machine that might suddenly start pouring out coins. It wasn't a huge problem when the reward didn't come, I liked the rush of pulling the lever, the possibility that I might suddenly win. I mean he had, at one point, smiled at me. And if it could happen once, why not twice? Tony Atwood writes:

> "Someone's kind act may be misinterpreted as having a more significant meaning than was intended. Due to impaired or delayed Theory of Mind abilities, the person with Asperger's syndrome may assume that the other person feels a reciprocal level of love, and may persistently follow around and try to

talk to the other person." (2007)

I didn't have a sense that for most people there were varying stages of liking another person. There might be a smile you give to someone who looks friendly, for example. There are many, many stages and levels which I personally didn't experience. There are subtleties required for almost every exchange and I knew none of them. I did develop in my understanding of the feelings of others, but in the meantime Neil was nice (not everyone was) about not being interested. He just avoided me. He could have been so much worse.

We are only taking in a limited amount of input at a time and thus, might only be focused on our thoughts or feelings and not those of the other person. This might account for moments where we've seemed insensitive. Where it appears we've just not bothered to think of the other person. The reality of this isn't that we've not bothered, but rather that expanding our circumference of awareness does not come as naturally to us as it does to others. Also, because many people on the spectrum are also diagnosed as hyper active, we may be talking or acting so quickly that we don't take the time to consider the other person.

Combine impulsivity with a difficulty for holding a broader awareness of the world and it makes senses that we may seem very insensitive or out of touch with the feelings of others. It can be that in the moment we don't think about how someone else might experience our behaviour or words, but then – upon later reflection – be racked with anxiety and guilt over how we've been.

This quick shift between total inhibition and shame can lead us to developing social anxiety as we become scared of ourselves and our ability to get it right with others. It's like I have difficulty seeing but an instinct to run, as a child I tripped a lot, and as an adult I was scared of just leaving the house for fear of all the shame and hurt I'd feel when I got it wrong.

After a few bad experiences with trying to form social relationships I retreated again. I made more of an effort to be quiet and go unnoticed. I hated classes like music and PE, which often involved group and performance activities, which meant that others were watching and I had to participate and could not just sneak off into my own mind where I was more comfortable. "Zoning out" was, and still is, a big feature of my Asperger's. But I was starting, at this point in my life, to become aware of the fact that others didn't "zone out" quite as often or as publicly as I did. And that they noticed when *I* was "gone".

I was becoming self-conscious about this, and so I did it less and less. I began to recognize that the things which gave me the greatest feelings of pleasure and calm in life were the things that made me look the most bizarre to others. I began to feel anxious about letting go, and found fewer and fewer moments when I could.

Writing and art were among the activities that still provided me with a passport to freedom: they helped me forget not to let go, and I could – without anxiety – wade into the depth of my thoughts where I was most comfortable. So it was that at the age of ten, sitting in art class, drifting aimlessly in my own imagination, I finally found a friend.

Zoe was the new student in the class, having joined mid-year. The start of our friendship was simple. Our class went down the hall for art. Zoe sat next to me. She needed to borrow some crayons. I had crayons. I'm reminded of that scene in *The Abyss* when the face comes out of the water – it was like that. Suddenly she was just there looking at me, and

I was looking back amazed to have discovered her. Amazed to have discovered the joy that others felt with each other. That elusive thing I had been sure was there somewhere.

Zoe's newness to the school gave talking a sense of purpose, which made everything safe and contained. It also meant that I could take the lead, allowing me to seem helpful rather than bossy, as I told her everything I could think of about our primary school.

Zoe was very emotive, responding with piqued interest to everything, "Really!?" or "No. Way!" or "Oh wow!" She was very good at making her feelings obvious for others, and her overt approval gave me an even greater feeling of comfort with her. Zoe even made irony clear, which I found hilarious. Most girls in the 5th grade were shy and giggly, but Zoe was tomboyish. She had saucer-shaped aquamarine eyes, a sprinkling of freckles over her cheeks and nose. Zoe and I exchanged phone numbers and quickly got on with the business of arranging sleepovers and going over to each other's houses.

Because of my narrow circumference of awareness, my world tends to evolve only around what (or who) I'm interested in. In short, when I do notice people, I have a tendency to get, a little bit, obsessed. So at the age of ten I decided I was *in love*.

Because Zoe was the first person, in all my years of life, to excite such intense feelings, I assumed that she would be the only person to make me feel this way. That made sense. It had never happened before, why should I believe it could happen again? So I told her exactly how I felt and that I wanted to marry her. She rolled her eyes and told me I was being weird.

After leaving primary school Zoe was sent to a private school and I went to a state-funded middle school. We weren't able to see each other every day but we were still together every weekend, wandering around the mall or the skating rink or the church. I preferred the latter two because there seemed to be a point to skating or activities at the church.

Just wandering around a mall and talking with people you knew from school felt pointless. When I was younger I hated having “the plan” constantly being changed, and in my adolescence I felt completely lost without having one at all. But socializing was becoming more about “hanging out” and less about doing things. Being a teenager was about being aimlessly cool.

An unintended by-product of my friendship with Zoe was that she gave me a group to be a part of. She translated social situations for me, sometimes with exasperation. More than one of my neurotypical friends has had what I would call a what-the-hell-were-you-thinking look. It has shown up on different faces throughout my life and is always a recognisable expression that I have grown to find amusing and have thus created my well-you-know-me look.

Fortunately, Zoe would turn the odd things that came out of my mouth into jokes or act as if my directness was based on confidence rather than lack of forethought. If I was to say that the cute boy everyone liked smelled bad, Zoe would laugh as if my statement had been intentionally cruel and funny; or if I went into the rest room to cut off half my hair because the tips were starting to tickle my shoulders Zoe would act like that was the coolest thing anyone could do.

Others seemed to be swayed by her reaction to me. As a young girl with no censor, having a friend whom others respected was a saving grace. If it did nothing else it protected me, at least a little bit, from being more disliked than I was. I still wasn't a member of the group, but having Zoe in my life was like getting a guest pass.

Within a short time I acted and spoke exactly like Zoe. This may sound very *Single White Female*, but it is a natural human behaviour. This act of mimicking comes from a childhood developmental stage called twin-ship. This is when young (younger) children start to become aware of the world around them and model the behaviours and interests they see in others. This osmosis is their way of establishing membership of the world. This is how cultures are established. This is why members of the same culture will share certain behavioural traits and accept them as normal.

Because Asperger's is a developmental disorder, we hit such stages later or perhaps in different ways. For me most people were one big cluster of indistinguishable faces. I didn't see people, I didn't identify with them; so while others were gelling and conforming to the norms of their culture – taking in multiple people, multiple personality traits available to copy, and discriminating between them – I twinned indiscriminatly with only a few select people who stood out for me.

On Sundays Zoe couldn't be with me because she went to church. My own parents had stopped taking me to church after their divorce. I wanted to be with Zoe as much as I could so I used my guest pass and tagged along. I loved the sermons way more than I had liked Sunday school; I liked that they offered actual information about God and morality rather than my just doing art projects. My only complaint was about the public praying.

I didn't actually dare to start praying when we were supposed to, because my conversations with God always lasted longer than the time they allotted. I usually started by asking God how he was doing, because that had been impressed upon me as the proper way to initiate a conversation, and then I'd wait so that he had time to answer.

After I thought I had given enough time I would move on to what was worrying me (I monologued a bit here) and what questions I had. Even though I imagined he knew everything there was to know about my confusion, I felt the urge to go through it all again and offer up different possibilities like a multiple-choice prayer.

“And if you are real, are you bothered that I ask you this? Or are you not at all bothered and others just get it wrong? And if they get it wrong what else do they get wrong? Why do they lie about Santa Claus? How can I know what to believe when people lie so much? How can it be fair that I would get in trouble for asking questions about you existing when people lie all the time and give conflicting information about you? Is this a test? How can you be benevolent and still give tests? ...” On and on and on.

Then I would sign off with, “Most sincerely, Kate. And amen.” I wasn't sure what “amen” meant but I knew it was the proper closing. Anyway, I couldn't pray like this in church, there was no time. It seemed safest just to sit there and wait to move on when prompted.

Sitting in the vast quiet church, when we were supposed to be praying, left my mind free to run wild. I often wondered what others prayed about. I'd sneakily peer at the people around me, wondering if my way of praying was normal and how everyone else managed to say and ask what they needed to in their prayers.

The 4th of July after I joined the youth group at Zoe's church, they planned an outing to see a firework display. I hated fireworks. I had difficulty with sudden booming noises: a door slamming, thunder, a book being dropped, fireworks. Many people don't like loud noises, but my entire person became hijacked by adrenaline when I heard them. I would forget about good behaviour and communication. Even if I understood what was expected of me I lacked the self-control to do it. All I had was the instinct to hide.

As a child I often had the extremness of my feelings and perceptions go un-validated, which can, and has for me, caused problems in later life. For a child, when their experiences go repeatedly unrecognized they stop understanding them. It's like a child saying, "I think I want a drink." and the adult saying, "No you don't." The child eventually thinks, *Oh this must not be what thirst feels like.*

I was constantly being told that everyone felt things the same way I did. A lot overwhelmed me that didn't overwhelm others to the same extent, and I was accused of being selfish, attention seeking, hysterical, a drama queen if I expressed my overwhelm. Sending the message that I wasn't as scared, or hurt, or put off as I thought I was. Causing me to detach from what I felt, and develop a secondary disorder known as alexithymia, which is the inability to recognize one's own emotions.

It makes it harder for the individual to communicate their wants and needs with others, as they themselves struggle to understand what they are feeling. They may seem passive aggressive or indecisive. They will likely fail to establish their own personal boundaries as they are constantly looking to others to know how they should feel or what they should find acceptable or unacceptable, leading to difficulties in establishing healthy adult relationships later in life.

So, I didn't like fireworks. And when it came time to discussing the 4th of July fireworks I told the young minister, Eric, that I wouldn't be going to the show. I was more than fine with the idea of not going, and I don't know why he felt the need to talk me into it, but he promised that I could stay in the van during the show if I wanted. Eventually, and on that condition, I agreed to ride along. We arrived near the site and drove into a vast crowded parking lot. Once we stopped everyone except me got out. I remained seated and waited for the others to say goodbye and head off, but they didn't. It was only Eric and Zoe who knew I had intended to stay in the van, and Eric began to look at me as if he was waiting for something. I reminded him of our agreement but he shook his head, as if he was surprised I actually expected to stay in the car.

"You can't stay here all alone," he said.

Zoe, eager to please authority figures, sided with him. "Come on, Kate, don't be stupid."

The others were just standing around waiting on me. I started to feel anxious, but I sat in my seat, not moving.

"You can come back to the car when the fireworks start. It's not even dark yet," Eric said.

"Do you promise?"

He sighed and said he did.

Finally I got out.

We spent a half hour walking around. I remained aware of where the van was parked in relation to where we were at all times. I'm not and never have been good with directions, but if I have one singular focus, no matter what it is, I can manage it. And getting back to the van when the fireworks started was my focus that night.

I kept track of how many street lamps we had passed and where the drink stand was in relation to where we were parked. Then suddenly the first boom sounded. Without thinking I clutched my ears tight to my head and ran for the van, covering the distance in only a fraction of the time it had taken us to create it.

I reached the van, but it was locked. I wanted so much to be in the vehicle – I had understood and prepared myself for hearing the noises from inside, but now I understood that the only way I was going to get that was if I made my way back to the group and got Eric to let me in. I'd have to walk away from my hub of security and back into the crowd. And so I did.

I went and found my group again and tried talking to Eric, my hands pushing my ears flat against my head as I spoke. Eric didn't hear me. I took one hand away so that I could tap his arm. He took no notice. Finally I had no choice but to expose both my ears to the noise.

I grabbed his arm and shook as hard as I could with both hands. Abruptly he turned, then smirked and shook his head and told me I was being silly. He said that if I went back everyone would have to go. We had to stay together as a group. "Do you want to ruin the evening for everyone?"

The booms kept coming as he spoke, and the ground seemed to be vibrating under my feet. I didn't think about the fact that he must have never intended to keep his word. I didn't even think about how much people would hate me if I ruined their evening. But if I had thought about it my answer would have been the same. I was that desperate.

"I'm sorry." I started crying. "I just want to go."

He just shook his head and turned away.

I thought he hadn't understood me. "Yes!" I screamed. "Yes, that's what I want. I want to leave."

I clutched my ears again, still staring at his head, waiting for a response. He didn't turn back. My mind switched off and I ran back to the car park, putting slightly more distance between me and the booms. When I found our van again I curled up on the ground next to it, hugging my knees and wishing I was inside. Later, when my mother collected me, the minister told her how I had behaved. She slapped me so hard that my braces cut into my lip.

Chapter 3

THE THINGS I LEARNED IN LATIN CLASS

The girl who sat next to me in my tenth grade Latin class, Taylor, had platinum blonde hair and perfect nails, but she had a natural beauty too. I particularly liked the indentation between her nose and upper lip which made her face stand out for me. We couldn't have looked more different.

When it came to clothes, every choice I made was motivated by personal comfort. I wore sandals in all weathers. I rarely wore undergarments, as I found them restricting and uncomfortable. I wore clothes that were loose. If something was comfortable I'd wear it until it was falling apart. My mother often complained that I looked homeless. Unexpectedly, Taylor kept talking to me, as if she couldn't see how different we were. Eventually she drew me out, I quickly grew to adore her and at 15 I declared her my second friend in life. She was a casually cool authority on beauty and social rules. She would tell me when I smelled bad, when I needed to wax my eyebrows, or other bits. She'd find a lipstick that was the perfect shade and buy some for me. Over the years, directly or indirectly, she would teach me how to be more feminine.

Latin was down the hall from Theatre Arts, which was how I met Adrian; he was tall and gangly, with John Lennon glasses and scruffy blond hair that was too long. I took one look at him and decided he needed me in his life, and because everything about how I interacted with him said *I expect you to like me*, he did. Adrian became my third friend in life.

Whenever we walked together he always put his hand on my back to keep me going in the right direction, help which I needed. His presence represented a strong feeling of security for me; we'd stay up all night having these marathon phone conversations until three or four in the morning.

I told him my life story. He told me his.

We discussed films and read scripts together; he'd read me stories from his favourite books, using his versatile thespian voice for the dialogue. Sometimes my mother would pick up the extension and tell me to go to sleep. We'd hang up for a moment, then I'd call him back and whisper, “Please finish.”

Adrian, like Zoe and Taylor, had plenty of friends, let me sit with him at lunch and took me to parties at weekends. But I struggled to pay attention or fit in within these group settings. Adrian used to point out that in these cases I only addressed him and tried to engage him in one-to-one conversations that excluded the others, and that I was often trying to leave the group. I found it impossible to have my antenna receptive to everyone at once. Tony Attwood explains this in his book, when he writes:

> “If a one-to-one conversation is a game of tennis, then a group interaction is a game of football. The delay in social processing means that the person can become out of synchronisation with the conversation and is liable to make conspicuous social errors or have to withdraw.” (2007)

The experience of having multiple friends was mind-blowing to me. Others would have taken having as many as three friends in their stride; I, on the other hand, felt giddy about the normalcy of it all. One day I was sitting in Latin class giggling with Taylor about something. We were trying to keep it down out of respect for Ms. Rektorik-Sprinkle, -Whom we all called Ms. R.S. for short - who was also talking.

Then, without warning, a heavy textbook was slammed down hard on my desk. We both jumped. Adrenaline flooded my body. "Ladies, I don't need this information. You do. I'm not talking for *my* benefit," Mrs. R.S. said in a soft, almost hoarse tone.

Mrs. R.S. was a woman of diminutive stature with salt-and-pepper hair which she wore in a bun, and glasses that were almost too large for her face. She had warned us on the first day of class that she couldn't speak loudly, so I understood that this was her version of yelling.

Taylor immediately said she was sorry and sat up straight. Her ability to change temperament quickly, to please whomever she was talking to, was something I both envied and resented. I wanted to leave. To cry. But instead

I sat there in a huff. My “fight” rather than “flight” simmered beneath the surface as I stared defiantly off into the corner of the room.

After a few minutes Mrs. R.S. said, very gently, “Kate, you're invited to re-join the class.” - “I don't want an invitation. I want an apology,” I said indignantly. “Well, you can keep waiting,” - “I'm done waiting.” I got up and walked out.

Mrs. R.S. called my mother that evening and I was literally removed from the house by the hair on my head. I stayed with Adrian for the next few weeks. During that time I skipped Latin class. I felt in some way that all of this made Mrs. R.S. the victor, that she would feel vindicated to know that my bad behaviour in her class had gotten me kicked out. I couldn't imagine that anyone would think anything different; I couldn't imagine that anyone would think anything other than that I deserved what I got.

Days later I was in the empty school hall, late for algebra, and at the far end was Mrs. R.S., heading in my direction. I veered to the left so that we could cross paths with as much space between us as possible. But as we got closer to the moment of passing she started crossing over to my side. I tried, not so subtly, to go to the other side. But eventually she was right in front of me, blocking me from trying to pass her.

"I miss having you in class," she said.

"Whatever."

"I hope you'll come back soon."

"I got kicked out of the house after your call." I could see the shock register on her face. I had wanted her to feel guilty, but I hadn't actually believed she would, and the moment she did I wished I could take it back. "It's not your fault," I sighed. "My mother does this a lot. It's her go-to consequence for my behaviour." Most adults would have responded by suggesting that I modify my behaviour. She didn't.

"Would it help if I talked to her?"

"No. Trust me, there's nothing you can do."

"Can I call her anyway?"

"If you want. But it won't help."

As predicted, Mrs. R.S.'s second phone call didn't undo the effects of the first. I suspect my mother felt frustrated that the same person who had complained about my behaviour a week ago was now disagreeing with how she had chosen to deal with it. I also called my mother asking if I could come back home; she kept saying no, that I wouldn't be allowed back this time. Towards the end of the second week I began to believe her. And then I began to accept it as the truth.

On the third week my mother called me and told me I could come back. I had found some sort of security in knowing for sure that I didn't have anywhere to go, so I told her no. At which point she called the police to tell them I had run away from home.

I was only fifteen so legally I could have been arrested and sent to a juvenile detention centre. I was fortunate that nothing was done. I can only imagine that someone asked why she had waited two weeks to report me as a "runaway".

I continued, for a while, to stay with Adrian and then with a friend of a friend. Everywhere I stayed was via the guest pass I had. But guest passes get worn thin when you use them this extensively.

Adrian's grandmother had left Adrian's mother her house after she passed away. Adrian's mother was letting her brother and his family stay in the house, so when she asked if they could let me stay in the converted garage they must have flt obliged to say yes.

In the mornings I'd often wake up to find the husband sitting on my bed. He never touched me, but I could feel him leering at me as he tried to make casual conversation about the coming day while I laid there wearing little beneath the covers.

A few weeks into my stay with them, Adrian's mother stopped by to check on how things were going. I could the wife saying, “Oh you know Tom. Boys will be boys. She just needs to go somewhere else is all.”

Nothing felt like mine. I never had lunch money, and I couldn't apply for free school meals because, at fifteen, I wasn't allowed not to be living at home and both my parents made too much money to qualify for free school meals. Mrs. R.S. had taken to coming to find me before lunch and giving me money. She'd tell me to come to her room after I had eaten, where she always had lots of oranges for me.

I should mention that for a long time in my life I had odd food habits. Not unlike how I experienced new friendships, if I found something I liked, I'd want only that for a few months. I had gone through different food phases such as baked potatoes with ketchup, or broccoli with pasta, or hummus with anything else. I mostly grew out of this weird food singularity as I entered my mid-twenties, but during the time when I was taking Latin, my circumference of awareness was orange-sized.

While I ate, Mrs. R.S. gave me extra credit work or simply let me correct my regular work before she put in a final grade, citing my living situation as a "special need".

Coming into the Latin room was like stepping into another world, far away from the chaos of life, which was why I had signed up for it in the first place. In the far corner of the room there were two gold sofas covered with stuffed animals and medieval-looking scrapbooks.

Choosing a class based on physical comfort may seem shallow and irrational, but I cannot emphasize enough the importance of my physical environment to my emotional and cognitive function. The effect is anything but shallow.

Sometimes, after lunch we would sit quietly, listening to Wagner play in the background. Other times we would talk. I told her everything, the way I would have told anyone I liked (without regard for age or social hierarchy) everything. I had no sense of needing to filter my language or accounts of my life for her. She was kind to me and so I trusted her; for me it was simple like that.

Within a few weeks she knew every last detail of my life. She never showed any signs of being put off by my over-sharing, she never suggested I talk to people my own age, and she never betrayed my trust. Then one day she did something that I hadn't expected. She started talking too. She talked about her marriage and about her siblings, her grown-up children and her own childhood. She talked about her mother and her grandmother and her parents' house in south Texas. At almost sixteen I made my fourth friend, who happened to be a sixty-year-old Latin teacher.

Chapter 4

WHERE STRANGERS END AND FRIENDS BEGIN

During my second week at university I took a job working in the international department, which oversaw cultural studies, as well as students who had come to our school to study abroad. One of my roles within the department was to tutor students in English as a second language.

It was through meeting Miya, an exchange student from Japan, that I learned I had a knack for connecting with people from other cultures. It was the cultural gap. She didn't immediately pick up on my quirks, my instinct for being direct and literal was usually helpful for her, and my lack of interest in meaningless conversation was appreciated.

Also, I felt we bonded over the exhaustion of feeling constantly lost in a strange culture. We were outsiders together. And finally, in this situation, there were well-established roles for both of us. With everything working in our favour we quickly became friends.

As I had done with both Zoe and Taylor, but not so much Ms. R.S., I started twinning with her. I mimicked everything right down to her accent. Her Rs sounded like Ls, and after a short time so did mine. Tony Attwood writes that he has worked with Australian children who speak with American accents because they feel more of a kinship with a character on TV than they do with any person in their lives.

It soon happened that if someone else spoke to Miya in English she would look at me, waiting for me to repeat their words, also in English but with a slight Japanese accent. It was nice for me to know and translate things for her, both literally and figuratively, as I could explain certain cultural norms I had grown to understand. But this was to be short-lived: it would be only a matter of months before Miya would surpass me in this area, making more friends than I had and knowing how to fit in and act American better than I did.

I loved my job in the international

department but, problematically, it started to eclipse most of my school work. This was only part of the problem. The other problem was that I only gave my attention to the subjects that really inspired me. I was either totally obsessed with something or my brain just couldn't take it in at all. There was no middle ground. I passed the senior-level classes I had signed up for, but then struggled to pass the required basics.

After losing my place at my first university, I moved to a university in Iowa where the focus was on meditation. It was *very* international, which meant that there was no shortage of cultural social gaps and I found multiple friends who were very tolerant of my eccentricities. I could talk to anyone as and when I wanted, but I could also retreat when I wanted and without warning. I could be direct or I could disappear and no one took offence.

Interestingly enough, the more openly accepting people around me were, the more calm and balanced I became, and the more happy to engage I was. Like a finger trap no longer being pulled at, my circumference of awareness had relaxed and I became better at connecting with people in groups.

After Iowa I moved to England. I would

spend my days pottering around in the front garden while my son, Michael played outside. He ran off a lot, and unexpectedly. Despite my repeated objections he would sometimes run into people's houses! In her book, Lorna Wing offers an explanation for such behaviour when she writes:

> "People with autistic disorders also have problems in understanding boundaries and relationships between objects in space ... They may be unaware of the boundaries between objects that to others seem so obvious. For example, they may not know where their house ends and the next one begins." (1996)

This can also account for getting too close to people, not seeming to be aware of personal physical boundaries. One day, Michael ran into a neighbour's home and went through the house and into the back garden, where the home-owner was smoking. My four-year-old son then proceeded to lecture this woman on the evils of cigarettes. That did not go over well, and I soon had a forty-year-old woman telling me that if she wanted to smoke in her own back garden that was her business and how dare this child tell her off for it. I could only apologize and concede the point, as she was, of course, completely right.

Days later, Michael ran into another back garden where the owner was knelt over, weeding. This was how I met Günther, a German research scientist. I was beyond mortified and ready for more yelling about my son's intrusion, but Günther was very kind about it. He shrugged his shoulders and said, “He's a kid.” As if that explained everything and nothing more needed to be said about it.

Michael decided he liked running into Günther's house the most. So he did it again and again, and would usually be returned to me by a jovial German man tickling and carrying him upside down. Günther always invited me to come in after Michael’s forays, but I can be uncomfortable in a stranger’s home, acutely aware of the smells and *their* mess.

As I gradually moved past my reservations I discovered that I loved his house. There was a herby smell in the air from his constant bread baking. It comforted me the way the Latin room had comforted me. Plants were everywhere. Books were stacked haphazardly on every surface, two deep in his cheap floor-to-ceiling Ikea bookshelf. It was like a library within a jungle.

"This one's very fussy," he said motioning towards one plant. "She needs extra looking after." He often applied genders to nouns, a carry-over from his German dialect. Plants, evidently, were women. *Mother* Nature and all that. Curiously though, a child of any gender was neutral, so he often referred to them as "it" rather than "he" or "she". Günther and I soon established the ritual of sitting out between our front gardens in the evening and watching Michael play. "It's getting better," he might say about Michael as he rolled by on his trike.

He always brought coffee in a cafetiere and it usually came served with his homemade bread. He complained that the Brits didn't know good bread so he had to make it himself. We talked about what it was like to live in England, the way only foreigners can. He had come to England to do a research project at Newcastle University, and after the initial project was over he got asked to stay on at the university and do some teaching. He was given his own office and to this day he still spends his time there applying for grants, publishing papers, tutoring students and playing solitaire.

Günther could make a funny story boring with the time he took to tell it, which often made me laugh more than the story itself would have. His personality had two notable offences: one was that he had the kind of sonorous laugh that would get your attention across a crowded restaurant; the other was that he cussed like a sailor. "The Tories think we all want to be bent over and fucked up the backside," might easily flow out of his mouth between sips of coffee.

He lacked any sense that parts of his personality might be found abrasive by others. In fact this is what made him safe. I never had to be curious about what he was thinking or where I stood with him.

He had this beautiful openness, that made me want to be careful with him, (to be my best self) the way someone might want to put a glass dome around a precious artefact to make sure it remains unchanged by the elements. But. More intriguing, was that he had never been sheltered from life, and he was still who he was.

I loved that someone could get a PhD, a job, buy a house, and in every other way *grow up* but still retain this wonderful lack of inhibition.

I had stopped counting my friends after university in Iowa. I was no longer sure where "stranger" ended and "friend" began, so I gave up trying to know. Still, I knew there were some people who stood out in my mind as being my favourites, and I loved Günther just as I had loved all my favourites, and, while I was learning that they didn't all stay forever, I planned to appreciate him for as long as he'd let me.

We watched the sun set behind the houses, making an indentation of light in the otherwise straight line of an A-frame roof. We must have sat through this ritual over a hundred times. Then one day I turned to look back at him and found he was already looking at me, his blue-grey eyes glowing and warm in the reflection of the sun.

The air was still and the birds were loud. I could rarely look for very long into someone's eyes, but I looked comfortably into his, as if I could just float there. Then, in that moment, there was a single silent thud, as if something quite large had just slotted into place.

My Home and Education Environment

"Who am I then? Tell me that first,
and then, if I like being that person,
I'll come up; if not, I'll stay down here
till I'm someone else."

LEWIS CARROLL, *Alice's*
Adventures in Wonderland
& Through the Looking-Glass

Chapter 5

THE STATUS QUO

My mother, who spent the first ten years of my life working on her master's degree in childhood development, tells me that her first concern that something was wrong with me came almost immediately after I was born. I had poor eye contact and difficulty focusing on objects. I always seemed to be "staring off", as she says.

In my infancy she took me to a paediatric ophthalmologist (an eye specialist for children) who told her I would grow out of this difficulty; then (years later), when the trouble persisted, she would take me to a vision therapist who would work with me to focus on objects.

I had my mother's colouring, blonde hair and green eyes with flecks of curiosity. Although therapy helped me to look at objects and not into mid-air, it didn't acknowledge or address my difficulty with *eye to eye* contact. It wouldn't be until my twenties that I started to work with myself on making and maintaining eye contact.

My father, a fun loving man disguised as a Roman Catholic, was more laid back and sure that my mother was making too big a fuss about things, that any challenges I had I would grow out of. But my mother couldn't be persuaded.

Her next concern came when I was around five weeks old and still hadn't started smiling or engaging with her. However, despite not engaging, I could not bear to be put down or left. I demonstrated severe separation anxiety, which is common to children on the autistic spectrum. When my mother tried to put me down I would scream. I had great stamina for screaming, and I slept far less than other children my age. As a toddler I wouldn't sleep for more than a three-hour stretch.

I'm told that in the daytime I was often off in my own world, “zoned out” or “day-dreaming.” As I got older, I would have moments of awareness of coming back from my inner world to realize that I had been singing or talking to myself or that people were simply staring at me oddly and I wasn't sure what I had been doing.

My inner life was rich. I could watch a movie in my head. I could have all sorts of experiences, exchanges. And then there was the chewing. As soon as I was physically able, I would put everything in my mouth. It was my most desired form of sensory input. As an infant and toddler I chewed the wooden bars of my crib to bits.

As is common for children with Asperger's, I struggled with my fine and gross motor skills. The term "motor skills" refers to the ability to use muscles for various activities. *Gross* motor skills rely on the larger muscle groups that enable us to walk, run, or play sports. *Fine* motor skills are needed for more intricate tasks such as using cutlery, holding a pencil correctly, being able to use tools.

As far as my gross motor skills were concerned, there wasn't anything too obvious to worry about. Kids at school would tease me, though, saying that I ran and walked funny. My gait was a bit rigid. Lorna Wing writes:

> "Children, especially those with the behaviour described by Asperger ... may not swing their arms appropriately when

walking and may walk with head and shoulders bent forward." (1996)

As an adult I've seen people recoil when I'm walking towards them. The way I sometimes carry myself, particularly when I'm stressed, comes over as aggressive or threatening even though I don't want it to. I was slightly less adept at sports than most of my peers; I was – and still am – fairly uncoordinated.

It's amusing to watch me in an aerobics class. I'm always walking into the person next to me. But other than a few laughs I don't think I got a huge amount of attention for this issue. The bigger problem, as I advanced in school, was my fine motor skills and more specifically my *horrible* handwriting, which, coupled with my poor spelling, made literacy an area of great difficulty for me.

Immediately following my birth my mother had started experiencing postnatal anxiety and depression. She had wanted to go to the doctor for help, but she was convinced by my father to keep it to herself. Over time her depression became chronic and as I grew, so did the strain on my parents' relationship.

My father had been an air traffic

controller until he went on strike and President Regan fired him along with 11,344 others. Times were stressful. As their marriage deteriorated, I remember them arguing at the dinner table – the fighting stands out in my memory although I've been told that it didn't happen that often. How true that is I can't say. It may be that my small circumference of awareness meant that it took up more room in my memory than it did in reality.

In any case I remember flying plates and shredded clothes and hitting. My early view of a marital fight, then, was of something very physical and vengeful. The night my parents finally told me they were going to divorce I was both relieved and devastated.

It was understood that we would all move away from the house we were living in, that I would stay with my mother, and my father would go somewhere else. I couldn't imagine what that would be like. Everything I had understood about the world was changing, and quickly.

It seems to be the accepted opinion that the love a parent feels for a child is greater than the love a child feels for her parents. I don't believe this to be true. I can see why people might think it though. We have babies in our adulthood. We experience a rush of love when we meet this new person who is so dear to us.

We don't experience a rush of love for our parents. We discover them as we discover the world. They are our constant; the security we get from them or don't get from them dictates how secure we are in the world. If they are there for us, there is no particular appreciation of this: that would require an understanding that it could be otherwise.

If our parents are there for us, that is all we know: the world is safe; we are safe. We are entitled to be safe. That is the status quo. We are completely trusting of this reality, and if it is broken we experience a pain so deep that we can't fully accept it. We cry. We beg for things to change back to the way they were: to regain the security that was once all we knew, and to be again ignorant of the alternative. The love for a parent isn't a rush, the love for a parent is *everything*.

So at five, I was experiencing my first heartbreak. I cried and begged for this man I loved not to leave me. He said, "It will all be okay." I clung to these words. For a long time after he said this I waited for it to be true. I waited for years for things to go back to how they had been. Or for this new reality to feel okay. But the divorce as an idea, a memory or life experience, never felt "okay" for me.

My mother and I relocated to a university town an hour away from where we had lived with my father. My father in turn moved hundreds of miles away in the other direction, to the coast, to open a restaurant with one of his brothers. I think he needed something completely different from the life he had been living, something to make the failure of that life disappear. I know he loved me and wasn't leaving me. Except he did. And I kept waiting for it to be "okay".

Unfortunately it doesn't take much to constitute a betrayal. My perception of a lie (which might have been a miscommunication, plans being changed without me being notified, or a "little white lie" meant to be nice) would offend me deeply and hold more weight than anyone else could possibly guess. Also, a betrayal didn't always have to be in the form of a lie. It could be an unexpected behaviour. My mother never seemed to change much. She was always anxious and overly direct. She was an equal opportunity offender, but she never lied and she never left.

As a child I had a limited understanding

about what was going on. What I knew was that my mother wanted the divorce and that my father did not. What I also knew – what I experienced – was that she had stayed with me and he had not. I wanted to love them both, but I couldn't reconcile the pain I was feeling with my desire to love them. So I took turns hating one and loving the other. I hated my father for abandoning me. Then I hated my mother for making him leave. Into my adulthood my anger towards them would continue to swing in one direction and then the other.

Following the divorce, my mother would put me on a plane to go visit my father in Houston. I had a little white and blue striped canvas bag that a flight attendant would put in the overhead luggage compartment for me. Sometimes they would give me a plastic copper pendant of an airplane to wear. When I disembarked the plane my father would be standing at the terminal waiting to collect me.

Today I have a terrible fear of flying. I talk to my therapist about it. I've told her about these trips, but I've said I don't remember being afraid. Other than the plastic pendant and my canvas bag, I don't remember the flights at all. I only know that I took the trips regularly and by myself. It didn't occur to me that this was odd or that there was anything to be afraid of.

"You were six?"

"Yes. But honestly I can't remember being scared."

"The same age your daughter is now?"

"Yes. I guess so."

"Can you imagine Grace not being scared if she was made to fly alone?"

"No," I said, taken aback. I hadn't considered that. "No, I absolutely couldn't imagine that. She'd be terrified."

"Can you imagine any six-year-old not being scared to fly alone?"

"No."

"Tell me about flying."

"Most people say they get more comfortable with it as they get older. I remember starting to feel scared in my teens and it seems to have only gotten worse as I've gotten older. People always give me statistics. They always make a point of telling me that airplanes are the safest form of travel. That doesn't help at all. I know they're safe. If I could be completely knocked out while I travelled, I'd do it happily. It's the feeling that bothers me. I hate the feeling of the bottom suddenly dropping out beneath me."

The panic I feel is physical. Not mental.

Except there is one thing that I keep pondering ... When I have nightmares about flying, I can feel that too: just as if I had really been there, even though I'm lying perfectly still in my bed, not moving at all. How is that possible? It makes me wonder about how real the things in my head can seem. If the panic is in my head, if a hormone is simply being released into my body when I perceive a threat ... could she be right? And if she would be right, after all these years of being afraid, could I change how I feel? Could I wake up and tell myself I'm actually okay? I don't have to be scared anymore?

My mother was the disciplinarian, my father wanted to make sure I enjoyed my brief time with him so he was rarely cross with me. He took me to the park and the cinema and always made sure we were having fun in one way or another. There were only a couple of times that I can remember when he got upset with me.

Once he got upset that I didn't want to take a shower. I can't remember why, or what I was feeling that made me not want to get in the shower. I didn't usually have a problem with it, but that evening I did. We were supposed to go out for dinner and he wanted me to wash up first. He tried negotiating, but I simply refused, then he yelled and I still I stood firm, then he reverted back into gentle prompting. "You know if you'd have gotten in the shower when I first asked you'd be half way through washing your hair right now."

Finally at some point my mind released it's vice like grip on the objection and I got in. The water ran all over me until I was completely soaked and then suddenly it stopped. I stood there, naked, under the shower head while the last drops fell slowly from the chrome rim. The whole apartment complex lost water and it stayed off for the rest of the night.

My father quickly rapped a towel around me and got me out. I started crying as he dried me off. He hugged me and he apologized for loosing his temper moments ago. We both knew he'd been right, that if I had gotten in when he first told me to I'd be half way through washing my hair. With suds on my head and no more water to get rid of it. Things like this, knowing to do or not do something, sometimes happened to me.

Something I was expected to do would feel wrong but I could never explain it to others, or it was the other way around. Something I wasn't supposed to do would suddenly feel necessary and only if I took a chance and stubbornly went against authority would the reason become clear later. I couldn't explain these moments, even to myself, which made it in many ways like all my other quirks.

My mother got a teaching position at my new primary school. I was starting first grade down the hall from her classroom. For my mother this was her first year as a single mom, her first year away from a man who had insisted that all my "quirks" were normal, that her own mental health issues did not need to be tended to. It was also the year when my academic struggles became more pronounced, and she was alone to deal with it. For me this was the year when what had been the typical discipline of our time and culture became something else. Something excessive and unpredictable.

My mother would hit me. With the palm of her hand across my face. With a belt. With our dog's leather lead. Sometimes she would hit me tens of times in one go, if she was having a bad day or if my crime was bad enough. She would hit me with whatever object was within reach. A phone book. A phone. Cleaning products. A shovel.

I would get punished for unintentional

things like forgetting to brush my teeth in the morning, losing my glasses at school, not remembering to spell a word correctly, or not correcting my lisp fast enough when we were practising my pronunciation. And certainly I would be punished for anything that included actual bad behaviour: sometimes being disruptive in class, not staying in my seat, forgetting to raise my hand when I had something to say, not staying on task; not staying organized.

As a child I assumed that all the shame and disgrace that came with my punishments or lectures was what I deserved. My life was tolerable as long as I accepted that. To believe anything else would mean believing that I was being denied an alternative and better reality, and recognizing that I was not going to get that better reality. It would mean experiencing a loss I was not old enough to recognize or grieve for, and certainly not while I was continuing the life I was living. So instead I recognized that what I got was love. And so it was. Of a type. Although I suppose what I mean is I recognized that what I got was the only kind of love there was.

I accepted that love was expressed through constant scrutiny. I accepted that love was sometimes blissfully nurturing and at other times scary. My mother was always quick to tell me she had had it worse growing up. Sometimes when I cried she would mock me and say, "Oh poor Kate. Everyone must feel sorry for Kate." She told me that I was at risk of turning into her own mother, someone she saw as an uneducated victim who had relied too much on men and public funds.

From the age of six she warned me against acting victimized or helpless or relying on men to take care of me. So I soon felt additional shame for my reactions of weakness to the punishments.

I once kicked a teacher for trying to give me a hug without warning. Considering that I would get punished for routine things such as shouting out in class or forgetting to brush my teeth, I was terrified of my mother finding out that I had done something worse. I would try, if I could, to intercept reports of my misbehaviour in class.

Although children with Asperger's have a reputation for being honest, and I am often clueless about when it might behove me to lie, I knew, though, from an early age what to expect from my mother if she heard that I was bad at school, and so from a young age I was a liar.

My mother hated lying and did not

contextualize my lies by remembering my age, or that I was scared, or thinking about how she contributed to my fear. So besides the physical consequences when I was caught misbehaving, my mother would also give me deeply emotive lectures about the moral ills of lying, about how devastating this was to my character. Telling me that only "low-class people lie". Letting me know that it was this part of me that she was most ashamed of.

I often had a sense that she was waiting for me to repent. And sometimes I would, only to find that my pleas were greeted with mistrust. She would say that I was only sorry I had gotten caught. Or that I only wanted her to stop talking – which was true, and which made my confession insincere. Crying was offensive. Admitting fault was inauthentic. So soon I learned to say nothing. I would pick a spot on the wall and stare, trying to leave the reality I was experiencing, as she ranted. Then she'd scream that I wasn't listening. But disassociation was my only chance of escape and I could leave easily.

I found living with my mother tense. I never knew when I could talk to her or how to talk to her. It seemed like the moment I would relax was the wrong moment to have done so. I might casually point out that there was a message on the answering machine and in return she might frantically scream that she couldn't do everything at once. It's that overproduction of adrenaline. Many people on the spectrum will perceive even the most routine or relaxed notifications as an urgent demand. In some cases these people will become avoidant of all demands ("Flight") in other cases they may greet perceived expectations with neurosis, anger and aggression ("Fight").

My mother seemed to live with a constant, oppressive, sense of urgency about everything. In situations where there is no escape, like school or motherhood, it is not uncommon for people on the spectrum to become aggressive and have regular meltdowns.

Once I was putting away laundry when a family friend from New Mexico phoned. My mother had me stop my chores to talk on the phone. I was putting the phone back in the living room when she discovered that I hadn't finished tidying up my clothes. For her this fact existed out of context. She did not associate my not finishing my laundry with the fact that she herself had instructed me to leave it and take the phone.

I could hear in the way that she said my

name – with a tone of accusation that made me feel guilty even before I knew what was wrong – that it was going to be bad. She reached out to grab me. I ran to the end of the hall, where she caught up with me and hit me across the face. I fell to the ground and she kicked my hip. “Get your lazy ass into your room!” she yelled. “Finish putting away your damn clothes!”

Chapter 6

24 HOURS OF SENSITIVITIES

At the end of a day, when the world was finally still, my mind would run wild letting out all the chaos I had collected. It was like I had a tape recorder in my head replaying audio from throughout the day. I would hear my name being said over and over again in the voices of my teacher, my mother, the kids at school. Sometimes I would hear repeated snippets of conversations. As I finger-painted in the kitchen, words would replay. As I shaped my hair into a Mohawk at bath time, words would replay. I would bounce, click my tongue or strum my fingers to release it all more quickly. For story time, the words took a pause.

As a young child I hated the work of reading but I *loved* being read to. My mother's more relaxed and affectionate side emerged whenever she read to me, which she did nightly – she was an excellent reader. She was good at inflecting her tone, which made the stories easy to follow. She would read to me for hours on end even though she complained that I insisted on fantasy books. Listening to her read was a pleasure comparable to putting warm socks on cold feet or eating a crème caramel: it made my mind go quiet and my body relax.

To hear situations described so clearly that I understood exactly what was going on was very powerful for me. The narrator only gave information that was important – movies and books were usually good in that way, they gave me a clarity that I missed and longed for in my daily life, where there was always irrelevant information to contend with. This clarity and lack of it had to do with understanding and anticipating what others would think or feel, and do, in different situations. This is called Theory of Mind.

A common misconception about people on the autistic spectrum is that we have a complete lack of Theory of Mind; in truth, this is simply another area of delayed development for most of us. Because I held details one at a time in my small circumference of awareness, I would see behaviours and emotions isolated from their cause, like my mother did; I would fail to connect things and thus struggle to predict the feelings of others.

As with sight-reading, I only understood the expressions I had memorized. The act of phonetically blending together behaviours and situations to understand what someone was feeling was an area of great difficulty for me. This is why I loved stories. Words, written or spoken, seemed more tangible. Something I could take in singly, one sentence at a time. With the help of a clear context and foreshadowing, I could guess at the internal experiences of many of the characters in my books. Being read to gave me a feeling of clarity and containment, of safety that I didn't feel anywhere else.

It also taught me something about how people were meant to emote when they spoke. Through the hours my mother spent reading to me, I developed a great vocabulary and a slightly artificial style of speaking. Lots of adults found it charming when this three-foot-tall child with pigtails and a gap between her two front teeth started theatrically mimicking the hand gestures and speech styles of fictitious, and more mature, characters. But what adults found charming my peers simply found odd; they would laugh and run off in a group, leaving me alone to myself. Which brings me to the other thing I liked about stories: the protagonist was usually a little odd.

During the school day I soon started to use books as a safe place to escape into. Even when I couldn't hold one in my hand, or have a story immediately read to me, I would be able to hear the stories in my head. I started to narrate my life as I went through my day. My internal narrator would talk about what was going on around me, isolating the important details for me. My narrator was a guide focusing me on just one thing from each moment to the next.

It was during that time in my life that I discovered the grounding effects of writing. When words were running around my head, writing made them be still. In my life, my lists, my journals and letters (even the ones I've never sent) have been the anchor of my reality. Despite my horrible handwriting and hideous spelling, writing has always been the thing that has made everything else real.

But then, lying in the dark of my bedroom, the words continued. So in the middle of the night, rather than sleep I would play in my room. I would dump all my Lego onto the floor and build towers at two a.m., or I would chew the feet off my Barbies, or I might just sing.

My mother, who needed her own sleep, decided to let me have a TV in my room, which was quieter than I was and kept me contained. I was given a TV, VCR, and a VHS tape of *Gone With the Wind*, which was four hours long, making it a good movie to fall asleep to. I played it every night for two years. I did that sort of thing with movies. Annie was the first movie I watched in the cinema and my mother tells me I got her to take me over twenty times. In his book, Tony Attwood writes:

> "Children with Asperger's syndrome often enjoy watching the same movie many times. This is a common preferred activity of typical children but the child with Asperger's syndrome may be unusual in terms of the number of times the film or programme is watched." (2007)

There is comfort in the predictability of a movie or show I know well. I can understand and anticipate what's going on in a way that I rarely can in real life. That comfort was the thing I needed to get relaxed and settled enough to sleep. And when I slept, different senses came alive for me.

I often had vivid dreams, sometimes precognitive dreams. I would dream about ordinary things like our bird escaping or our car having trouble or having a supply teacher at school the night before it would happen. In the day, too, when I was zoning out in class, I might have moments of remote viewing, seeing things that were happening somewhere else, like my dog tipping over the water bowl, and then coming home that afternoon to find it that way.

In her book *Nobody Nowhere*, Donna Williams writes:

> "I dreamed that it was again my birthday. The three of us stood around a dining table that was draped in an antique lace tablecloth. We had all raised our glasses (crystal glasses I had later been given by a friend). "Happy Birthday," these two had said ... Two years later the dream came true, exactly as I had seen and described, down to the last detail." (1992)

In his book *Autism and the God*

Connection, William Stillman writes:

> "I also used to see things move out of the corner of my eye, or have prophetic dreams like the one in which I picked countless pennies up off our front lawn and, the next day in reality, did just that." (2006)

I believe there is a wholly natural explanation for what I have experienced, that will one day stand up to the scientific method. But for now, without being able to prove it to anyone else, I simply know what has happened to me.

In the mornings I'd arrive at school early with my mother; we'd leave our coats on while she switched on the radiator in her classroom and unpacked her hold-all. The room was large and crammed with art supplies, toys and books, most of which she had bought with her own money at garage sales. Behind the softening effect of my mother's efforts was a plain room which hinted at the poor neighbourhood we were in.

The walls were painted concrete blocks, most of which were hidden by the many educational posters and displays of children's art. The windows had chicken wire embedded in the glass. The floor consisted of hard grey tiles covered in rugs, beanbags and pillows. My mother was always working on her classroom, adding or rearranging things. I'd sit at one of the desks, pencil in hand, tired, wrapped up in my coat, which felt teasingly like a duvet, gazing into the openness of the room while my mother busied herself with her tasks.

Morning light streamed into the room between artwork on the windows, illuminating every speck of dust in slanting streaks. My mind would drift in and out. Sometimes I would work and other times I would sit there in awe of the beautiful dust. My senses could be both a gift, allowing me to pick up on details others had missed, or a hindrance, pulling my attention away from what I was meant to be focused on. If my mother saw me staring at the air she refocused me on my worksheet. She never wasted a minute. Her mornings were busy, busy, busy. Go make copies, re-stick a peeling poster, remind me to work, get a diet soda, correlate handouts, chat with the teacher across the hall, remind me to work.

At eight a.m. the bell would ring and I would head into the crowded hallways to narrate my way to class. The world seemed so busy and chaotic for me that making simple statements such as "... and Kate finally reached her classroom" helped to keep me focused on what I was meant to be doing. Because really Kate *didn't* just reach her classroom. A mosquito buzzed near the florescent lights, while older kids rough-housed at the far end of the hall, a male teacher with an auburn moustache and shiny loud cowboy boots told them they needed to get to class, and some girl with a ponytail so tight it would squeak if you touched it walked by, and a woman wearing a nauseating perfume and a big chunky necklace smiled at the man with the moustache, *and Kate finally reached her classroom.*

My typical school day ran on adrenaline. To make it worse, a major side-effect of adrenaline is tunnel vision – a *tighter* circumference of awareness – which means Asperger's traits become more pronounced when we're anxious. Our hyper-focus becomes even finer. What we are taking in is more extreme and what we aren't taking in is more easily missed. Because general instructions often fell outside my circumference of awareness, I would ignore any guidance given to the class as a whole while I did my own thing. For this reason, throughout my school day, there was little that I could keep up with.

My desk, which had a cubby beneath it, was home to every assignment and scrap of paper I'd ever gotten and *for*gotten about. The idea with this cubby was that books and binders could slide neatly in and neatly out. But there are no words to explain the extent to which this did not work for me. Things were crammed into the aluminium storage compartment; papers were often getting caught and torn in the slits between the cubby and the desktop.

I was routinely asked to clean it out – while the class watched – in order to locate some lost piece of work. The students would snicker, and my face would grow hot, partly due to the physical exertion of pulling out such tightly wedged-in papers and partly due to the humiliation, and the teacher didn't discourage the snickering. Sometimes it even seemed prompted. She might say something like, "Isn't it sad that we all have to take time out of our day to wait for Kate to go through her desk again?" Or, "I've never seen such a messy desk in all my years of teaching." Sending the message to all that, in fact, I was particularly defective.

Chapter 7

NOT ALLOWED *NOT* COPE

The summer I turned eleven, my father arranged for me to fly out to Florida to visit my aunt. The day before the flight my mother went out to run some errands. My job while she was gone was to pack my bag, call my father, get my ticket information from him, and then call my aunt to tell her which terminal to pick me up from. These were the sorts of jobs that I was notoriously bad at in school but in the quiet of my own home I could do.

As soon as my mother left I called my father and asked him for the information I would need. He told me that he could call my aunt himself and I should just focus on my packing. He confirmed that he would be picking me up later that evening, and that I would spend the night at his house before he took me to the airport in the morning. By the time my bag was packed, everything seemed to be in order.

Later that evening, before my father came to pick me up, the phone rang. I was sitting next to my mother obliviously entertaining myself with a tissue as I awaited his arrival. Totally submerged in my own mind, I wafted the thin paper back and forth in the air; it became a princess dancing at a ball, a mermaid swimming, a bride walking down the aisle. Then suddenly I felt a blunt and intense pain on the side of my head.

I had no idea what was happening or why. (My mother had picked up the base of the phone and hit me over the skull with it.) She screamed, "I told you to call your aunt!" I was crying too hard to respond. In any case it was already too late to spare myself the punishment. She finished her phone call and went to her room.

The pain was bad and I continued sobbing and shaking for a long while after she had left the room. I tried to stop. I felt embarrassed – stupid for being zoned out when I got hit. I didn't want my father to see me like this. I was almost eleven. Eleven-year-olds weren't supposed to be punished like this anymore. But when my father came I was still crying. He asked me what was wrong and I forced out the words that my mother had hit me.

"Where?" he asked.

"On. My. Head," I said between jagged breaths. "With. Phone."

He felt my head, which now had a large bump on it. He yelled through the door at my mother. Then he said, "Come on. We're going to the police."

"No, I don't want to go," I said, quickly sobering up and pulling myself inside, away from him. The idea of going to the police scared me more than my mother did.

"Come on, honey. It will be okay."

He didn't understand. I was deeply, deeply ashamed of how stupid and lazy I was. I could imagine that the police would look at me and laugh that I was a badly behaved child who was just feeling sorry for herself. And if not, if my dad was right, then what would happen to my mother? I was standing on a precipice of uncertainty.

We stood on either side of the door, him pleading with me to let him report my mother, me begging him not to destroy me in that way. I agreed to go with him but only if he wouldn't make me go to the police, if we could just go straight to his apartment. Eventually he agreed.

In the morning I got on a plane and flew to my aunt's. My father already had some idea of what I went through with my mother, and had on occasion asked if I wanted to live with him. I always said no. I would have felt too ashamed to say yes. For my own sake I needed to stay with my mother rather than become one of those women who allowed themselves to get rescued by a man.

What I didn't understand, as a child, was that her words were the words of a person who had never had someone look out for her. Who had been taught that she was not entitled to be taken care of. Who had been taught not to ask for support, and not to need it. Someone who had not, herself, been rescued.

The following autumn I started middle school. I had six classes a day and they were spread out across the campus. My locker was in the main building, which meant I had to *get to my locker* multiple times a day, coming from across the grounds. I had to remember my locker combination, which direction to turn the lock in, what books to take out for my next two or three classes, and do all this in the middle of a crowded hallway. The corridor between classes was much worse than anything I had experienced at primary school.

Amid the chaos, everyone was simply in charge of getting themselves where they needed to be, with whatever supplies they needed to have, with a time limit of six minutes to complete the mission *and* get to class. I would almost never end up getting the books I needed for class. I could rarely open my locker when the hallways were so full of people. Sometimes the teachers would ask why I was late, and I gave an honest answer, that I couldn't open my locker or that I got lost trying to find the classroom. Even months into school I would still get lost. Then the teachers would ask why all my classmates seemed to be able to make it on time, and why no one else had trouble opening their lockers, or why no one else got lost. I had no answers.

I lived in a culture where accountability was valued to an unhealthy extreme. Where complaining and asking for help too much was frowned upon. Where dependency, needs and excuses were considered bad before they were even evaluated. The few times I attempted to explain my difficulties, I was greeted with the statement, "That's just an excuse." This often left me confused, as it was often the same people asking who were refusing to listen.

People would tell me to calm down and just be myself, and then tell me I was doing it wrong. I wasn't really supposed to be lost or confused or even authentic. I was meant only to slot neatly into the hole society had allotted for me, and that was it. For any child, the experience of being repeatedly given tasks they can't handle and then being chastised for not coping ingrains in the mind the message that they are not allowed to not cope. In her book *Ten Things Every Child With Autism Wishes You Knew*, Ellen Notbohm writes:

> "President Kennedy urged us to 'never accept difficulties as an excuse.' I would turn that around and say, 'Never make up excuses for difficulty.' Really look at this statement: 'He just doesn't want to. He could (behave/sit still/cooperate) if he wanted to.' See how it lets the speaker off the hook, excuses him or her from the harder work of finding an underlying cause?" (2004)

No one told me that fireworks weren't loud or that I wasn't scared. No one directly said, I wasn't getting lost or having trouble with my locker. It was simply that, like with many other things, I was expected to cope better than I did. It had always been that way. Everyone else acted so convinced that I wasn't trying hard enough, that I too became convinced. I felt ashamed of my "lack of effort". I had mounting detentions for my lateness.

Most of the teachers didn't like me because I was late, and when I did make it to class (often without books) I would sit and "zone out" while I recuperated from the chaos in the hallway. When I'm exhausted and overspent I stop taking in words. If I fight very hard I can bring myself back and hear words, but even then my brain may not make any sense of what I'm hearing. I remember quietly sitting at my desk and writing stories in my notebook. Writing grounded me, but it was also an escape from a reality in which I was drowning.

My mind had become my place to revive and prepare to try again. As an adult I call this "sensory repair work". It's my down time and my body *needs* it. I couldn't have articulated my experience back then, mainly because I had no way of knowing it was different to anyone else's experience. I understood that, in comparison to others, I was lazy and undisciplined. I did not understand that, in comparison to me, their brains could tolerate more stimulation than mine could. And that in the right environment I could even excel.

Unfortunately middle school didn't lend itself well to kids who needed such frequent and lengthy breaks. Classes were only forty-five minutes long, and if it took me half that time to collect myself I had usually missed out on the instruction portion of class, and teachers tended to be averse to repeating themselves for children who weren't paying attention.

The class in which my lateness and lack of books affected me the most was Earth Science. This class was inside a brown metal trailer at the far end of campus. It was as far away from my locker as it possibly could be. I would have to be one of those people who could open their locker on the first try and then grab my books and run. Or I would have to be one of those who had the forethought to carry the relevant book with them to their previous class so that they could then go straight to Earth Science without stopping at their locker. I was neither of those people.

I usually got to see the book courtesy of the person next to me, but when I looked at the photographs, which were on every page, I was lost. I didn't know it back then, but I strongly prefer illustrations, graphs or charts to photographs, which can't help but contain irrelevant information.

I would look first at the photo with its many details (like sand on a beach, perhaps, but also pebbles and ocean and blurry people in the background and sky and clouds and that was all meant to accompany a chapter on erosion), and then beneath the picture I would see lines of uniform words. The words became fuzzy, I became dizzy, inertia set in.

It was like being in a vast space with no sense of direction. Which sentence was going to be *the* sentence that would explain the point of the picture and anchor my attention? Tony Attwood describes this in his book where he writes:

> "Children with Asperger's syndrome are often distracted and confused by irrelevant detail and they don't automatically know what to look at. They

> may need specific instruction as to exactly what to look at on that page." (2007)

One to one instruction was something I didn't get in that class. I made a zero in Earth Science that year. Other grades such as 15 or 27 or 45 would have been considered horrifically failing grades (a pass is 70 in America). I made *no* grade. I had not put one answer on one worksheet or test at any time during this class.

One to one instruction would have been ideal, but was hard to get. I remember my history teacher that year was laid back and would repeat things whenever I asked, giving me the information when I was ready to hear it. That was the one class I managed to pass. That class was around the corner from my locker. If I didn't have my book he would send me to get it, which I could do quickly and easily when the halls were empty. Although this is not to suggest that my every failure or success was exclusively down to the teachers. There were definitely times when I made *choices*.

I was good at geometry, although I didn't pass. Our work was often in the form of equations written on the board. We were meant to sit and listen to the lesson before beginning, but I would just set to work. Like I had done with the block patterns before they were facing my direction, I didn't do this to be defiant but because I got such a rush out of being good at something that I couldn't wait to show off. The teacher would see me scribbling away and ask what I was doing. When I showed him my almost completed assignment he would unceremoniously make me throw it away. *Then* I became defiant. I would throw away as many as five nearly completed assignments before he was done talking on any given day. By the time he said we were allowed to begin I would stop working and turn away.

I didn't want to sit there next to everyone else competing to get the answers down first, competing to be the best. I had already gotten the answers down first. He couldn't change that fact by leaving my work in the bin and refusing to acknowledge it. He would sometimes pull my work out and go over it to tell me that I had a perfect mark. That if I could only follow the rules he could record the mark I had earned.

I found it patronizing that he expected me to perform for him, in fact the whole system of teachers grading students seemed like a discriminatory class system I didn't agree with. I didn't understand why so many of my peers tolerated it. In any case I decided whether or not my teacher acknowledged my work was between him and the school and their arbitrary grading system did not affect my intellect.

So science was bad, history was okay and math was my fault, but I at least expected to enjoy my elective, Home Economics. I always liked crafts and cooking in a creative, hippy sort of way. I often wore sun dresses my mother had made, or clothes I had creatively modified for myself, paired with my favourite sandals and toed socks. Unfortunately the teacher of this class liked crafts and cooking in a 1950s-housewife way. Everything had a particular way it had to be done. Which meant the class was more about replication than creativity.

Our teacher liked everything neat and pretty, and my work (whether a paper assignment or a sewing project) wasn't neat or pretty. She used to take off an automatic thirty points for frayed edges on the ends of the paper. Since 70 was the pass mark there was no room for a second mistake after that.

One time we partnered up to make pizzas. I stood to attention in my apron, with my hair pinned back, as I awaited instruction.

But the girl I was meant to be working with turned on the oven prematurely. The teacher saw that our oven was on, came over and yelled at me. Even when the other girl spoke up and said it was her fault the teacher still only looked at me and addressed me.

After the teacher walked away, my classmate whispered an apology to me. It was clear she felt bad, and said she couldn't understand why I had been the only one to get told off. I understood. This was becoming normal for me. Between being late, unprepared, zoned out, defiant or handing in messy paperwork, teachers didn't like me. Even when I genuinely tried the damage was already done.

Chapter 8

IN HERE WE SAY, THE FIRST STEP TO RECOVERY IS BEING HONEST

A few months into middle school, my father did what many parents might have done when watching their child's grades take a nose-dive and their detention slips rocket skywards. He took me to a drug rehabilitation centre. He simply showed up at my school, told the office I had a doctor's appointment, and took me. The psychologist I met with there was a middle-aged man in a grey suit. He wore glasses and a full beard, both working to hide his face. My father had stayed out in the waiting room while I went in to his office.

The doctor asked many questions focused

around drug usage. (At this point I didn't actually know where I was, why I was there, or what this man's speciality was. To me he was just another psychologist asking questions. I had done all this before. I liked psychologists. They were safe.) He wanted to know if any of my friends were using drugs and if I had ever tried them. I told him that the girl next door smoked cigarettes and that I had tried smoking with her once but didn't get the appeal.

After our talk the psychologist called my father back in and explained that I was getting into a world of drugs and that in his experience if a person admitted to "just trying" something that meant it was usually much worse and I needed rehab. He said all of this right in front of me. Angrily I restated that I didn't even like cigarettes and had never done anything else. I was eleven! I didn't understand what else I could say to make him believe me. He just nodded and gave my father a look. Before the appointment was over the doctor gave me a lecture, saying that he saw kids like me all the time and that I needed to take responsibility for my actions.

"In here we say that the first step to recovery is being honest. And I think you need to be honest with yourself first. Nobody can take responsibility for you but you."

"I'm a minor. My mother and father are supposed to take responsibility for me."

"You won't get better if you can't first be honest."

"But I was honest. Am I better now?"

There was another look exchanged between the two men.

"It's time to go, Kate," my father said quietly, which I understood to mean he was embarrassed by me for speaking to an adult like that.

Luckily that was my one and only appointment at that facility. As soon as my mother found out where my father had taken me she shut down the idea that my difficulties had anything to do with drugs and that was the end of that. But I have to wonder – if it's true that the doctor saw children like me all the time, how many young people on the autistic spectrum had this man put into drug rehabilitation?

After a certain amount of detentions had piled up for my lateness, I was given the additional punishment of being sent to in-school suspension (ISS) for three days. I told the principal that it was unethical to punish someone for having already been punished.

Then suddenly I had *five* days of ISS. I hated the stigma of having been so bad that I belonged there, but I actually liked the calm of being in one room for the whole day without worrying about my locker or the busy hallway.

Lunch was served in the room and I could eat and work and not have to worry about the crazy cafeteria chaos. I was in a room with only five other kids, none of whom teased me. The room itself was not so nice. The high-pressure laminate top of my desk was peeling off at the corner to reveal particle-board, and there was a burn mark in the plastic of my chair. I tried to imagine how that came to be there.

I discovered that, without having to do anything to attain it, there seemed to be some status that went along with being one of the "bad kids". So there I sat – amid dried-up bubble gum and the ancient engravings of pencil graffiti from students past – finally getting my work done. I worked so much that I finished all my assignments well ahead of schedule and my kind history teacher sent down extra credit work for me. Which I enjoyed doing. But somehow that productivity only served to validate the idea that I must be intentionally avoiding work when in the mainstream school.

Upon my return I heard comments from the teachers that they knew I *could* work because I had managed to complete assignments while being in ISS.

In the space of a few months, since starting middle school, I had become very jaded. I started to think there was no reason to play by the rules because I got in trouble either way. Being bad was somewhat cool, and I was easily "bad", whereas I was not easily good. I started skipping classes to be by myself in the middle of the day. I would go to the library and write in my notebook. If I looked busy no one questioned if I was allowed to be there. Sometimes I would skip the whole day and just stay home while my mother went to work.

One day I woke up insisting I was sick. I wasn't. "Do whatever you want," my mother said in a defeated tone before she left for work. That was exactly what I did. I microwaved one frozen pizza after another. I turned on MTV to full volume. I sat sideways on our arm chair dropping a tube of nail varnish into a glass of water just so that I could hear the 'kerplunk!' it made as it hit the water and sank to the bottom. I'd squish my hand into the glass, fish it out and repeat.

Until one time, when I felt a very slight, almost non-existent pain on my middle finger. I looked down to see that the glass holding the water had split and had gone inside my finger. There was blood all over the place. Terrified, I ran out of the house and over to a neighbour, who called an ambulance.

A nurse called my mother to get my insurance information; the glass had cut through to the bone and I was going to need several stitches. Unfortunately my mother had taken my name off of her insurance policy the month before. My father's policy was due to pick me up *next* month, so someone was going to have to pay out of their pocket for what I needed.

The nurse came back in the room with a concerned look on her face and asked if there was someone else I would like her to call because my mother had said she would not pay for the local anaesthetic. She told the nurse that the doctor could stitch me up without numbing the area and she'd cover the cost of an aspirin afterwards. I gave my father's details to the nurse.

A week later I was in the garden raking leaves, and then I was being hit over the back with a shovel. I fell to the ground, not knowing why I was being hit. It was my mother. When she stopped she demanded that I get in the car. I ran to the car and crawled into the back seat as far away from her as I could be. I was scared. I was trying desperately to control my crying, which I knew would antagonize her even more, but the more I tried to repress my emotions the bigger they got.

It wasn't until we were halfway to my father's apartment that I started to understand what had happened. My *mother* had gotten the invoice from the hospital, which included the expensive anaesthetic; But even as I started to understand what had upset her I was still too scared to speak. I didn't know what I could safely say. What would make her stop or what would set her off again.

At last as we were exiting the highway I timidly started to tell her that my father had said he'd pay the hospital bill. At which point she screamed louder, accusing me of not speaking up sooner because I wanted her to feel bad. “Oh poor little Kate. Everyone needs to feel sorry for poor Kate,” she mocked loudly.

My feelings of fear had not been contemplated, or reached for, or used to punish her. That was just how I felt when I was attacked. How could it not have been? My mother dropped me at my father's for a few hours, but then came to collect me later that evening. When I got home my bedroom had been filled with new clothes, notebooks, sports bottles, tape cassettes and other items a teenage girl would like. I looked at the new things in my room and said, "Thank you."

I worry that sharing such stories about my abuse might mean that people will attribute my challenges to the psychological damage rather than to Asperger's. I wanted to make a clean break between any messy childhood experiences and my neurological disorder, but this break can't exist in anyone's life. And it needs to be known that, actually, dysfunctional living situations *are* more frequently found in the lives of children with developmental difficulties than in developmentally typical children.

In 1998, Patricia M. Sullivan and John F. Knutson published a study on child abuse and neglect and their correlation with disabilities. The findings were that:

"Children with disabilities are 3.4 times

more likely to be maltreated than nondisabled peers."

This is likely due to the combination of excess stress in the home and, in many cases, shared genetic difficulties between child and parent. What's important to remember is that these are common *coexisting* factors which explain social challenges. One does not negate the other.

I spoke to my mother about why I wanted to put all this in my book. She said I could write about everything with complete freedom and then she said she was very proud of me. My heart aches when she says this. I wanted to save her, to keep quiet and gloss over it, because I don't blame her any more. She was a woman who, like me, grew up with a condition she couldn't understand and an abusive father who likely had the same condition which *he* couldn't understand.

Today I see the wonderful grandmother that my mother has become, and the hurt child she once was, and I feel deeply angry for that little girl who wasn't cared for the way she should have been. And that's the thing: regardless of where abuse comes from, it begets anger and resentment. It's easier for me to blame the grandfather I never knew for mistreating my mother than it is for me to blame my mother for mistreating me, but the anger is there, and stays there, coming out at the wrong times and in the wrong situations. As Louise Hay writes, "*We are all victims of victims*."

When I spoke to her about this, I asked, "Mom, do you know you're allowed to call what he did to you abuse?" "I wouldn't call it that. That was the way it was back then." But I feel certain that not everyone had it that way. I feel certain that even if they did, that still didn't make it right; and I feel certain that she'll never accept that as true, which is unfortunate because a person can't avoid bad behaviour if they don't allow themselves to identify it as wrong.

The other day, on social media, I came across a quote. It read, "Your abuser's trauma doesn't justify them abusing you." This single sentence was repeated nine times. I understand this point. What bothers me about this sentence is that it was repeated nine more times, as if to say, there is nothing else to say. But as someone who has been abused, been angry, struggles with her own emotional regulation, I feel I'm entitled to ad something to this statement.

Just because someone has been hurt, or even because they have a chemical imbalance, does not make it okay for them to hurt others. Of course it doesn't. However the sentence implies that people are responsible for containing their own pain, even when their pain has been more than what most have had to deal with. What is needed is compassion and support in processing pain.

I haven't been able to contain all my pain all my life. It has spilled over, turning into bitterness, being taken out on others. Some people have left me. It's the ones who have stayed and forgiven my ugliness that have helped me to heal and stop passing on the hurt. We can distance ourselves by taking a "no excuses" attitude, or we can recognize that we are all connected and have the opportunity to heal each other.

I am not sharing details about my relationship with my mother so that anyone can feel angry on my behalf. I have had my own anger, no one needs to have it for me. She is *my* mother. I am *her* daughter. The relationship is *ours,* and we have made peace now. Of course abuse isn't justified. Sometimes what it unjust can not be rectified. Sometimes it can only be forgiven. And sometimes not. Each person must come to what's right for them.

In primary school there had been movies and talks about abuse, insisting that we must tell if someone is hurting us. But then we lived in a culture that accepted spankings as discipline, where even schools were rumoured to administer paddlings as consequences. The messages were mixed and the lines unclear.

For a long time my mother insisted her punishments were not "abuse" and if I viewed them that way I was just feeling sorry for myself. But I knew what had happened with the shovel was not okay. What had happened with the phone was not okay. Having things thrown at me was not okay. So the next day at school, hearing my mother's voice criticize me as I did it (telling me I just wanted pity, telling me I just wanted to blame someone for my bad behaviour, telling me I didn't know what real abuse was), I broke my silence.

I went first to the ISS teacher, the one adult I felt most comfortable with, as we had spent whole school days together. I walked right up to her and said, "My mother is abusive." There was no segue. No hesitation. No negative emotion.

It is common that children (even neurotypical children) are often not distraught when reporting abuse. I was emotional when getting hit: in the moment I was feeling basic animal fear and physical pain, and I was responsive to both. But the next day, to feel sad over it was unnatural. How I was treated was just part of my reality.

When a child grows up with a certain kind of treatment, the idea that it is wrong is not internalized; instead it's a theory that originates from the outside world, it's something people say but doesn't actually feel true. This meant that telling someone about the abuse felt like performing a ritual from another culture, one I didn't entirely believe I was entitled to participate in, because I didn't feel truly entitled to be treated better.

In 1978 Dr. Pauline R. Clance and Suzanne A. Imes wrote about a condition called Imposter Syndrome. Many minorities suffer from Imposter Syndrome, it is the feeling of being in some way a fraud, that any success was an act of affirmative action or luck or pity, and that at any moment someone is going to stand up and yell, "Fraud!" But this term stretches beyond simply not feeling entitled to success. It can include not feeling entitled to support or understanding. This condition is common amongst women, minorities, amongst abuse victims and people with disabilities, particularly ones that go unseen.

In my life I was regularly told my difficulties were purposeful or nonexistant, a message that had been and would be reinforced many times over by peers, caregivers and clinicians. And the repercussions would be that I would speak out less about my difficulties or maltreatment at the hands of others, I would be reluctant to seek help when I needed it, I would even stop saying when I was confused, I would miss opportunities for friendship and academic success for fear the truth would come out. That I was not deserving.

Logically I knew what I was saying about the abuse was the truth, but somehow it still felt dishonest to call it that. Telling a grown up I had been "abused" felt fraudulent. An appeal for support I wasn't entitled to. At home when I cried I was accused of being manipulative and so being emotional felt like an act of manipulation. When telling this woman at my school I tried to be an adult, to simply get the words out of my mouth. To see if "telling someone" really made any kind of difference to my life. It didn't. The woman from ISS told me that I was spoiled.

While, as a child, my candour with adults often endeared them to me, as a teenager it had an opposite effect. I was frequently thought to be disrespectful for not exhibiting the right demeanour with them. This woman reiterated my mother's sentiment that I had no idea what real abuse was. I hadn't gone into detail. The details were humiliating. I hadn't mentioned the shovel, or the dog's lead, or the phone, or the random items she grabbed when she was angry. I may not have felt deep sadness, but I felt deep shame over sharing the specifics of what had been done to me. Those were the words I couldn't speak.

I quickly felt stupid with the first woman. I didn't fight for her to listen, and I was told to go to class. I disobeyed, and went instead to the school counsellor's office. The counsellor had seemed interested in what was going on with me. In the past she had interrogated me endlessly about my odd behaviours as I sat across from her, sinking into my chair, having nothing to say for myself. She might have already been fed-up with me before I went to see her that day. The ISS teacher had followed me to the counsellor's office. The two women exchanged looks before I ventured into the office and told her the same thing I had told the first woman.

The counsellor told me I was making a serious accusation. That I didn't understand the seriousness or the consequences if she followed it up. That I should give my mother fewer problems and then maybe my home life would be smoother. I stopped trying to tell people after that. A month later, I got into ISS again. This time it was for skipping class. That was when my mother had finally had too much and sent me to live with my father for good. I begged her not to send me away. I called her from my father's house asking when I could come back. She unplugged her phone for a few weeks so I couldn't contact her.

"My Son's psychiatrist said 'I'm a fab mum and I'm too nice. That I don't speak up enough.' He said this in front of everyone in the room." I laughed. "They must have thought he was crazy."

"Why is that?"

"Because I'm a bitch. At least when it comes to getting things for my children. There wasn't a person in that room, maybe except for him, who's life I haven't made miserable. I'm that mom who get's talked about in the teacher's lounge. How can he say I'm too nice?"

"You keep that side of yourself from him."

"Yes."

"You like him."

"I trust him."

"So he gets do be human. He gets to make mistakes without encoring the wrath of Kate?"

"....."

"They don't."

"He's earned it."

"So people have to earn humanity?"

"I'm angry."

"I know."

"Maybe I am a 'fab mum' but I'm a shitty adult. I can't let anyone relax and do their job with my
children. I resent those who try to help. I feel like, why the fuck do they pretend to care now."

"They weren't there for you."

I start to cry. "I'm so angry."

"I know."

My father's apartment only had one bedroom so I slept on the sofa. Despite the lack of space, I found my day-to-day life with him calmer than how it had been with my mother. I was now living in another town from my school, but my father allowed me to stay put, and drove me back and forth in the mornings and afternoons. Until, that is, my mother called him and told him that - at the age of 11 - I was sneaking out of school during the day, taking a bus to her house, and going to her house and pulling up the flowerbeds in her garden. My father believed her and had me transferred to the school nearer his house.

After the move, when the destruction of my mother's garden continued, she placed a camera outside her house and found that a boy from the neighbourhood was doing it. He was years younger than I was, and neither my mother nor myself had ever met him.

Gradually I was allowed to visit my mother on the weekends and our relationship got rebuilt. In the summer my mother told me I could come back to live with her. I told her no. She was angry and told me that living with my father would be bad for me, that he didn't care about my academic success and she wanted me to succeed. “As long as you're ready to be a serious student you can come back.”

The options, as I understood them, were for me to be responsible and move back with her; or to admit I didn't *want* to be responsible, and stay with my dad. I felt wretched and small for saying I wanted to stay with my dad; but the sting of that only lasted a moment. As soon as I admitted that, deep down inside, at my very core, I was just plain lazy and didn't really care about myself, I could be free. So that's what I did. Then I hung up the phone and sighed my relief.

Chapter 9

ROUND AND ROUND

I lived with my father for two years in his one-bedroom apartment, before we moved into an old farm house with his new girlfriend, Carol, and her daughter, Haylie. The house had no air conditioning, which was bad for Texas, where the temperatures could reach over 100 F as early in the year as April, but I had my own bedroom again. Our closest neighbours were a couple of acres away and between our houses there was a giant field of sunflowers that stood taller than I did. There were thousands of them.

Tens of thousands of golden pedals stretched out around beds of brown velvet, all of which turned to face the sun and thus faced my room in the evenings. At dusk I would stand in my room staring out at the field of sunflowers beneath the cobalt sky. It was stunning. I quickly developed an obsession with sunflowers, a typical girly obsession to have.

Like lots of girls on the autistic spectrum my obsessions were typical to my peer group. I liked sunflowers, writing and boys; these things didn't strike others as odd. They went quietly unnoticed and so did I as I followed *this* obsession to Holland to see Van Gogh's sunflower paintings years later.

I watched as my father's demeanour changed from his everyday personality into something much more charming. I could see that while his divorce from my mother had hurt him and devastated his idea of how his life was supposed to be, his new partner, and her beautiful young daughter, offered him a second chance at that life. Haylie was easily affectionate. She clung to my father and called him “Dad”. I was jealous that she felt comfortable doing that when I didn't.

Trying to copy her for the sake of keeping my father endeared to me would have felt hugely demeaning though, so I never tried; I simply stood back and watched as they formed a bond we never had. It was around this time that I retreated and took the first sabbatical of my life.

I always felt that every few years I needed to go into hiding, which I call my "sabbaticals", to purge the build-up of excess emotional baggage. Without knowing I had Asperger's, I was always trying to figure out and cure whatever was wrong with me. I was most likely only dealing with my latest mood disorder. Overcoming my PTSD. Dealing with social anxiety or a fear of abandonment.

I often experienced spurts of development during my periods of retreat, bringing me each time a little closer to the social maturity of my peer group. This was in part because of the effort I made to investigate myself, but also because during my times of retreat I could relax and allow myself to integrate what I had learned whilst out in the world into my behaviour.

I was "piecing together the islands of my puzzle, getting a little closer to understanding the full picture." Although this first sabbatical was short, and less about self-exploration than exploration of the abandoned chicken coop and our new rural environment, it did have a huge effect on lowering my stress levels, and this was reflected in most parts of my life, especially at school.

Unfortunately social anxiety or any stress

can further inhibit the development of theory of mind. In order for someone to attune to the feelings of others, there must be a degree of inner calm and self trust. Reflecting on social exchanges *can* aid in the development of theory of mind, but it's tricky because it's easy to experience great anxiety over social mistakes and then have that anxiety get in the way of any development that could have come about from the reflection.

It's crucial that we are not shamed over our mistakes and it can help if some of our faux pas are normalized by another person like a career, friend or therapist. My son often wants a number on a scale to get a sense of "how bad" something was. If he is very anxious over having said the wrong thing I can tell him to relax it was only a 2. We also use self forgiveness exercises to let the anxiety go. The aim is that we still feel safe enough in ourself to trust ourselves as we learn so that we feel brave enough to use that learning in new social situations as they come along.

I would take sabbaticals in my life, often during the summer when I could get away with it, and always, when I emerged people thought I had changed significantly in how I related.

These were times of great social development for me, despite the fact that during a sabbaticals I spent most of my time alone. I was being self reflecting, but also self soothing and forgiving. I would tell myself that I was okay and that I *could* do better. When I came back to the world I could attune to people better and seemed more empathetic as a result. My capacity for empathy hadn't changed, just my ability to: slow down, pay attention to and interpret what others were feeling.

Despite my ownership of the idea that I preferred to be lazy and irresponsible my grades in school started to improve. I discovered that while I was horrible at earth science I was decent at biology, which I suspect is because my biology book was full of focused illustrations rather than vague photographs.

After my first year at high school I was on the honour roll, and despite my *still* hideous spelling and my slightly improved handwriting, I had been moved up to advanced literature. Again I had another kind history teacher. He was a short, bald Italian man who was always willing to give me extra help whenever I asked for it. I took to slightly stalking him between classes. I pestered him to quiz me about our readings and upcoming tests. It was a little extreme but that was how my brain worked. I either made something an obsession or I failed. I quickly averaged 100 in history.

The Saturday before spring break was over that year we went to a party Carol's employer was throwing at a hotel in town. After an hour of staring at disco lights downstairs in the main hall, I found Haylie dancing and asked her for the room key so I could go up. By the time I got up to the room the thoughts in my head were swirling. Aggressive and overwhelmed, I picked up an empty water goblet and threw it at the wall. The crash provided a moment of quiet in my head. But when I closed my eyes I could still see the disco lights. Everything started moving again. It was like being on a ride with no way to stop.

I opened my eyes and stared at the glass, remembering the day I had cut my finger. I had barely felt anything. I had just looked down to see blood everywhere. Then suddenly a dark idea materialized in my mind. I have long suspected suicide is a common thought amongst people with Asperger's, but until just recently I could find no statistics on the matter. It was as I was finishing this book that the first study on Asperger's and suicide ideology was finally released. Dr. Sarah Cassidy and Professor Simon Baron-Cohen of the Autism Research Centre at Cambridge University led a study finding that:

> "Compared with the general population, adults with Asperger's syndrome were nearly 10 times more likely to report suicidal thoughts."

What's interesting, though, is that this same study also showed that the number of people with Asperger's claiming to have depression is much lower than the numbers of those claiming to have considered suicide. In other words many people who *wouldn't* say they've felt depressed have considered ending their lives. This makes perfect sense to me: the anomaly is to do with our small circumference of awareness. Everything we experience or think or feel takes up *all* of our awareness from one moment to the next.

We may not be depressed in general, but if at one moment we find ourselves with an intense need to escape, that's all we know. That is all there is. There is no past or future. There is no, *I was happy yesterday, surely I can find that again at some point*. There is no tomorrow. There is only, *I want off this ride. Now!*

I hadn't made up my mind about religion and life after death by that point. I didn't really buy into everything I had been told. I worried a little about Hell, about an eternity of solitary confinement (which was how I pictured Hell, thanks to Sartre). I considered it for a moment, and then I said out loud in the empty room, “If you're really there, then, the one thing I'm sure about is that you'll understand.” The worst case scenario was that there was no God, that I would die and there would be nothingness. And nothingness was certainly better than an eternity of disco lights. So I picked up a shard of glass and put it to the inside of my elbow as I prepared to make a long cut down the length of my forearm.

Just at that moment Haylie and one of her friends walked in the room. Haylie ran over to me to and tried to grab the glass. In one quick movement I pointed the glass at her. “Stay away.” I hadn't meant to point the glass at her. It was a reflex. I was trying to keep her from grabbing the glass away from me. Her friend ran out of the room. Then my father and Carol appeared in the doorway. Their focus was on getting Haylie out of the room and away from me. They were scared for her.

Then I was left standing alone in the room with the glass still in my hand. I could finally do it. Only I couldn't. I had, for a second, escaped my overwhelming instinct for survival, but now that moment had passed. The intensity of being interrupted had shaken my resolve away, the bars on the ride came back down on the ride and I found myself bound again by my fear of death. I put down the glass and went to take a shower. When I got out my father was sitting on the bed.

"Do you want a car?" he asked.

This was the oddest question he could have asked me just then, and the oddness of it scared me. "Why?"

"You need to go."

"..."

"I'll give you my old Buick as soon as I get it fixed up. But for now you need to go."

"Where do I go?"

"To your mother's. If that doesn't work out then you'll have the car." The implication being that I could sleep in it if I had to.

The next day, without calling my mother or preparing her in any way, my father took me to her house. When we pulled up at her driveway I refused to leave the car; I told him he had to explain things to her, I couldn't just show up on her doorstep to stay for good. He yelled at me to get out. I was scared of him, but I was more scared of her. I sat there until finally he left the car, slamming the door behind him and went to her front door. Their screams carried out to the curb. “I don't want her!” “Well I don't want her either!”

I left the car and ran to a nearby petrol station, where I hid behind the shop crouched between two trash bins. Half an hour later my father found me. “Get in the car!” he demanded. “No.” I said. “Goddamit Kate. Get in the car right now!” “I'm not going with you.” I said. He was so angry I thought he might drag me into the car. Instead his voiced softened. “I'll take you to Zoe's.” Slowly I got up and went with him. Minutes later we were *passing* the turn he'd need to take to Zoe's.

“Where are we going?” I asked. He didn't answer. I didn't know what was going to happen next. He was so angry, that white quiet kind of angry. I wouldn't have been surprised if he had taken me to the middle of nowhere and just left me, or worse. I thought about *Of Mice and Men,* which we had just finished reading at school. I was terrified. But he simply took me back to his house. He told me I had to wait in the living room and not to go back to my old room. I was not to get any ideas that I might be allowed to stay. He took the phone into his bedroom and sorted things out with my mother.

I sat there in the living room, awkwardly quiet, as Haylie and Carol came and went without acknowledging me. I had not been an easy child, and in my adolescence I could be a downright terror. And then pointing a piece of glass at Haylie – Carol couldn't have someone in her home who had threatened her daughter like that. I think she had suggested to my father that he move out *with* me. But finally the man who had once tried to save me had had enough. He was choosing normalcy for himself.

By the end of the day I was sitting on my new bed, in my new room, at my mother's house. It was the room I stayed in for visits. It had pink and beige striped wallpaper and flower prints in gilt frames hanging on the walls. Except for my ages-old tote bag, there was no evidence of me in this room. Everything I had built for myself in my last year and a half of high school was gone. My good grades, the debate team and other extra-curricular activities had all just been withdrawn from my life.

Once I was back with my mother I tried to hang onto my success. At first I felt it slipping away as everything in my life had changed. My environment. The topics being covered in my classes. The masses of people surrounding me. And then came my mother's dismay. Her threats of consequences, groundings, if I couldn't keep up; and all at once I was overwhelmed. My mother yelled about my grades, her main argument being that if I wanted to be okay in life I'd have to work hard. I yelled back, “I tried working hard. I was on the honour roll! All the good that did me.” “Oh poor Kate, everyone must feel sorry for Kate. She's had it so hard.”

I was not allowed to call what I had been through in my earlier childhood “abuse”. I was not allowed to blame my dropping grades on being suddenly moved. I was not allowed to blame others for the problems in my life. We had gone from, “This is not abuse,” to, “You have to take responsibility for your own life.” There was never a moment when any of us simply stopped and said, “Yes, actually what you went through was wrong. It shouldn't have happened.”

For both my parents, the moment something had happened it was "in the past" and only the good things were worth remembering. There was never a time for grief or processing. There was only moving on. But, allowed or not, I did grieve. Exactly as it had been in middle school, my life became about looking for opportunities to escape and situations to exploit.

My mother had bills and bank statements that needed organizing. It had been recognized that over the last year I had become compulsive about organisation and lists. This was seen as something cute and girlie and was liked, because in many ways I was not traditionally girlie. As with everything, when I decided I was going to do something I became rigidly, emotional-breakdown-pending obsessive about it. So my mother put this neurosis to good use and asked me to organise her filing cabinet.

I obliged happily. Her filing cabinet looked like my desk had in primary school and I enjoyed taking over and getting everything sorted out. Also, I was shocked at all the personal information I now had access to. This woman – who would sometimes wake me up screaming into my face that she knew I had been into her make-up *again* and where the hell was her hairbrush – had no problem trusting me with her deepest, most private information.

I had access to account numbers, passwords, birth dates, her social security number. And so, at fourteen, in her office, I gave birth to the idea that if I was angry or creative enough I could take advantage of her and get my denied retribution in one go. Allowed or not. Justified or not. My anger was there. But I filed my anger and ideas of revenge away with everything else and closed the cabinet drawer.

Chapter 10

MY MODUS OPERANDI

As soon as I turned sixteen I got a one-room flat across town. My father offered to let me come back to his house, which I refused. Then he lectured me about the difficulties of trying to live alone. I was openly indignant about his lecture, considering how I had come to be living on my own. Furthermore, Haylie, who was a few months younger than I was and still living at the house, was due to have her first baby, so I wasn't particularly interested returning to a house with no air conditioning and a baby. Reluctantly my father seemed to "get it". He co-signed my first lease and started giving me regular financial support to pay my rent and buy groceries.

My first jobs were in fast food restaurants. I couldn't have explained it back then, but the brunt of my social difficulties – in every environment – was my difficulty with attuning to those around me. Constantly *trying* to pick the right demeanour to exhibit I would often be in the wrong one. I would be playing it cool and casual when upper management stopped in for an inspection. I would be peppy after we'd all been lectured about poor performance. I would be direct when subtlety was required. But the social problems only compounded my other difficulties.

My jobs were a whirlwind of sensory experiences and social transactions amid mundane tasks. It was like trying to open my locker in junior high, but for eight hours at a time. And like in school, I was given to understand that my perception of the world was essentially the same as everyone else's and that I was not allowed to not cope. But that didn't mean that I could cope. I would struggle to stay organized. I was once fired after three failed attempts at putting lettuce, tomato and pickle on in the correct order. If that sort of thing was my only problem maybe it wouldn't have been the end of my job, but I was the weird one. I was ditzy and awkward, I think people felt entitled to not like me.

If I didn't end up getting fired I would burn out either emotionally or mentally. I would work until one morning I'd wake up with no energy left and I'd end up hiding in my apartment for a few weeks. And where I would once have gotten detentions for missing classes, I now got fired for missing work. From the age of sixteen to thirty eight there was no job I held for more than three months. Working as a psychotherapist, a job where I was aloud to focus on one person at all times, was the first job that got me passed this barrier.

After a summer of living on my own and trying to hold down jobs, I had become someone else. I sat in first period on the first day of my senior year of high school listening to some students talk about an upcoming football game, the person behind me passing a note to the person next to them. In second period the teacher asked if anyone went anywhere nice over summer. In my third class I realized that I no longer belonged there.

Running away and quitting things had become my modus operandi. It was one thing to be kicked out of my homes and then choose to stay gone rather than go back, but how often could I fail at school or lose a job and blame it on something else? I had no idea what was wrong with me. Except the obvious: what I had been told. I was lazy. I didn't put in the effort that everyone else did. At some point I had to accept that the one common link between me and all my failures was ... me. Even as I was walking out of my third-period class that day, I knew this. I felt sick to my stomach and hated myself for quitting again. But I couldn't stay, I couldn't do this for another year, even if it was supposed to be the last year. I went to the office and asked the receptionist for the form to withdraw from school.

I filled out the forms and handed them back. It was real. And surreal. I felt dizzy. I had no idea what would happen next. If I couldn't hold a job *at a fast food restaurant* how could I possibly do things which were held in higher esteem and which, in my mind, meant even more difficult? But as I started down the hall to leave school I wasn't worried about my crumbling future. I was worried that I had let Mrs. R.S. down: she had been watching out for me for the past year, feeding me, appealing to my other teachers for support, getting spare books when I didn't have mine. Now I was throwing all her efforts away. I felt like a fraud, but whatever ounces of character I had laying around I would pull together and give her a proper good bye.

"Are you okay?" Mrs. R.S. asked, after coming into the hall to see me.

I stood there staring at her necklace. "I just dropped out of school," I said.

She took a step closer. Getting right in front of my face, like she had in the corridor that day, so that I had no choice but to meet her gaze before I could dart my eyes away again. "You had to," she said in earnest. This was not what I expected from a teacher. I honestly expected that to be the moment she got a jolt and realized what a worthless cause I was. "This isn't the place for you," she continued. "You are very strong and you have come so far considering what you've had to deal with. I'm so proud of you."

I'm so proud of you.
I'm so proud of you.
I'm so proud of you.

Her words echoed in my head. It wasn't something I had heard much in my life. And now, at the very moment I had dropped out of school - doing the thing my mother had always told me I would one day do: give up - here was Mrs. R.S. telling me she was proud of me. This moment reminds me of the part in Les Miserables, where the police have dragged Jean Valjean back to Monseigneur Bienvenu to show the Monseingneur that Jean had stolen the silver. That, after all, he hadn't been a worthy cause. Rather than take back what she had already given me, she gave me more. *You forgot the candlesticks.*

In that moment the person I would one day become changed. This is the way in which a teacher has the power to save a life. I didn't not drop out of school, I didn't immediately become a different person, things weren't suddenly easy, but she had planted a seed that, over time, would grow into something resilient that would nourish me when everything else was dying.

I started crying and she wrapped her arms around me. "I thought I was going to disappoint you," I said between sobs.

"So what's next?" she asked as I wiped my tears away. "Have you taken your SATs?"

I shook my head.

"Okay. Well, you need to do that and get your GED." GED means general education degree, which can be used in place of a high school diploma to get into university. “Do you know where to take classes?”

Again I shook my head.

“Okay, leave it with me. I'll find out what we need to do. I have a feeling you'll be much more comfortable at university.”

I just stared at her, stunned. She really didn't seem to have any doubts about me. I was always waiting for a hint that she was acting. That she was simply trying to make me feel better. How could she look at me and see someone capable of going to university? But I trusted her more than I trusted myself, and she seemed to honestly believe I had a future.

“I love you.” The truth of the statement dawned on me as I said it. I suddenly became aware of the fact that I was keeping her from her class. My love for her made me look at her needs. “I should let you get back.”

“I love you too,” she said. “And I'm *so* proud of you.”

Again these were sentiments I couldn't imagine were true. Or that she would maintain. Sometimes, however, I am quite simply ... wrong. Mrs. R.S. would end every conversation we had for the next eighteen years with the statements: “I love you” and “I am so proud of you." She said them until I understood that, no matter what I did, they were – and would always be – true.

A few years later my mother started taking medication for mood management. Sometimes "antidepressants" are used to treat anxiety. Because anxiety will naturally restrict the circumference of awareness (something that is already naturally tight in people with Asperger's) medications that treat stress can soften the main autistic traits. As it often happens, by trial and error, my mother found something that worked well for her. Neither she nor I knew about autism back then, but the medication changed her life.

When I was eighteen we rebuilt our relationship, although we both suffered from a past we couldn't understand. We couldn't talk much about the past without arguing, so instead we bonded over old activities that we used to enjoy: going to the cinema, the theatre. And new activities: decorating my apartment; having conversations in which we would right all the wrongs of the world.

Despite our turbulent history we shared a common perspective on most things. We shared a strong dislike for social games, a strong work ethic and strong sense of morality. We talked about the OJ Simpson trial and Princess Diana's death and what the world was coming to. Then one day I woke up to a knock on the door.

Mrs. R.S. was standing outside with a university application in her hand. “All right. So you've done this,” she said motioning around the town houses. “Now it's time to go back to school.” The application was for her alma mater, a prestigious private Catholic school in San Antonio, Texas. She said she still knew people there and would make a phone call once I sent in my application.

I figured the odds of me getting into her old university were as uneven as the rest of my academic journey had been. This school was clearly out of the league of someone who had failed their last year of classes before dropping out of school. On the other hand, Mrs. R.S. being who she was – someone who seemed to have amazing powers of persuasion – might, I realized, give me more of a chance with them than with some anonymous state-funded university.

I sent in my application. A month later I received my acceptance letter. I spent the last weeks of the summer hanging out with Taylor as much as possible. We would just drive around in my very used pick-up truck screaming the lyrics to our favourite songs. We would do this until the sun was setting and often end up at the local airport to sit and watch the planes take off.

Chapter 11

THE EMERGENCY STOP

Surrounded by ignored stop lights, traffic jams and peeling Spanish billboards was my new school. The main building, which was attached to a chapel, had a steeple that towered over the surrounding area. This would keep me from getting lost when I left the campus. I would only have to look for the steeple to know where school was. If I was very far away I might just see a needle touching the clouds.

Choosing to go to another town where I knew no one was the bravest thing I had done so far in my young life. It was my attempt at independence. But being brave wasn't my concern. I was good at one-fell-swoop grand-gesture-style declarations of strength. It had to be like that, all at once: Saying no to returning to my mother's house, walking out of school, moving to San Antonio. Each time it was me trying to leave behind all the places I didn't fit in, hoping that I could find my place if I just started over. And so I would over and over again.

I would take a leap and hope to maintain it. Most times I would feel triumphant for just a moment and then quickly fall face down on the hard ground like a cartoon character that forgets about gravity when running off a cliff. Because no matter what I learned or how strongly I felt that I had *finally* conquered my challenges, there were always new ones. Either that, or they were the same old ones: my obsessions, my difficulty with over-stimulation and exhaustion, my temper, my inability to *hide* my temper, my bluntness, my lack of understanding or value of conventions. I kept learning how to behave better, but with every fresh start the problems would still be there, just less obvious or taking longer to show up.

What was particularly difficult for me was my living situation on campus. I lived in the dormitory and was required to have roommates. The room I was put in was large and square, with stark white walls and a shiny linoleum floor. Against the far wall was a single bed and against another wall was a pair of bunk beds. I was the first dweller to arrive. I quickly chose the bottom bunk and hung sheets from the top bed's slats. This gave me a small thin square of solitude within the room.

One of my roommates was a beautiful Hispanic girl with lots of friends and a framed picture of her boyfriend from back home. The other was a fashionable, stick-thin Taiwanese girl who loved techno music. Living with them was like being in an elevator with strangers while trying to pretend they didn't exist. It was exhausting and without relief.

Over the next two years I would do everything in my small 6x3 square, from sleeping to eating to writing. I never truly had any down time after classes. During the day I tried as best I could to tick all the boxes for being normal. I tried to be perky and cheerful for as long as I could. But even if I didn't shock someone by doing or saying the wrong thing, at some point I would eventually just run out of energy.

I started experiencing times of going mute and of not feeling as though I was physically capable of talking or of making any kind of social effort. Because I was almost never alone, my body and mind had no choice but to seek rest among people. These experiences only came during the years I was at this school and haven't recurred sense. Indeed the experience of being publicly mute seems so bizarre and so removed from my life now that I have to wonder if it was real. But it was.

On days when I felt such extreme fatigue and couldn't make words, I had to figure out how to communicate this to others. I remembered in high school that some of the drama students were given the exercise of being silent for a day. They would carry with them a slip of paper that let others know they weren't talking. I quickly decided to use this technique for myself. I would write "I'm in silence" on a piece of paper and show it to people if they tried to make conversation. I thought it was very Zen and got me off the hook from having to speak. It had been totally acceptable for the thespians in high school. But it was not acceptable for me, not in this place.

One day an instructor told me I was just doing it for attention. It was the height of hypocrisy to suggest that my muteness was a form of vanity, while at the same time assuming her attention was something I desired. I was supposed to not be attention seeking, just be myself, but all of the ways in which I was myself (being overly direct, overly sensitive, going mute, losing my sense of touch) were seen as being an act I was putting on for them. As always, I wasn't being myself in the right way.

By my third semester I was already on academic probation, so in an effort not to fail any more classes I had spaced everything out to give myself down time between each lecture; that meant I had around an hour between each and no more. This became a problem when I needed to leave campus to go to a doctor and could not make it there and back within the time of an hour, which I had allotted myself for resting. My only real option was to miss a class.

I had been failing the basics as I passed the more advanced classes I chose for myself. I chose to miss art class and not something I cared less for because I knew I needed more the subjects I cared less for. A more socially-minded student, however, might have considered the teacher's flexibility rather than the academic practicalities of what they could afford to miss. This instructor was particularly strict and had a no absence policy. I was dropped from the class and ultimately ended up losing my place at school after that day.

Without having any practical plan for what to do after school ended, I found an apartment across town in a suburb of San Antonio. Near my new apartment there was a cluster of shops with a café, a book store and an import store; I applied everywhere and got hired at the import store. The shop had soft lights, a gentle oak floor, and scented candles everywhere.

The job had the usual stresses of costumers and co-workers and multiple tasks, but my senses were constantly being soothed by my surroundings. My favourite task was opening the boxes from other countries. We would get shipments in a couple of times a week and the employees would all meet at the store before dawn to unload a truck; then, at around eight, we would retreat to the sofas for an hour before the shop opened. If not the sofas, I had also found a comfortable spot on a huge bag of Styrofoam in the back warehouse, nestled in between stacks of towering boxes, my own secret hideaway.

My second university – which allowed me to have my own dorm room – was known for integrating meditation into the curriculum, and teaching in blocks. I would take and complete one class at a time, one after the other. Each class lasted a month. In a semester, then, most students would complete five classes, the same as if we had done them concurrently. Because of this block-style learning, I was in one class for the whole day, which meant I only had to go to one building throughout the day and my daily schedule never changed. Even at the end of the month, when my class changed, the daily schedule was still the same. I appreciated the consistency of the routine, and *adored* the meditation.

8 a.m. – Morning meditation
9 a.m. – Breakfast
10 a.m. – Class
12 p.m. – Pre-lunch meditation
1 p.m. – Lunch
2 p.m. – Class
4 p.m. – Afternoon meditation
6 p.m. – Dinner
9 p.m. – Recommended sleep time

Despite everything now working in my favour, I failed my first class, The Science of Creative Intelligence, which is an intro to meditation – and no one *ever* fails this. But I did. There were two instructors. Each instructor taught half the class. Mine was a Russian woman, and I couldn't understand her when she spoke, but I was not allowed to not cope, so I did what I had been doing for the past decade whenever I found myself in situations in which I felt lost. I pretended not to be.

Every day when I arrived in class she would say *something* to me in her thick accent, and in return I would smile and nod and take my seat. I later realized that she had been asking for my *homework*. I was aware that we had assignments to do, but I honestly hadn't understood that we were meant to hand them in. At my last university many assignments were given for the students to do at their discretion, to practice or review the materials. An example of an assignment for this class was to draw a picture of the levels of consciousness. Our assignments were so simplistic and subjective (which is why no one ever fails) that I couldn't imagine they really wanted to bother collecting them.

I had seen other students handing things in from time to time, but I did not connect this to myself. Nor did I connect the act of one person handing something to another person, to the concept of handing in assignments. Each person was a separate individual preforming this act one at a time, each out of context in my small circumference of awareness. This was exactly the sort of thing I had missed all my life, the sort of behaviour that has caused others to think I was ditzy and lazy. Because my mind did not connect, what to others would have been obvious links.

After the class was concluded, other classmates were shocked to learn that I had actually failed, which made it all the more devastating. I worried that block-style learning (which I was new to back then) might only lead to faster failing because there was simply no time to be confused. Fortunately, though, this was not the case. That was the one and only class I failed at this school. After that my grades were either As or Bs.

The single-mindedness of doing just one class at a time and having my own space where I could calm down afterwards made everything better for me. I felt smart there. Which is good, because I was. It was my dearest hope that I could just keep everything like that until I finished school. Maybe I could even live there in that town and be Zen and calm and still for the rest of my life.

Three years later I was living in the north-east of England. *Still* trying to finish my BA. I was taking eight online classes at once and actually doing okay with it. Considering I couldn't manage to pass five classes at the same time at my first university, I was surprised to be doing so well with eight senior-level classes, but I was. Sitting alone in my office, left to my own devices, relying on myself alone to stick to a routine, I was totally fine. Also, senior-level classes were all specifically focused on my major (my interest), unlike all the subjects I had been required to take in the beginning. I've heard (and witnessed the truth of it) that for some people academia will actually get easier at higher levels. My grades were decent, and after years of loopty-loops I was *finally* almost done with my bachelor's degree.

Because my classes were online I had to go to London to sit my exit exams, but like everything else in my education this was not going to be a straightforward event. The day started with me missing the train that morning. I literally got my nose to the doors as they were shutting. Then I had to pay another eighty pounds to get the next train. Once in London it took me two hours on the crowded underground and further searching to find the right building.

Finally I was sat at a computer terminal

writing essay answers to test questions. Four hours in, I was interrupted for lunch. I explained that I didn't want lunch. What I didn't explain was that, for me, lunch in London meant being surrounded by more crowds of people. Their noises. Their smells. Them brushing against me as I walked down the street. The test centre was more comfortable for me. But I was told that the staff needed a break.

Fourteen hours later, with every muscle in my body tense and my senses overloaded, I set out on the train back home. It was late in the evening when I got near to my stop, Dinnington. That was supposed to be my stop. I thought. It was either Dinningon or Darlington. *Oh dear.* One was right after the other and I couldn't remember where I was supposed to get off. I started to panic. By the time I finally got my ticket out and read "Dinnington" The train started moving away – we were about to leave the platform! But I couldn't leave the platform; I had to get off at the right stop. That was the only thing I knew in that moment. I had no awareness of other options. No awareness of other people. I just needed to get off. Now!

Frantically I looked for a member of staff, but there was no one around. Then I saw a green lever which read Emergency Stop, and ... Yes ... I did.

I pulled the lever before the train got past the end of the platform. *Then* many staff members came running. I explained that this was my stop and could they just open the doors for me. I identified this as feeling like an emergency, and I had followed the instructions on the lever for emergencies. The train had stopped. But they said that they couldn't open the doors; that they weren't allowed to let anyone off once the train had left the platform, and that we had left the "official" platform, which looked identical to the slab of concrete outside the window but was in fact ten metres back.

I sat back down and stared out of the window as I felt the train come to life and we started moving again.

The Emotional Nebula

"Alice opened the door, and looked down
a small passage, not larger than a rat-hole,
into the loveliest garden you ever saw.
How she longed to get out of that dark hall,
and wander about among those beds of
bright flowers and those cool fountains,
but she could not even get her
head through the doorway."

LEWIS CARROLL, *Alice's Adventures in Wonderland & Through the Looking-Glass*

Chapter 12

A LEAF BOBBING ON WATER

An autumn leaf fell to the lake and bobbed like a bath toy. The floor beneath the water's surface – a Monet of richly coloured stones – looked deceptively close. Longing to be at eye level with the leaf and push it around with the tip of my nose, I quickly freed myself of my clothes and jumped in. My parents were focused on setting food out when they heard the splashes. Seeing my overalls and sweater strewn on the bank, they realized what I'd done. My father rushed over and grabbed me out of the water.

While any three-year-old child might have a general disregard for their behaviour, a child with a more focused circumference of awareness can be oblivious to it altogether. I hadn't hesitated about jumping in. We are more likely to see only what we want and no other options. I loved the water. Whatever the reason, whenever I had the chance, I preferred to be in the water rather than out of it.

My mother went to look more closely at a painting and I stayed in the middle of the gallery – there was more space in the middle of the gallery, but there was movement there too. My body had already started to feel stiff as I stood there amid all the people. I could feel my chest getting tighter and my breath becoming shallower. I felt the prickles of tears behind my eyes. I felt the overwhelming need to let out a long, loud scream. Inside I was already screaming. I could feel the scream rising up in my throat.

Then, just when I most needed it, I noticed a courtyard in the middle of everything. Separated by glass walls and doors, right in the middle of the vast room, it was an oasis of nature and solitude. There was grass and a bench and not even one person; everyone was packed inside as if this reality beyond air-conditioning and artificial lights was somehow invisible to them.

I walked swiftly through the doors, desperate to be swallowed up by the fresh air. And I was. Like a great rush of relief, with my first breath all my tension was all gone. I sat on the bench and wondered about what I had been feeling. Why did no one else seem like they were on the verge of hysteria? What would everyone have thought if I *had* screamed?

Sometimes in a crowd my senses would simply shut off. The noise around me would fade into a white buzz. If someone was trying to speak to me in a busy restaurant I wouldn't be able to separate and hear their words from the background noise. In a shop I wouldn't feel the people brushing past me. If one of my children tugged on my arm it would take me a long time before I'd notice. This loss of sensation has to do with irregular endorphin levels (regulated by the GABA neurotransmitters) common to people on the autistic spectrum.

Endorphins are released when a person experiences pain, stress or pleasure. Because endorphins have pain-killing properties, when there is an over production senses can shut down. A lot of children on the autistic spectrum experience long delays in toilet training due to the fact that they struggle to feel their bodies. Even after a child is toilet trained accidents are still likely to occur when the child is heavily engaged in an activity they enjoy, or in the middle of class (a potentially stressful environment for someone on the autistic spectrum). While there may be more than one explanation, the most frequent explanation coming from children is that they didn't realize they needed the toilet. This is only one example of how a loss of sensation can leave someone vulnerable.

In middle school, in the chaos of the crowded hallway, one day I looked down to find that a boy had his hands on my breasts. I pulled away and he laughed and ran off. What was odd and scary to me was that I could see him clearly, if I happened to be looking, but I couldn't feel myself being touched. It was as if I were looking through a window at my own body. I went to the principal to complain. I didn't mention that I couldn't feel what was happening. I was ashamed of myself for not feeling my own body. I felt stupid for not knowing when I was being touched. Other people would have known. Why didn't I?

On the wall of the principal's office was a poster of Eleanor Roosevelt with a quote underneath which read, "No one can make you feel inferior without your consent." I felt hideously inferior and had to wonder how I could now withdraw my consent. I relayed the event to the principal as I had experienced it. I didn't know who the boy was, but I tried to describe what he looked like as best I could. I struggled to differentiate between faces.

Difficulty with facial recognition is another common problem for people with Asperger's. Like with the block pictures from my IQ test, I tended not to take in a face as a whole. People who wore glasses or had facial hair or piercings were easier for me to distinguish because I could recognise singular unique features. My good friends usually had one striking feature I could hang onto. Zoe's aqua eyes, the sharp indentation in the subnasel fold of Taylor's mouth. Bone structure, skin tone, skin texture were things that made up the whole face and varied subtly from person to person, which kept them from being, to me, finite. They were abstract and hard to hold in my distinct-detail-loving mind.

My problem with faces was another thing I couldn't explain. And actually because I didn't know it was different for anyone else I didn't think much of it. All my life I've heard people make statements about how they were terrible with faces. In the same way that they would say they'd only had a few friends, or also disliked loud noises. I just thought I was one of those people and there was nothing new to say about it. But it affected me more than it did others. I could never identify (even just for myself) who might have previously hurt me in some way. I never knew, at nursery, which child was knocking over my dominoes, or which one had teased me.

The assault by my locker became a recurring incident. Sometimes it happened multiple times a day. And so multiple times a day I would head to the principal's office to report it. Soon I could see the roll of the secretary's eye as I approached *again*. I was clearly intelligent, and people often expected me to be able to take care of myself, so they would get exasperated if I had too many problems which perhaps to them seemed avoidable.

The principal finally started asking me what I wanted him to do about it. I didn't know what to say. "I want you to make it stop," but I thought that was obvious. I had the sense that his question meant something other than what it denoted directly, so I asked him what he suggest I do to prevent it from happening again. If he would tell me, then I wouldn't have to complain all the time. I simply wanted him to give me some other option besides standing there and being molested by this boy. He sighed and told me to continue reporting the incidents when they happened.

I began to understand; like being lost and late to class, I was expected to figure out how to take care of myself. I went back to the principal far more often than anyone else probably would have, until eventually I learned that it did no good and felt convinced that I was doing something wrong, both in being molested and complaining.

Even when I'm mentally present, in a crowd, I'm withdrawn from others, preferring to keep to myself. This was often been interpreted as me looking down on other people. In middle school, "Snob" was the first label that became common for me. As an adult I am overtly apologetic and meek so that I cannot be accused of thinking too much of myself. But as a teenager I didn't know how to do that.

Classmates were always accusing me of somehow having the wrong look on my face. Teachers would often ask me what was wrong, while some of the more aggressive children would accuse me of looking at them the wrong way and challenge me to fight them. To go with my unintentional facial expressions, I was also unapologetically direct.

I didn't see the point of self-deprecation, which was a big thing for middle-school girls. If a group of girls were in the rest room pointing out their "flaws" – the lumps of fat that showed up only when they grabbed at their flesh and forced it to appear, or their microscopic clogged pores – I would likely just say, "Okay," to acknowledge I had heard them. I had been taught to acknowledge people when they spoke. My first instinct was to say nothing unless I was asked a direct question. I had been told this was wrong, but evidently saying "okay" when someone is calling themselves ugly is even worse than being non-responsive.

It feels odd to contradict someone when they are downgrading themselves. It is not because I share their opinion, but because I can't determine if the bigger insult is disagreeing with them or agreeing with them.

The biggest bully I had at middle school was Kirsten Blackard. Never did I so much *want* to be lost in the crowds of the hallway, but the moment there was a gap in the sea of students, if Kirsten was around, she would just start screaming wildly. Everyone else would stop what they were doing and stare, creating a gawking wall of teenagers around me and her. I suppose people either didn't like me, or simply had no sense of responsibility because they were part of the masses, and if no one else was doing anything then why should they?

Even some of the teachers didn't help; they would see the crowd of kids gathering and walk back inside their rooms, or watch but say nothing. Many of the teachers thought I didn't care about school and that my odd behaviours were purposeful and perhaps I needed to learn some peer-administered social skills.

I have heard some professionals say that it is the peer pressure at school that teaches social skills, that some degree of shame can be a good thing. I won't argue against the idea that peer pressure may teach social skills – I know it does – but I firmly believe that shame usually does more damage than good. Especially for people with a fine circumference of awareness, for whom shame, even at "optimum" doses, *cannot* be small or contextualized.

In school I was always learning from a place of extreme anxiety. Having adrenaline routinely pumped, in overwhelming doses, into the blood stream does more damage that good. It conditions a person to be socially anxious rather than socially confident. There are more positive ways for adults to teach social skills, than to simply stand back and let the bullying happen.

Going home from school on the bus was another arena in which I was very vulnerable. Vanessa Hastings would sit behind me to pull my hair. I would sit there while she yanked furiously on my hair, not responding, hoping that she would soon get bored and stop. She would often jerk my head all the way back onto the chrome bar that topped the vinyl seats. The harder I tried to ignore this, the harder she pulled.

Other children asked why I didn't just hit her, but - besides the fact that I had asked the bus driver if I was allowed to hit her and was told no, - I was also scared of retaliating. It wasn't unlike my uncertainty about any transaction. What to say? How to say it? When to stop? Only hitting felt more scary. It felt wild and uncensored and I could see myself hitting her, but I couldn't see myself stopping.

If I turned around and grabbed her face and smashed it against the chrome bar would I break her nose? Would once be enough? What if I stopped and she came after me more? What if I kept going and did worse damage? How do children fight without seriously hurting each other. I really didn't think I could. I was going to *really* hurt her or be a coward. So I chose the latter. Except it didn't feel like an honourable choice. Whether I was afraid of the bullies or afraid of myself, all I knew was that I was afraid. All I felt was repressed and pathetic.

A major autistic trait – at the root of demand avoidance (flight) or rage (fight) – was that I couldn't handle the uncertainty of where my action or words might take a situation. Would I get it wrong? How wrong? Could I handle whatever the consequence was of being wrong? The uncertainty wasn't just painful, at least I could chose to face pain. It was more like fire, adrenalin flooded my body and I ran from it every time. Another possibility is that the abuse of my peers rubber-banded me back to the terror I felt at the hands of my mother.

When it was between me and my mother I truly was powerless. Although I may have been physically capable of taking care of myself when it came to my peers I had already been conditioned to feel extreme panic over physical threats. As is common with PTSD I was easily paralysed, later in my teens I would stop being repressed and start raging. Choosing fight.

A difficulty with regulating emotions is a feature both of Asperger's and those with a history of abuse and, as mentioned, abuse is more common amongst those of us with developmental delays. Although, in either case, the therapeutic work would still be about helping the person to practice self soothing and become emotionally bigger than the uncertainty, so that they can make conscious choices in the moments of stress.

Aside from the unwanted touching from that boy near my locker, boys were one area where there was an almost guaranteed lack of hostility. In middle school I kept chopping off my hair and had braces, but despite these things boys were still "nice". I'm not sure if this was because I was pretty or because I was naïve, all I knew is that they were kind to me – and because this was such a contrast to the publicly shaming, hurtful, torture girls bestowed, I was grateful to them.

I quickly became reliant on the kindness of boys. I adored anyone I felt safe with. The bullying was so bad and the relief of finding allies so great that I couldn't distinguish between the pleasure of relief and the pleasure of attraction. I would get into relationships where I felt a genuine sense of affection (gratitude for finding someone I felt comfortable with), and then, when that person wanted signs of affection, such as hand-holding or kissing, I would start to feel anxious. Hostile, even. That was often my first *clue* that I had no real attraction towards someone, although I rarely understood it to mean that.

I struggled so much with recognizing and respecting my own feelings that I discounted such clues. I would either force myself to be affectionate or avoid such situations, making up excuses to them and to myself. But while the male contingent of students was nice – or at least neutral towards me – most girls became even more aggressive and started calling me a slut. I was a "slut" a year before I even plucked up the courage to kiss a boy.

"Did I ever tell you how I lost my virginity?" I asked my therapist one day, a year into our work together.

"Would you like to tell me?"

"I was twelve. It was after my mom sent me to live with my dad. Every day at school was just a painful black hole in my life. After a while the abuse stopped being shocking. People were just a wall of hatred surrounding me. But then one day this boy wrote me a note. His name was John. He was one year above me and a football player. He said he thought I was cute. He kept sending me notes and he would bring me little presents. And finally we started meeting in the park after school. Every time I met him he would ask me to kiss him."

"Did you want to kiss him?"

"No. I hadn't kissed anyone yet and I was scared I would do it wrong. Then after a week he said that if I didn't kiss him he'd break up with me. And he did. He had been the one kind person in that place, and now he was leaving me. And I had made him leave. I had so much regret over my choice. I couldn't imagine a pain worse than losing my one friend. I could feel the aching in my chest. In my muscles and my stomach. It was horrible.

A few weeks later he told me he'd give me a second chance. We met again at the park and this time, when he asked, I kissed him. Then he asked me to have sex with him. I knew what would happen if I said no, so I had sex with him. Then he broke up with me anyway. I hated him.

After school ended he moved on to high school while I remained in middle school. Then I met Robin, my next boyfriend, that summer. We would have sex and swim in the day while our parents worked. He was mean. He used to call me 'stupid' and a 'fat git'. I cried terribly when he was mean but I couldn't imagine anything worse than being alone. The sex kept him around for some time. When he finally ended things I met another man. He was twenty-two. I was thirteen."

"*Kate*."

"I know. He lived in my dad's apartment complex. I liked going to his apartment in the evenings. He was so nearby that his apartment felt like an extension of ours in a way. Being with him felt safe. I hated being alone."

"Safe?"

I didn't say anything. I just thought: she's right. It was odd that sex with an older man felt safe. But it did. The weight of him on top of me felt grounding. The smell of him reminded me of my father getting ready for work in the mornings. There was a relief in having someone acknowledge me. My existence. As he said my name. As he penetrated deeper into me. For a few minutes, with him, I mattered. For a few minutes I was the most important thing in someone's life. For a few minutes I wasn't alone." My voice broke and my own tears started coming. "If any man touched Grace I would murder him," I said, feeling, for the first time, that my parents had let me down in this way.

At thirty-six the realisation that this just *wasn't* okay, that I *hadn't* been to blame, was finally real. As a child I didn't have any sense of entitlement to protection. I didn't have a sense that adults were responsible. I had been told that I had to take responsibility for myself, I had gotten this message over and over again and understood it to be the shared opinion of everyone around me, but I had never learned how to do it.

I had shame for not looking after myself better. A shame for wanting acceptance *so* desperately that I would trade my body for it. I couldn't understand how other people kept from being so desperate. I had shame for liking the sex in a basic physical way for what it was. My mother would tell me repeatedly that a woman should never have more lovers in a lifetime than she can count on one hand. I had more than that by the time I finished high school. "I would kill him." The words coming out low and deep from the back of my throat, as I decided how I would respond to someone who took advantage of my child in this way.

"I know you would."

"A thirteen-year-old can't consent. There

is no such thing," I declared. Defending the girl I was talking about as if she wasn't me. As if I could fight for her now.

Chapter 13

AN ATTITUDE PROBLEM

After my father moved us in with Carol, he adjusted his work schedule so that he could be home in the evenings. Our family had suddenly become important and suddenly seemed to function in the expected way: with family dinners, family talks and house rules. Boundaries were suddenly put in place where there had not been any and I resented them all. Our new neighbours, long-time friends of Carol's, would pop over unannounced for no particular reason. It seemed expected that the whole of our family would be friends with the whole of theirs. I resented this too.

Vicky, the mother, was a voluptuous woman with frizzy blond hair and tattoos. Her husband, Tom, had long strawberry blond hair and drove a shiny black pick-up truck that always made me think of a commercial where the vehicle is bouncing over rough terrain while classic rock plays in the background. I would often feel uneasy in other people's homes. Their smells and noises. If homemade food was offered, I approached it with caution and a face that didn't entirely hide my scepticism.

One day Vicky and Tom were having a BBQ. After a wrinkly-nosed refusal of Vicky's ambrosia, which everyone called "Green Stuff", Vicky, whom I had known for a few weeks at this point, pulled me aside and in a stern voice said, "I know you've been through a lot lately but you need to drop the attitude. We're all here for you."

While most children my age didn't like me, there were many adults who seemed to approach me with the equality-degrading attitude that all I needed was some touch-love to break down the walls that were keeping me from emoting the way they thought I should. I could imagine that Vicky would welcome me telling her my life story and having some cathartic moment when I dropped my "defences" and started crying.

I could imagine she'd already heard all about my mother from my father or his new girlfriend, which only made me feel protective of my mother and angry at my father for turning her into gossip. No one seemed to understand this. My mother had done horrible things to me, but I loved her. She had an ugliness in her, yes, but there was something very deep and good in her too. People missed that. And I felt protective of her against them. Angry at her myself, sure, but no one else was allowed to feel that with me or on my behalf. She was mine to know and understand. Not theirs. And the idea of sharing something emotional with this person I barely knew made me feel intruded upon. "We could be your friends if you'd let us," Vicky said.

"No thanks," I said.

As if struggling for restraint, she said, "If I had a child like you I'd send them to a boot camp to get an attitude adjustment."

People would often take my honesty as a complaint or deliberate rudeness. I couldn't understand why stating an honest positive was okay but an honest negative was rude, and why lying to make something sound better than it was, was often considered polite. Pretending was like lying, and lying was supposed to be bad. It seemed all very inconsistent to me. I would lie to avoid trouble, but it didn't seem fair that if I was caught I got in trouble for lying; but then I was considered rude for being too honest. It was like trying to play a game but only learning the rules when my opponent used them to their advantage.

I often didn't know what others wanted of me, and (even when I did know) to make the deliberate choice to be a people-pleaser still felt uncomfortable. Wanting me to emote was another demand that made me freeze. I could not cry or be vulnerable on demand. It would happen that, weather I wanted it or not, people would decide I was a “miserable cow” and they would then be ready to interpret any future miscommunication as further evidence of this.

In the years to follow Vicky's two daughters, each in their own way, treated me with disdain, I couldn't help but feel there was a sense of permission they must have gleaned from their mother, the way that students in the hall had understood that teachers wouldn't intervene or the students in my primary school understood I was a scape goat for their behaviours.

The psychological term for this is “The Hated Child”. It comes from a sociological idea that every tribe or group of people will identify one person as being the vessel for their angst and frustrations. The sacrificial lamb, so that they don't have to acknowledge their own darkness. They often appoint someone – usually less couth, disabled in some unsympathetic way, a person deemed morally corrupt, or perhaps in some way foreign to the group – to be the bearer of their hated. The reason can be as obvious as the colour of ones skin or as subtle as the lacking of social skills.

If you've ever noticed the phenomenon of one person being criticised for actions that another would get away with, then you have witnessed what I'm writing about. What bothers me is that many adults in these groups often don't stop to contemplate the power of their role. They find the child difficult and allow the bad treatment to exist and grow.

A week after the BBQ Vicky phoned the house. Everyone else was out so I took the call.

"Hello?"

"Hi, Kate. Is Carol or your father home?"

"No they've gone shopping."

"Oh. Is Haylie there?"

"No she went with them."

"Oh well ... can you tell them I rang?"

"Sure." I put the phone down.

A few hours later I was in trouble for "hanging up" on Vicky. I kept saying that the conversation was over. I had understood that our exchange was over, I had seen it in films:

two people are on the phone and they both know the conversation is over so they just hang up. It might be like, “Okay, I'll see you tonight.” Click. I thought that was normal, but no one could be convinced that I hadn't been deliberately rude.

Even to this day I hate being on the phone; I'm very goal-orientated with verbal exchanges, I want to know why someone is calling or get to the point of why I'm calling. I was once yelled at very badly by a guy I was seeing, because when I called him I hadn't started the conversation by asking how he was doing. Evidently I *never* asked how he was doing, and finally he yelled that I was selfish and didn't care about anyone but myself and he didn't want to see me again. I was devastated and cried for the rest of the night. So now, whenever I'm on the phone, I'm scared of getting it wrong.

Even asking the question, “How are you doing?” made me anxious for a time, because what if the other person could tell that I was only asking them to avoid being rude, and then they determined that I didn't really care and yelled at me for only going through the motions. That has happened too; if I say the thing I'm supposed to say but with the wrong facial expression or tone of voice I get accused of having a bad attitude. Early in life I found shallow social exchanges to be a minefield, which I quickly became terrified of trying to navigate.

My new high school was small and well maintained, and no one from my old middle school was going there. There was no Kirsten Blackard or Vanessa Hastings. And no one who had witnessed their bullying of me or my cowardice. No boys who knew how desperate I was for approval. It was a fresh start, but I had already had a few of those and I didn't hold out much hope that things could be different here. I had been disliked in so many different situations that I now understood this was not environmentally dependent.

It was immediately understood that in my new school the athletes were the superior class, and half the students were into some type of sport. On any given school day half the student population would be dressed in blue and white: blue and white cheerleaders, blue and white basketball players, blue and white fans, all roaming the halls. Within that large group, there was still room for a hierarchy, which seemed to range from gods to part of the "in" crowd. Those of us *not* involved in sports ranged from acceptable to a walking joke. Variables that affected this, on both sides of the athletic division, were fashion, physical beauty, family or local ties, and of course social skills.

By the time I reached high school I was not only done with boys, I was weary of them. I stayed away from them. I didn't look at them. I desexualized myself as much as possible. I kept my hair short. I did not wear make-up. And so, after a few months at my new school, I was given a different label. Lesbian.

People accused me of staring at girls' breasts – this wasn't the first time it was brought to my attention that I didn't look people in the eyes. There is something very intense about looking into someone's eyes; it's because I can see them looking at me and I have no idea what they're thinking but I get the feeling they can see more than I can. I tended to avoid faces altogether. And the closest I would get to the face was the chest region.

I hadn't even thought about being a lesbian or not. I wanted to find it amusing, going from being the school "slut" to the school "lesbian". I wanted to laugh at the ignorance of people and at how they judged others based on such trivial details, but of course I couldn't, because it was never funny.

I wasn't sure how to respond to this new label. It was the early 90's in a small Texas town, it felt clear that the other students meant this as an accusation, as if I were guilty of committing a crime. Although, to me, the word lesbian was not an insult, and to have hurt feelings, or accept that it was, felt like going into cohorts with them. The most obvious defence, to say I wasn't a lesbian, would have felt like I was agreeing that there was something wrong with it, when I didn't agree with that at all. For months I said nothing. If someone would have asked, I could have answered.

Teachers and staff knew about the harassment, but most of the teachers doubled as coaches and most of the bullies were either playing basketball or baseball or cheering for the school. Nothing was done about *them*. Instead the families of those children called the school to complain that they didn't want their daughters sharing a locker room with me in PE.

One afternoon a group of boys in a truck followed my bus home with a big sign that read, “Go home Lesbian.” We went through neighbourhood after neighbourhood. Most houses were flying the American flag in declaration of their patriotism since George Bush Sr. had declared war on Iraq. I rode past all those flags, in all those green yards, most of the way home until the truck finally turned away.

There was no one at our house when I got home that day; in the kitchen there was a tin of cooling muffins sitting on the hob. Sweet and warm. An image of normality. An image of a life that had nothing to do with me. I grabbed the muffins one by one, screaming and squishing them into a pile of crumbs on the floor until they were gone, and collapsed on the floor next to them sobbing.

My unhappiness within the family and at school suddenly starting coming out in spurts of rage. Part of my rage was about having had *enough*. There was no way around that. I was reacting to a horrible living situation, but also I was starting to experience hormones typical of puberty. Except in an atypical way.

Many young women report struggling with premenstrual tension, but studies have found that up to 92 per cent of women on the autistic spectrum struggle with a more intensified version called premenstrual dysphoric disorder. Premenstrual dysphoric disorder has been said to mimic borderline personality disorder, which gets its name from *bordering* on psychosis.

While 92 per cent may sound like an incredible statistic, it must be realized that this is in a group of women already diagnosed with ASD, a disorder that makes most parts of life more extreme. For the same reason that our senses are far more acute, and mood disorders materialize more easily, our hormones are also being experienced in the extreme. My emotions were so big that they hijacked my brain and during those times the only thing I could do was to seek relief. By crying. By screaming. I simply couldn't handle everything going on inside of me. I made my father and his new family miserable with my behaviour.

When I raged I yelled profanities and other nasty things. I was stepping into the abyss that I had always known was there. I left everyone uncertain about what to do with me. How to control Kate. If anyone at school started to bother me I would go crazy; I stopped holding back, I would just go ballistic. And very quickly. Everyone. Backed. The. Fuck. Off. Teachers were just as complacent when it came to dealing with me as they had been in dealing with the others.

I can understand wanting to be left alone so bad anything would be worth it. I can understand the teenager who commits suicide or the one who walks into a school with a machine gun. I don't know if it was cowardice or resilience that kept me from making those choices, but I entered my own kind of crazy. And like a wild beast who just wanted to be left alone, once I had scared everyone away, I retreated again.

It is often said that people on the autistic spectrum lack the ability to empathize. I cannot stress enough how untrue this is. Like everything else in our lives, our capacity for empathy is huge and intense, but I often couldn't understand what people were feeling and why, and it is that understanding which needs to happen before empathy can occur. If the information isn't there, then of course empathy can't happen.

I feel like the lack of knowing was often because I was overwhelmed and anxious, I simply lacked the calm and time to be or remain attuned to those around me. If I had a need, weather it was an anxiety (a desire not to mess up) or a strong want (to do a certain activity, discus a certain topic) that would take over my circumference of awareness and I might miss what other people were feeling.

When I think of attunement I think of a choir that needs to be singing the same song, but also at the same pace. I could be good as part of a duet. I struggled with trios and quartets, those cliques that most people enjoy being a part of, I rarely had in my life. It's through attunement we sense when it's our turn to talk, to listen, when it's best to leave a topic, or give someone space. It is about the subtleties in connections and it is a more abstract concept than empathy.

Empathy is something we can do *too* well, we can know what someone is feeling, and feel strongly on their behalf, but not know how to help, when to leave them alone, when to hug them, what to say. What's too personal, or not personal enough. These things can depend on who the person is, and who they are with us, and these are the details we may struggle with. Sometimes our empathy is so strong we retreat rather than engage, sometimes we become so concerned over someone else's negative feelings we smother them with our own worry and inability to relax about what they're going through.

About a year after we moved in with my father's partner, a young girl about my age, known by Carol and Haylie, had to go to court to testify that she had been abused by a man in her life. There was an abundance of sympathy around her for what she had gone through, as was right. She had a mother and father who went through the process of pressing charges with her.

My mother had always told me what I went through was not abuse and that others had it worse. I understood that what I was witnessing was an example of someone who had been hurt worse than I had. That the discipline I had experienced was considered okay in our culture, but sexual abuse was unacceptable. And with regards to the sex she, unlike me, had not sought what had happened to her. Unlike me, she was beautiful and emotive in all the right ways, and she was entitled to seek justice. If I'm completely honest I resented her.

I felt angry standing so close to someone who was being taken care of, while I had become someone ugly, who was now hard to love. We went to see her the day she came back from court, but I felt no resentment then. I could see she was upset. Her emotions weren't for show or a skill to be coveted. She was just simply devastated, and I felt infuriated on her behalf. I wanted to undo the damage. But I was at a loss as to what I could do. I couldn't imagine what might comfort her. So I did what I usually did. I kept my distance.

Suddenly someone looked over at me and said, "Look. Kate's crying." They all looked and, for a moment, they seemed to regard me with some affection as they realized that, contrary to what they had thought, I cared about other people, I didn't lack feelings. It's lonely to have people not know that. It's hurtful to have them look at you and actually think the exact opposite.

Chapter 14

THE MAKEOVER MONTAGE SCENE

The summer I turned fourteen I took to being alone as much as I could. I went into Carol's abandoned chicken coop and journalled for hours at a time; I walked down the long country roads until I couldn't take the heat. My spirit was in a place of charred devastation from the past few years. I was scared of people, always ready for them to hate me, ready for them to pounce. But as I had already learned, being frightened didn't save me from them, and my rages meant I was alienated for a different reason. All I wanted was to coexist with some peace.

It was at this time in my life when I decided I'd learn to do what others expected of me. I made understanding their wants my project. I read my mother's old university psychology textbook, and as an adjunct to the psychology book I read gossip magazines. I read articles about *The 5 Friends Every Woman Needs*, and *How to Deal with the Bitch in the Cubicle Next to You*, and *How to Get the Guy.* It was all very informative and the best was the horoscopes: they gave me a way to categorize people, and a set of "rules" by which I could predict their behaviours.

Studies show that boys on the autistic spectrum tend to have a higher intellect than girls on the spectrum; this is because a fair comparison cannot be made. High-functioning girls with autism use their intellect to conform – it's not that our male counterparts are smarter, it's that smart autistic girls are hiding. I began to smile constantly, I adopted some of the local Southern patois; even teachers seemed more endeared to me as my speech lost its formality and correctness. The moment I understood the other person's perspective, I adopted it as my own. I *believed* it was my own.

Everything in my life became about pre-empting negative judgement. I was so eager to please that I stopped knowing what I wanted at any given moment. I didn't pause to consider the validity of my own wants and needs; instead I agreed to, and even suggested, circumstances that I thought would make the other person happy just so that I could hide how deeply flawed my own instincts were. I started doing what was expected of me as quickly as I could and without question, in the hope that no one would notice that I had ever had a different idea or had not known what was right. Once I was visiting a friend at university, and his eight-year-old niece, who was with us at the time, suddenly snapped, "Sit!" I sat so quickly that I didn't realize she was talking to the dog until after.

For me, making an effort to get along with others was like trying to walk around confidently without the glasses I badly needed. I tried to present myself as knowing and understanding everything the way I perceived others to. What this meant, though, was that I never allowed myself to openly *not* know something. So I couldn't stand silence, moments when it was okay to just be. What if I was supposed to be the one saying or doing something? What if everyone was quietly thinking how stupid I was for relaxing when I was supposed to have a sense of urgency?

Even in situations where I was new and *expected* to be clueless and receive guidance from another, I often assumed the role of the leader, or at least that of an equal. When I was older this would get me into jobs quickly, as I came off as being a go-getter who was comfortable in new roles; but people would be sorely disappointed with me when I couldn't back up my fake confidence with any *real* understanding of what I was meant to be doing.

The problem was that after a while I wasn't making a conscious effort to fake anything: my persona had become an automatic defence response. Like in the hallways of my old junior high, the noise surrounding me was so loud and constant I had lost awareness of myself. I had already been referring to others to help identify my feeling, only now I did that not just to understand myself, but to gain their approval as well. It became not: *What am I feeling?* But *What would you like for me to be feeling?*

This was a period of huge social development in my life, as the latter question meant I sought and learned to recognize social cues I had previously been missing. But the trade-off was that I was more deeply insecure than ever. It's one thing to learn how to play the game; it's another to be constantly terrified of losing. There was no rest. There was no quiet. Tony Attwood expresses perfectly what I was going through, when he writes:

> "We need to recognize the degree of mental effort required by people with Asperger's syndrome to process social information. Using cognitive mechanisms to compensate for impaired ToM skills leads to mental exhaustion." (2007)

As I entered my second year of high school, people were already starting to treat me differently. Despite my huge social anxiety I submerged myself into, and tried to navigate, the chaotic world around me. I had grown out my hair, I started wearing make-up and took up Catholicism and tennis. Despite my subtle difficulties with coordination and gross motor skills I was okay with tennis, and what I lacked in natural grace I made up for with obsession.

As with academic ability, there was also an imbalance between hyper-vigilance and total disengagement. The trick I had learned was that I could pick my focus. I started checking my weight fifteen to thirty times a day. Each new endeavour was born from the same desire: to fit in, for my ugliness, my childhood abuse, my promiscuity, the publicly shaming bullying I had endured to all be washed away like some unfortunate stage in my childhood, like braces or acne which were completely gone and could no longer be seen by others. Every second of every day was about making myself clean. I joined the debate team, I got on the honour roll. My father bragged to our extended family that this was my best year yet, and it looked it.

After reading everything in the magazines I turned my bedroom into a floor-to-ceiling collage of pictures from their pages. I picked archetypical females who I felt I could emulate in some way. I used these pictures in the same way I used the people around me, I looked to them to tell me who I was, or was trying to be. The difference with the pictures was that I had chosen them, so in a way they were me making a statement of who I saw myself as capable of being. They were my idea of beauty. They were my way of referring to myself. There was the bohemian hippy, the angsty Goth, the tomboy; I always felt I related most to women on the fringe of culture.

Putting pictures on a wall might seem

typically girlie, but my expression of this ritual was extreme. My most consistent source of calm came from my solitude; my bedroom was my place for sensory repair work, my private retreat, my ongoing art project, and my place for self-expression. But unfortunately what was a calming haven of solitude for me was a wonderment to others. One day Haylie took a friend of hers into my room. I suppose standing in there was a bit like standing inside a cubed collage – it must have been quite an experience for someone who hadn't created it.

They were marvelling at my work when I walked in on them. Had this happened today I might have felt proud and safe knowing they couldn't really see the pain and loneliness behind it. I might have felt free to let them stand there and look, understanding that what I had created was extraordinary. But that day I felt invaded. They touched nothing, they were only looking, but still it was a crime. It was as if they were reading my diary; the words these pictures spoke were of my lostness and my desperation to find my place in the world. No one else in my family would understand how I felt about them staring at my bedroom walls. It would seem like what I did next was an over-reaction, like I was being ridiculous.

I started screaming and ripping my collage off the walls. I smashed my lipsticks onto the walls. I grabbed the clumps of rouge and smeared the colour over my face and head. My father came home, hours later to find me, skin and hair covered in red, trembling, amid the wilderness of my shredded collage.

The next week I started seeing Dr. Smith, an adolescent psychologist. Sitting in a small office warmly decorated with teal walls, sturdy mahogany fittings and two potted palm trees, I told Dr. Smith about my life. I told him that recently I had been trying to conform but despite my efforts I would still feel overly upset about things; that a rage would come on so quick I didn't even know it was coming. The doctor told me I was amazingly articulate and insightful for my age, and that I was exhibiting clear signs of being bi-polar.

I went back to my mother's psychology book to read up on my new diagnosis. I was hoping desperately to understand what was wrong with me, but psychological disorders were a little like horoscopes: most of them could apply to most people at least some of the time. Asperger's especially, because it's about an intensity of perception and reaction, tends to mimic many psychiatric disorders, so unfortunately we do tend to get misdiagnosed quite easily. The real annoyance here isn't that the most appropriate label is missed, it's that our life experience is missed. The reasonableness of our response to life is missed. As Lorna Wing writes in *The Autistic Spectrum:*

> "The first type of error is mistaking an uncomplicated autistic disorder for a psychiatric illness. Adults of borderline, average or high ability with undiagnosed autistic disorders have been wrongly labelled as suffering from any and every psychiatric condition." (1996)

It is likely that during adolescence, when transitioning hormones are taking their toll on males and females alike, that those of us on the spectrum are most at risk of being misdiagnosed as bi-polar. While I would continue to experience sensitivities to my hormones throughout my life, for the most part it was at its worst in my late teens and early twenties.

Although bi-polar disorder (Like ADHD) can coexist with Asperger's, a true bi-polar disorder does not settle with hormones, making this almost certainly an incorrect label for me. Also, the extremes experienced in a bi-polar disorder are often longer lasting (going on for days and weeks of one then the other) than the reactionary behaviours of an Aspergian woman at that time of the month. After my misdiagnosis of bi-polar disorder, I was put on lithium for the next four years.

Chapter 15

WHEN EVERYTHING IS JUST RED

A few months after I had met him, Adrian graduated from high school and prepared to start university. Selfishly, I was nervous about losing him to another environment. For different reasons I had many anxieties around being rejected or abandon by people I loved; hence, when my feelings for Adrian intensified so did my fear of losing him, and I began exhibiting behaviour associated with borderline personality disorder, a personality disorder often triggered by experiences of abandonment. I was terrified of losing the people I loved. Convinced that if I gave them any space they would disappear, I was willing to go to any lengths to keep them close.

If Adrian couldn't be with me when I wanted, I became distressed. If he didn't respond to my distress, which he quickly stopped doing, I'd threaten self-harm. I felt I meant it every time. The first time he responded by staying. This shocked me. I couldn't have imagined that anyone might care enough to give up their own plans to keep me safe.

Being shown that I was *that* important to someone else was like getting a drink of water when I was dying of thirst, but only enough to sustain me for a little while. I reached for the water again and again. My threats of self-harm became a commodity, but it didn't come from a place of contemplated manipulation. It came from an instinct for emotional survival. A desperate and painful need to not be left again.

I am reminded of a movie I once watched about mountain climbers. In the opening scene three people were hanging onto a rope, the rope started to fray and everyone was going to fall to their deaths. The middle man on the rope took out his knife and cut the rope, causing him – and the man below him – to fall to their deaths so that the person above them could have a better chance of survival. He had taken responsibility for his own weight. He knew that hanging on was an act of selfish cowardice with no reward for anyone. Watching that scene gave me a sense of shame because I knew that responsibility and selflessness were things I lacked.

When I was desperate for love I clawed at it and gripped it and refused to let go, no matter how bad it was for the other person. With Adrian I had become a neurotic and frightened mess, constantly seeking clarification about what we were to each other and how he felt about me. To make it worse, as I became this clingy person his friends started to see me as controlling and manipulative. There was this if-it's-meant-to-happen-it-will-just-happen attitude.

I never understood how anyone could be so calm and relaxed about these things; I couldn't imagine how much safer other people's lives had been than mine. If there was some universal grand plan, I at least wanted a print-out of the itinerary. And finally, somewhere between our friendship and my clinginess, Adrian became my boyfriend. My behaviour left me feeling sated but pathetic and unworthy of the love I got.

Puberty is said to start and end between the ages of ten and seventeen. In my life that was a time of many physical and emotional changes after which I was supposed to be biologically mature. But for me this “maturity” was like a second childhood: I was free to recklessly test the boundaries of my own limits and the limits I had with others. I discovered in sometimes thoughtless and other times timid ways what I could cope with and what I could inflict upon my relationships without losing them or myself. After leaving high school Adrian and Taylor and I started looking for a place to live together. Living with them was difficult for me, and for them.

While I could be bad at planning, I was worse at letting things just happen. In a day there would be plans I had made with Adrian and Taylor, and there would be the plans I had made in my own head - trivial ideas I had about how things were meant to happen. Once I had it in my head that something would happen a certain way I needed it to happen exactly that way. This is why I couldn't walk away from the dominoes when I was younger. I needed to complete my plan, but dominoes didn't mind how rigid I was or how many times I'd start over until I got the outcome I wanted. People were different. They couldn't be controlled. When I tried they would usually leave. My frustration when they did this was unbearable.

Taylor was an overly generous free spirit who would be hours late to our plans because she had picked up someone stranded on the side of the road and had driven them an hour out of her way to their destination. One time she showed up at our apartment with a father and his son whom she'd found stranded in the airport. I was blamed for my inability to cope with the unexpected.

I was seen as narcissistic, controlling and just plain rude or uncaring. Sometimes crazy. My ability to communicate my feelings was another source of great uncertainty, which I avoided with Taylor (because I loved her but wasn't sure I could hang on to her.) for fear of getting it wrong. A quirk of my relationships has been that when I love someone, but aren't sure they'll stay I hold back. When I know they'll stay I let loose. When they survive that – and few have – we often get along really well. It's not fair and it's not the way I want to be, but it's the way I have been.

With Taylor I'd avoid mentioning my upset until I couldn't stand it any more and finally I'd bring it up, often weeks or months later. Making me seem more crazy and passive aggressive for ruminating on a tiny detail.

Which was another thing. Details that bothered me could be large or small. I could stay silent far too long about something large. I could make far too big a deal about something small.

My difficulty with explaining myself meant that, to others, I seemed hugely unpredictable and irrational and bitchy. But my actions didn't feel chosen, they felt big and overwhelming and they happened so fast I didn't have time to make choices. I would very quickly find myself in a place of not caring what I lost or destroyed. Then I'd come to, only to be surrounded by regret, wishing I could take my words and actions back.

I don't want to shrug off all accountability because that's not fair. It's the job of each person to manage their own emotional calibration, but it's hard to explain how out of control I felt. I could have tantrums without a moment's notice. Most of what we fought about was control. I wanted to control everything about my environment, from when they were there, to who they brought over and how the house looked.

And when Adrian and I were in the midst of a fight (or when I was simply in the midst of a meltdown) I would become all the more rigid about how I needed him to navigate us out of the suffocating darkness. It was like my mind became a maze and only certain moves could get us out of the argument. One moment at a time. Each one fragile. Each move had to be correct. I needed a certain amount of apologies or an exact set of words to clarify that he understood my pain.

I was selfishly ugly about my painful insecurities, and rigid about the way in which I could accept love. The rules dictated that I could not tell Adrian what I felt or needed, because if he didn't know on his own, he mustn't really love me. He had to guess right. Or better yet, understand. Turn left here and right there – and even if he made every move correctly, better than anyone else might have done, and we were almost out of my crazy labyrinth of rage, it would still only take one wrong move and we'd be right back in the middle of it.

I was a terror. I didn't mean to be. I was still waiting for a parent who would come along and magically see into my soul, understand what I needed at all times and meet those needs or at least care enough to try. I was in as much pain as I put everyone else through. But everyone else could just leave, and most people did. Taylor quickly moved out. Adrian's friends grew to hate me. I was that unhealthy relationship that one friend will try to get another friend out of. But Adrian never left.

Finally there seemed to be a moment when I hit rock bottom, when I admitted I was miserable. I sobbed that I was lost. That I hated the lithium I had been taking, and that I *knew* – despite my horrible, inexcusable behaviour – that I wasn't bi-polar and this wasn't right. I was asking Adrian to *just* be my friend again, not to want anything more from me, but not to leave me either; I couldn't handle being left, and I wanted him to let me (the craziest woman he had ever known) go off my meds while he stayed. And somehow, without any reason to, he looked at me and said, "Okay."

We started to make a project of monitoring and investigating where my emotions were coming from. One issue we could see was that I was more likely to have a meltdown if the house was overheated. Heat was a trigger, and humidity was an even bigger one. If I am physically uncomfortable I find it very hard to focus on anything else or feel anything else. Everything will be about me expressing my misery.

In some cases, like with temperature, it can help to do positive reframing: to associate the heat with something I enjoy. I started to make a conscious effort to think, *Oh great I can wear my shorts and flip-flops,* whenever it got warm. It worked, and after a while I had an automatic positive association to warmth. Another trigger was the wrong kind of work.

In the three years since leaving high school I had gone through many jobs (including: working at a newspaper printing press in the middle of the night, picking gum off the underside of bleachers, working as an orderly in a retirement care home, working in a gas station, working at countless fast food restaurants). Most of my jobs were stressful, monotonous, shift work. Adrian allowed me, for a time, to stop working, with the agreement that when I went back to it I would look for something less stressful. With much effort and reduced stimulation – and without the lithium – my temperament began to improve.

Still, there were other times when I got upset and it was more difficult to understand what it was about. Times when it seemed not to make sense and I couldn't verbalize, even to myself, what I was feeling. This can come from the over-intensity of feelings. This intensity is again related to the circumference of awareness.

I might see a big blob of red but not know what that red is a part of, and I'd have to zoom out to see that it's a red balloon at a circus. Because when something takes up the whole of your awareness it cannot properly be seen. It cannot be measured. It doesn't have a size or weight. It doesn't matter where it came from or how trivial it may seem to others. It simply is. Everything is red. I may know I'm feeling excited; but good excitement or anxiety? They often feel a lot alike. And often when everything is just red, that's when there's a meltdown.

I can get particularly upset during special occasions. Giddiness = Stress = Cortisol = My most exacting and rigid self = Misery for myself and everyone around me. When I was little I was deeply hurt that things often didn't go to plan, especially when the plan was important. And so my birthday was a great source of anxiety and I spent the day worrying that everything would go wrong. Year after year I would have the worst behaviour on my birthdays, and as a result no one wanted to be around me.

By the time I reached my twenties I thought the day was cursed; I was completely missing that my sensitivities were greatly heightened on this particular day, that *I* was the one ruining it. The solution, I would later realize, was to not try and have a big celebration. Plan something small and simple. To put my attention on one detail that was very unlikely to go wrong (like spending the day with my best friend) so that whatever else happened was just a detail.

Chapter 16

"AM I THE BUNNY BOILER?"

Adrian and I transitioned back into friends. For a year I journaled and reflected. I felt pathetic about the desperation with which I loved people and about how I tried to control them. Everyone else I knew seemed more able to let go, to accept some degree of unpredictability in others. They had multiple interests and relationships, so that no one person meant the world to them. My relationships were all sparse, my social abilities unpredictable. I had a history of problems I didn't understand.

In my everyday life I looked to others for guidance, and so during my year of self-reflection I looked at myself through the eyes of popular psychology. I looked back over my childhood and examined the way I had been treated by my parents. I grew to thoroughly believe they were the source of my problems, that - knowing this - I could now fix everything about myself and move on and be someone completely different.

I declared that I would never again hang on too tightly to another. I expected that, with sheer self-control (something that is not my strong suit), I would be able to follow this rule. Next time I fell in love I wouldn't cling. I would do from the beginning what I had waited until the end to do with Adrian. I would let go. But I was so bad at this.

At university I had a slew of very brief, very turbulent relationships. I dated a lawyer, an electronics shop manager, a psychiatrist (who told me I had a social deficit). All my difficulties within relationships were still there. I would try to pace expressions of interest to match their own; it was hard. Other people seemed to exchange multiple phone calls a day with the people they dated. There must be a way that the rhythm of calling and effort making is established, but who establishes it?

My confusion in this area wasn't very different from my confusion about how to make friends in primary school. It was all about how to get the connection I wanted. What if the guy calls once a week and I'd like to talk multiple times a day? How is this changed? Do people talk about it? Or is their a subtlety to it? I know from my work as a psychotherapist that it is not only women on the spectrum who ask these questions. But like a dislike for loud noises, and a problem with faces, this was on another level. And so was my neurosis when it came to dating. One problem was that the people I dated often had boundaries where I still had open wounds.

While I was at my first university I dated a professor, he was in his mid forties. I liked that he was mature and grounded. I believed what we were doing was really dating, but looking back I realize he never took it seriously. He would never have told anyone about me. I remember early on that he told me women his age didn't think sex was such a big deal, that they would want sex from the very beginning of a relationship, and so I went to bed with him from the beginning. I would spend the weekends at his house, like it had been when I was younger, it was nice to have somewhere to go. Foe me it was an escape from my crowded dorm room. For him it was always about the sex though.

I got left a lot, but in many cases things were not ended properly. Most of my partners would either stop calling and stop taking my calls, but if I did manage to get a hold of them they would insist they had simply been busy. If I asked if they still wanted a relationship with me, they would say yes, then dodge my calls for the next few weeks. Sometimes a man might say he wanted to "take a break" but not that we were over. Like anyone I could ignore the signs, when I wanted to, but if someone didn't say we were over, I had no closure. I needed things to be clear and real. I didn't interpret behaviours that conflicted with words because it made no sense to me that a person would find it difficult to be honest.

What made dating worse – me more self-conscious – was that there was a prevailing attitude that something was *more* wrong with me for not reading between the lines. There is a common view – shared by men and women – that "boys will be boys". Which means that forty- and fifty-year-old men will be boys. Because most other people seemed be okay with communicating things in subtle ways, and accepting that men had an agenda while women had to be the gatekeepers of morality. This meant that, at 20, I was "stupid" that "I didn't have my head on right" that I was guilty of not taking care of myself, rather than a forty-five year old philosophy professor was abusing his power.

One partner who inspired more self reflection was a man named Andrew, whom I was particularly hung up on. In this relationship I was my most neurotic self. I was always trying to pace my behaviours to match his own. I called when he called. If he left a message I could return the call the same day, but if he called and we spoke then I needed to let the same number of days go by before I made the effort to call him. Using this method we only spoke twice a week. Once to arrange a date, and once to confirm. I wanted more. More phone calls, more attention from him, for myself to feel relaxed.

The relationship was brief, about six weeks, which was normal for me, (not unlike employment) but there were things he said during our time together that impacted me more than others. Once, during an argument he called me "exhausting". I immediately responded, "At least you can leave." The words came out before I knew how much I meant them. Before I understood that "exhausting" was the perfect word to describe how I was feeling and had been feeling for years.

Most of what I understood about my

feelings still came from others – like a child needing to have her feelings named – often others didn't quite understand what I was going through. It's a powerful feeling when someone says the word that describes the feeling of another. It causes a vibration. This word shook me. He was right. I was exhausted. How had I never realized this?

His ability to understand me and explain me to myself was intoxicating. I was young and all I really knew was that I had lost everything else that was stable in my life and I was pretty sure what I was feeling was love. I had said, "I love you." to basically any man who was happy to hear it. Falling in love happened way more times than I can actually remember. Literally. I'm sure there are people who I've been certain I wanted to spend the rest of my life with, whose names I've completely forgotten by now. Only this had never really bothered me before Andrew.

My constant falling in love and having my heart crushed into a million pieces before moving on had never really worried me to this extent. Despite my efforts to act normal, or act the way he acted, I think my feelings were obvious because of the anxiety I must have exhibited when I was with him.

I had said, "I love you." too much to too many. And that fact alone made me not want to *ever* say it to him. I realized I was holding on to a completely overused sentiment which I did not want to give and he did not want to receive. So I never told him.

In the end the relationship fizzled away. He grew more and more distant, I had dated enough men to translate what his behaviour likely meant, and I ended the relationship as, at least, doing so gave me clarity rather than confusion or false hope. We agreed to stay friends. Then, I thought, happily, that being friends meant I didn't have to worry about "behaving myself" any more and I began calling with abandon.

One day Andrew called me back and whispered that I was calling him too much and did I not know he could see the caller id. Again, what's too much? I could call Miya, Taylor or Mrs. R.S. as often as I wanted, multiple times a day and never be whispered at. And actually the thought of caller id hadn't even crossed my mind. Like lots of things in my life, this was brought to my attention as something most people would have thought about. I felt ashamed for not being more self-aware (or other-person aware).

Writing about this, along with many other parts of my story, brings old stuff back up for me. It's all fresh again. The attractions, the hurt, the embarrassing behaviours. Only this time I see it through the eyes of my thirty-six-year-old self, who feels very protective of my twenty-two-year-old self who didn't understand herself or the world around her. Today when I'm uncertain about something I ask my husband for his opinion. I tell him about my ex-boyfriend and I ask, “Is calling twice a day too much?”

And he says, “Yes, calling twice a day is too much.”

Oh. I was hoping he would reassure me and tell me it was perfectly normal and Andrew was just being weird.

Then he continues, “It might have scared him a bit.”

I'm scary? “Am I like that woman from *Fatal Attraction*?”

“What's *Fatal Attraction*?”

“You know, that movie?” No. He doesn't. “Okay, so there's this guy who sleeps with this woman and then she gets obsessed with him and won’t leave him alone. Then she breaks into his house and kills his pet bunny.”

"Oh my god, that's horrible," he says with the shock-horror of a person who's hearing the story for the first time.

"Yea! That's what I'm saying. Am I the bunny boiler?"

"No. Of course not. You would never kill someone's bunny."

"That's not what I mean. I mean do I scare people like *that.*"

"I would never worry that you would do those things, but you can be scary. You scare me sometimes."

"I scare you?" Suddenly my self-esteem plummets to a new depth.

"Sometimes." He looks at me. "Why are you concerned about all this? I'm in love with you and the rest of it happened fifteen years ago."

Oh my god, he's right. A few months ago I even got upset about my first-grade teacher who made me miss my playtime because someone said I knocked over the crayons when I didn't. (For about five minutes I thought about writing her a letter to let her know how much this had affected me in my life.) *What's wrong with me?*

"So why are you married to me if I'm so scary and neurotic?"

He looked at me again, seeing that I was now in the foetal position, and let out a loud laugh. He kissed my forehead and said, “I have an early lecture tomorrow. I can’t stay up all night listing out all the reasons I love you.”

Okay. I get that. I'm now extremely conscious of my tendency to push myself on others, and don't want to do that here by keeping him engaged in the conversation longer than he's prepared for. In an attempt to wrap this up quickly I say, “So what you're saying is that the good stuff outweighs the bad stuff?” Notice how this is a simple yes or no question.

“You are one of the most kind people I know, you are generous and sexy and honest and loyal and ...”

Urgh! “So is that a yes?”

“Yes.”

“Okay. I'm done with you for tonight. Go to sleep.”

Chapter 17

MY SUMMER OF ZEN IN SAN ANTONIO

The room was still and quiet and I stood there still and quiet with it. I could hear the evening birds outside my window. I wondered for a moment what it was like to be a bird, to not have to worry about anything; there must be bliss in living such a simple life. Standing in the stillness, I let my mind go in all different directions, trying to get a sense of my immediate plan, to stay or not to stay. After some thought I came up with a plan for a summer of Zen reflection, a plan to be less reactionary and more trusting, another sabbatical. After that I got my bedding and lay down on the floor.

My special dreams had been coming more

vividly in the past few weeks and I had become frightened of sleeping in my bedroom, so I lay there on the floor of my living room. I knew experiencing my feelings was going to be a part of this plan: I meant to start a long and exhausting journey. There's that word again, “exhausting”. I supposed I could either expend energy to hide, energy to panic while feeling lost, or energy to change. And finally I had chosen the latter. Either way, tonight, at least, I was going to rest.

As I lay there I thought of a swing at a playground rocking back and forth, and whenever my thoughts tried to drift into the dangerous dark void that surrounded this singular thought I forced them back to the swing. For me that was an accomplishment. I had never *forced* myself to focus, I always followed my imagination wherever it took me, but not that night. That night I was certain there was nothing safe to think about, so I focused on the swing until sleep relieved me of my efforts. That was my first experience with meditation.

My first sabbatical had happened after my father moved us in with Carol and her daughter, after everyone at school had started calling me a lesbian; that had mostly been about getting away from people and discovering the relief of being alone. My second sabbatical had started as I was leaving Adrian. That had been about trying not to cling to people. Each time I had taken to being alone I had sought to understand myself. I would make decisions about how to be in the world.

As a teenager I decided I would be happier if I could just conform. As a young adult I decided my parents were responsible for most of my difficulties. Conforming had its good points. Processing my childhood abuse had it benefits. But I never found that one answer that would make my life easier. That would make me normal. This time I was going to try a different approach.

My third and favourite sabbatical came on the heels of losing my place at my first university and breaking up with Andrew and feeling very alone and lost. This wasn't a new feeling: my temporary success at fitting in got me into relationships and jobs, but again and again I kept losing these things. Others my age had families they were close to, or a stable group of friends, or were doing well in school, or even working on their careers. My sparse attachments and the lack of stability in my life made it hard for me to feel safe in the world, which made my anxieties and needs very heavy.

Being a vulnerable woman was no longer politically correct, and I didn't want to be one anyway, I wanted to be someone confident and independent and socially savvy. But I had deep insecurities. I had entered my young adulthood with a history I was ashamed of and couldn't explain. I had spent the last eight years of my life being exhaustingly neurotic about getting everything right. Doing penance for my mistakes until I would run out of energy, until I went mute at school, until I had a meltdown.

The thing I most wanted in life was to have someone else approve of me, and I honestly felt my only chance of finding that was if I disowned the me that was still scared and hurt. The me that was completely and utterly desperate for love. I kept hoping that if I hid long enough I would one day really be someone different. But even when I was in hiding I was still getting hurt. Whether my broken heart this time was about the end of another relationship or about something that had been missing far longer, I knew I couldn't keep going like this. I had to explore what I had been doing wrong.

I needed to understand how my behav-iours had contributed to my repeated experiences of rejection. That is not to say that I take responsibility for all the mistreatment that came at the hands of others. The abuse. The bullying. My personality, while it may have made me odd, did not give people the right to treat me badly. But I wanted to understand what, specifically, my quirks were and where they came from. As I started to look at this I felt a deep sense of insecurity mix with memories from the past.

It was hard to be objective, hard not to just be angry and blame, and hard not to go in the opposite direction and hold everything that I had been through as my fault and be totally insecure and ashamed of myself. It was clear that I was going to have to *first* deal with the opinions of others, the ideas they had about why I acted the way I did (which lingered in my head, continually telling me that it was all on purpose and I was attention-seeking or snobby or lazy or whatever), before I could honestly see my own explanations as something separate. I would have to dismiss all the internal criticisms so that I could hear my own voice and give myself an honest answer to my question. What am I doing wrong?

I thought about how I had become scared

of people in the last ten years of my life. It was really since starting middle school that this fear had grown and changed me. I suffered from PTSD, although I wouldn't have called it that back then. Not because my feelings were undeserving of that term. They certainly were. But being bullied in school was treated as something that "everyone" went through; even corporal punishment was regarded this way. And the people who didn't get over it by the time they reached adulthood were further stigmatised as not wanting to move on and as wanting to blame others for their misery in life.

Because I didn't want to be further stigmatised, I tried to shake it off, to pretend none of this had the huge effect on me which it had. I tried not to act scared of others, or scared of myself. I tried to hide the damage that was there – which caused more damage, the way it would if someone insisted on trying to walk on a sprained ankle.

I declared to myself that I *had* to acknowledge my feelings of hurt and examine the past so that I could properly heal. Doing this didn't come from a desire to blame others, but from a need to stop blaming myself. Never letting go of my anxiety and anger meant that it kept coming out at the wrong times and with the wrong people. I decided that dealing with my emotions, however far back they were from, was a valid (if not totally necessary) thing to do, not just for my own self-indulgence but for anyone I would interact with in the future.

So in my barely furnished apartment I sat down on my rug with my notebook and started to write out the words in my head, to make them real so I could challenge them, the phrases that echoed again and again whenever I messed up, whenever I wanted to hide or cry, whenever I wanted help or understanding. "Oh, poor Kate. Everyone must feel sorry for Kate."

Much of what I had internalized came from my parents, but it also came from my teachers and my classmates. "How come everyone else can do it?" "Isn't it a shame we have to wait for Kate?" "Why don't you defend yourself?" "Are you retarded?" Their cruel words were theirs, but without wanting to I had been carrying all of it as if it was my own. I needed to sit down, remember, and examine everything I was carrying; pull out what was mine to own and keep, and give everyone else their crap back.

In the weeks to come I would journal a lot and write long emotive letters that I was never going to send. Then I would climb into the shower and let the water wash away all the emotions I had brought to the surface. This was a crucial last step for me: the processing of the past was necessary, but I tended to have circular thought patterns.

Many a time trying to release emotions would only bring them into my awareness, where I could not move on. Having a shower was my way of affirming that I was now done. After processing, I would take a walk in the sun, surrounded by hibiscus flowers and the waxy blue-green leaves of tropical shrubs. I recuperated in the beauty of nature, affirming to myself that I *was a part of* this nature, that I was entitled to a place in this beautiful world.

After several days of venting by pen every hurtful and shameful experience I could recall, I very gently started to wade through all the hyperbole and judgement and look for the common bare bones of what everyone was saying and what I honestly thought to be true amongst it all. My biggest, most obvious issues were my hyper-sensitivities and difficulties with staying organized, which I didn't understand myself. My other big issue was that I was often seen as being self-centred and uncaring about how others felt. I was always missing what others needed or expected of me. This is called Theory of Mind, and was what I was most embarrassed about.

With lots of self-love and reassurance, I decided to let go of my defences and start the search for how I might change to improve this. I came up with a formula to help me start looking at people's emotions. I turned what I wasn't getting into an equation where I had to fill in the missing value.

Formula

SITUATION

+

(UNKNOWN EMOTION OF OTHER PERSON)

= BEHAVIOUR.

Like:

4 + (X) = 6

What must the value of X be?

What was the other person feeling?

For the most part I could see the situation and I could see the behaviour. Again this had to do with my circumference of awareness. I was holding the two visible parts of the equation separate from each other. If a child broke something in a shop, that was the *situation*, and the parent might *respond* by yelling, or they might respond by speaking to the child in a vaguely affectionate but condescending voice, "Oh *dahling*, not again ..." Or they might quietly reassure their child that it was an accident and apologize to staff and offer to pay.

I could see the two visible parts to the equation: the situations and response, but guessing at the emotion meant connecting them to each other and me to them. Not an easy task for someone who sees the world in bite-size chunks.

I would take the two factors I could see: Situation + X = Response. Then I would imagine I was in that situation and ask myself what feeling would cause me to get that response? What was the value of X? I concluded that the parent who yells is feeling insecure. And the grandiose parent is feeling too insecure to even acknowledge their insecurity so they are having an inauthentic reaction. And the insecurity likely came from their own upbringing or neurological make-up, so I couldn't judge them negatively for it. But the parent that doesn't yell but helps their child is confident that others will be understanding, which is also likely a result of upbringing or neurology, which is something no individual gets to dictate, and so in a way mental balance is as fickle as physical beauty.

After a few recorded observations, I decided that how we feel about ourselves, our place in this world, is often what determines how fearful and anxious we are of it. We either know that we are good and deserving of happiness and in that case we have an inner expectation of security, or we don't know these things. If we are a parent standing in the middle of a strange shop and imagining that we are being judged by all the more-valid people around us, then the world is a scary place.

I definitely didn't have an inner sense of security, I didn't have a consistent group of people in my life giving me approval, I had tons of situations where I was judged for my odd behaviours; and for those reasons and others I was very fearful of the world. And this affected my ability to have relationships or believe I could sustain any of the self-growth I managed. I was afraid of failing, and I wanted to stop being afraid of that; I wanted to know that I could *give myself* the approval and love I longed for whether I managed to do anything else with my life or not.

I wanted to be one of those people who seemed to have an internal reservoir of self-confidence. I wanted - in the future - to be one of those parents who don't need to yell or put on a show, whose only job is taking care of the needs of their children. Maybe, like physical beauty, it was something that could be worked towards. I started practising meditation, reading books around mindfulness and overcoming PTSD.

Like most of my projects, I took this to the extreme: on days I worked I would meditate for four hours; on days I didn't work I meditated for seven. I quickly felt more emotionally balanced, but at the expense of being almost entirely withdrawn from the world around me. I could feel my anxieties from the past begin to dull, and I stopped feeling that I had to put on a constant act to avoid being hated, which made me feel less resentful and defensive; and when I was around people I found them less abrasive.

As I made advances I embraced the world and forgave the past. I was feeling emotionally open and ready to go out and try again. With practice I found understanding the feelings and needs of others became more instinctual. I no longer had to pretend; I could simply be my authentic self and use my growing anticipation of others in how I interacted with them. The response I got when I was able to show someone genuine understanding was a sense of membership that I had never felt before. The wall was starting to slide open. I was becoming part of the world.

As if I had just learned to drive, the thrill of all this intrigued me and made all people more interesting as each one presented an opportunity to practise my new skill. I started to recognize defensiveness and self-consciousness; I started to know what to say to reassure someone, and understand what was too personal or what was *just* personal enough. It took a lot of forethought for me, way more than I suspect a neurotypical had to put in, but during this time in my life something in my brain was changing too, all my efforts were gradually becoming instinctual. Like learning a new language, it started just coming to me.

I didn't instantly become hugely popular and have tons of new friends, and I wouldn't have wanted that. But what did happen was that I *connected* with people briefly, and remained true to myself. Exchanges were far less scary when the emphasis was on the other person, and as long as my attention was on what the other person needed I was far less worried about what they thought of me. Most people simply wanted to feel that they had been heard and seen; and working on giving that to them was all I needed to do: I didn't need to agree, I didn't need to pretend. If I listened, they liked me.

When the summer was over I returned to the town where I had been living before. I would see people who had known me just a couple of years earlier, and from them I would hear many comments on how much I had changed. One person even flat-out said, “I didn't like you before. But I do now.” The problem, though, with having a heavy-going reflective programme like the one I had been on was that, while it can be great for making huge strides forward, it's usually not sustainable long-term. And for me this sort of routine (because it's such a big effort) is the first to go when life starts getting stressful again. I have learned that it's better to adopt small sustainable habits that can be kept up with even on the busy days. Especially on the busy days.

After I left San Antonio my pendulum started swinging again. Some of my growth around Theory of Mind stayed in place, but I was left with a new vulnerability. I had gone from being overly scared of people to *realizing* that I had been overly scared, and in response I had become overly trusting and vulnerable again. At first, social interactions went better for me: people seemed to regard me as someone with confidence; but I was still sensitive to being over-stimulated. I had almost forgotten about how sensitive I could be when I wasn't meditating for multiple hours a day.

Chapter 18

CALLING IT 'RAPE' FELT MELODRAMATIC

I still struggled with basic life skills like staying organized, paying bills, getting places on time. In this I acted cute and ditzy, copying certain slapstick characters off popular sitcoms, so that I seemed to be playing down the importance of things rather than struggling to cope. But in reality I was twenty-three and couldn't keep up with life the way that other people my age did. Despite my multiple sabbaticals for self-reflection life was still much more exhausting for me than it seemed to be for others.

I changed jobs three times in three months; at my third job things seemed better. I met a couple of people who I started hanging out with, who had a social circle which I was invited into. One night there was a party at someone's house. I wore a light blue cotton sundress; it hid my muscular calves, which I hated, and showed off my collarbone, which I loved.

When I was overwhelmed by people I still fell back into discounting my discomfort and pretending to be fine, but I had gotten better at acting chilled out. Being detached was my new strategy for surviving anything that overwhelmed me; it was slightly different from "zoning out" because I chose it. I didn't feel embarrassed or concerned that I should be saying or doing something. I simply chose to not care. I made an art of seeming detached from any social concern, which was how confident people seemed to be. Parties and group gatherings still made me anxious, and, as I usually did, I quickly drank too much and got nauseated. One of the guys at the party offered to let me sleep in his room. I crawled between his sheets and as my stomach settled my fatigue got stronger.

I woke up in a state of disassociation. My dress was around my waist and a man was inside of me. It wasn't like sex. It was like watching someone engaging in the completely solo act of relieving themselves in my body while I just lay there motionless. Only it continued happening even as I gradually regained consciousness.

As the reality of the situation dawned on me, so did the fact that it was already too late, and in an attempt to hang on to my sanity I clung to that disassociated state. I stared at the pattern on the sheets and allowed myself to be lost there. Wandering around in a mental daze, I tried to contextualize. To rationalise. To do anything but experience what was happening in the moment. But the feelings crept in, slow and muted. Not like the clear screams one would expect in a moment of such violation. *I don't want this*, I thought as he penetrated deeper into me.

I wish I could write here that I screamed. That I fought back. I wish I had been the girl with the dragon tattoo. Except I didn't want that. I had worked so hard to convince myself that people weren't scary. I didn't want to spend my life being angry. I didn't want *more* to process. I couldn't deal with more. I wanted to be Zen. I would fight for being Zen. So I very aggressively clung to my passivity.

But sometimes Zen just isn't possible. No matter how I tried to convince myself I was okay I just wanted for that moment in my life not to be taking place. But then there was another thought that kept me from responding. I had had so much sex in my life with people I hadn't really cared for. I had bartered it for friendship. Then just for company or a safe place to be for a few hours. I had enjoyed it despite the fact that I was often using it as a tool to keep men who didn't love me from leaving. It seemed unfair to say that, *this time*, because I did not enjoy it, and did not want it, I was entitled to complain. Was I really allowed to care about sex now?

I had used it as a tool so many times that now the issue of consent almost seemed like a matter that didn't apply to me. Like the right to care about my body was something I had given up and was no longer entitled to. Like the right to report my childhood abuse did not apply to me. To complain I was raped would have felt hypocritical. I had been hurting me longer than he had. I had to get through it quietly. Not make it a bigger deal than it was on its own. My only escape was if I could really believe this wasn't important. Then I could move on. Tomorrow I could be someone else. Tomorrow I would be someone who took care of herself. Who was clean and entitled to respect. Tomorrow the world could start being safe.

After he was done, I went home and showered and went to my own bed. I lay there trying to convince myself that it was over. That I had left it behind in that room. But really I had brought it with me. Regardless of my choice to not let it affect me, it was there. At the core of me. In a most personal place, growing like a fungus, moving from his bed onto mine. Taking over everything. I felt disgusted and so many other things. I felt anger, fear, grossness, sadness, loss, and fear again. More fear than I had ever had. And most of all I felt ashamed for letting it happen. Why hadn't I screamed?

Voiced or not, a scream was there in my throat making it hard to breath; so instead I cried. I lay there crying and gasping for breath until I fell asleep. When I woke up, the events were still there playing over and over again in my head. I missed work that day. I didn't call in because I didn't know what to say. I knew I would be classed as a “no-show” which meant an immediate termination. It didn't matter, I couldn't think about anything but what had happened. The man had been friends with others at the party. I had been there on a guest pass. No one had heard me scream, since I hadn't. Everyone would be on his side if I tried to speak up.

They would say that I was flaky and awkward, that no one knew me that well. Or they would *think* that and then say something more discrediting. Maybe they'd say I was a slut. It would be harder for the authorities to help me than not help me. I'd have to give personal details about everything. Why had I been drinking so much? Why had I been in his bed? Why hadn't I been wearing underwear? Did I honestly think this was his fault when I made the choices that I made? Wasn't this mess really mine? Did I honestly expect someone else to clean it up for me?

As I lay in my bed processing and feeling everything, the question came down not to what was right and wrong but what I could live with now. I had learned how to process old traumas, things in the past that were over and I could evaluate from a safe distance, but I didn't know how to sit with the darkness of uncertainty and hold myself together while taking care of myself. The only way to have certainty about this was to decide it was over, to keep quiet and avoid feeling.

I thought also about the very real

possibility that I would be blamed for drinking to much, for passing out. I thought of the teasing in high school – that supposedly everyone went through and was just “kids being kids” that I was too whiny. There was the abuse of my childhood. Being told that it was my behaviour that was the problem. And I knew that being blamed for your own suffering was a trauma in itself. Not telling was the only way I could protect myself now. I didn't know how to be an adult, I only knew how to hide the child that I still was, and so that's what I did. I no longer had a job or the means of making my rent, and I no longer felt safe in my apartment. So I packed up most of my things and, leaving my bed behind, I moved out.

Chapter 19

"OH, SO YOU'RE GOING BY KATHERINE NOW?

Seen from the outside, I had just lost another job and moved out from another apartment. My life had fallen apart *again*. And even I saw it like this. I just couldn't figure out how to grow up. I kept expecting that at some point I'd snap out of this latest funk, that I'd soon be able to live the way everyone else my age was living, hold a job, work enough hours to pay rent, get along with a roommate, know how (or who) to trust while also being careful with myself. Deal with things without totally shutting down.

But even the daily anxiety that everyone else coped with I couldn't handle. I couldn't process everything fast enough to be that balanced person I wanted to be. I had gone from being devastated and anxious to simply feeling numb; I was a lump living in my mother's office – but underneath the numbness I could sense the pain. Waiting. Ready to overwhelm me the moment I faced it. And I wanted to do anything other than that.

I could easily claim that it was the abuse from my childhood that incited me to do what I did next. I had anger over our past. But that wasn't why. Our history, in my mind, gave me permission. But the real reason was that I was desperate to have things I didn't have and hadn't earned. I wanted to be a grown up with security and comfort, the person I imagined I should have been by then, the person I had planned to be. I wanted a life I was starting to think I might never figure out how to get. That's why I did it.

I applied for a credit card in my mother's name. I went into her filing cabinet got the information I'd need and I filed an application online. I was staying at her house so it was simple. When the card came in the post I went shopping. When I was shopping I became one of those real people. Unblemished. Grown up.

New shopping strips were opening up all around. All the shops were made to look

European and rustic, all the products were gourmet and environmentally friendly and expensive. I bought cushions and toiletries: expensive soaps and shampoos, things suggestive of what I was craving. Care, comfort and renewal. I adopted an air of entitlement as my life took on a glutinous melancholy of artificial comforts. My shopping didn't go unnoticed. Eventually my mother looked in my wallet, found her unfamiliar credit card and told me not to come back.

While, in light of how the last party had gone, it seemed like I should have stopped going to parties, I did just the opposite. I crashed on people's sofas, stayed for a few weeks here and there, I left owing money for food and rent, leaving a trail of enemies in my wake while I went looking for my next escape.

It was one thing to have people not like me because they didn't know or understand me, or because they themselves were just mean. In those cases I could always think to myself: *I would have liked me. I would have understood me.* And then eventually I could get over it and move on. What was more difficult was when I knew I wouldn't have liked me either. I would have kicked me out too. I might have taken care of a good friend going through something, acting out of character, but not a stranger. And to most people that's what I was. This was all they knew about me. I was a stranger and a burden. So I did the only thing I could do, I decided I didn't care.

When I burnt through all the friends of friends - and had nowhere else to go - for the first time in my life, I did what my father had alluded to years earlier, and I began sleeping in my car. The brakes were going but I managed to drive it, without incident, to a university parking lot in the next town. I chose to park near a dormitory because it had a communal toilet and wash room. I would wake from the passing lorries at 5a.m. and very badly need the facilities.

The first morning I discovered that the doors were locked from midnight until 6 a.m. only *after* running across the parking lot, at which point my need to urinate had become way more urgent. The car park was empty but also vast and well lit. I tried to imagine squatting over the gravel but I couldn't bring myself to do it.

Just then a house keeper came by. She scanned her ID and let me in. I relieved myself in the wash room. Before walking back out I noticed a TV room with a sofa. I wondered if I could get away with laying down there for an hour. I was the same age as the students sleeping in their rooms upstairs. The air-conditioning was an alluring contrast to the muggy morning air outside, but I didn't try it. I went back to my car.

On future mornings when I woke up too soon I would lay in my car knowing that if I moved it only made me more aware of my bladder. When it was time I would go and pee and wash up. No one else was up at six so I never saw anyone. Or no one saw me, which was more the point. After a bit I would return to my car and read or sit and stare out at the rising sun. The car park would get full. People would come and go. And I would sit. Then one day, a few hours into the morning, a random passer-by tapped on my window. “Turn on the radio!” he shouted and then walked away. Confused I did what he said.

It didn't take a second for me to understand. A plane had just crashed into one of the Twin Towers. I didn't know anyone in New York. I couldn't feel anything. About *any*thing. I didn't want to feel anything. I put a

CD on. I listened to Jewel singing one of her slow sultry lullabies And then, like a flood, it all came. I rested my head on the back of my seat and I cried. Openly. Unconcerned that people passing by might notice, knowing that just now, because of the news, it wouldn't even seem so out of place. I sobbed. Out of extreme sadness. Out of extreme fear. I didn't know what would come next. Nothing was as it had once been and it would never be the same again.

I wanted to go back to my summer of Zen. That had been the best version of me so far. In the last half year I had become someone very different. Someone I didn't recognize and wish I had never met at all. And yet I knew I had the possibility of both people inside of me. I told myself I could just flip the switch back. I could just decide, out of sheer will power, to walk out of this hole I had dug. Only I had no money, no address, no friends or family left. I made a plan. The way a robber plans one last heist when they are ready to get out of the business. I still had an old *empty* checking account I hadn't closed in San Antonio.

I drove to my new bank and I wrote myself three $500 cheques for cash. $500 was the limit for how much they would cash on the spot without waiting for the cheques to clear. I went to three branches and walked out of the last branch with $1500 in my purse. I used the cash to put down a deposit on another apartment and pay the first and last month's rent, after which the money was gone. I, then, decided I *needed* one last thing for my fresh start. I bought a new bed. In my mother's name. I got caught and quickly. Whereas my bad behaviours would once have earned me a detention or cost me a job, I was now going to jail.

The detective who took me in kept calling me Kathleen; I corrected him and he said, "Oh so you're going by Katherine now?" Then he looked at my face and asked why my eyes were red. I had been crying. *Obviously*. "Are you on drugs?" The message of the moment was that everything about me was suspicious, I was totally untrustworthy and he had no sympathy for me. He seemed, for the hour or so that he questioned and processed me, to get some sort of perverse satisfaction out of being nasty to me in any small way he could.

I spent a night in jail. The next morning Mrs. R.S. paid my bail. I had been avoiding her since that night at the party, dodging her calls for the past few months while I went on my crime rampage. Even after she got me out of jail I didn't tell her about the rape. I still didn't think of it as that and so I didn't tell anyone.

Eventually my mother tried to withdraw the charges that had been filed against me. She said she hadn't actually wanted to press charges when she phoned the police, she had simply wanted them to scare me and make me stop buying things in her name; but when she explained this to the detective, he said that it was too late. Since he knew of the crime, and because identity theft under all circumstances was a felony, he had no option but to pursue it. My mother wasn't pressing charges. The state of Texas was.

I spent the next year hiding from my parents and ended up living in a large house in Dallas, with five other people. One night, not long after I'd moved in, there was a party. I met a guy named Sam. He was the first person who didn't trigger any immediate reaction of fear or anger. It was such a difference from how I had felt towards men for the past year that I had to acknowledge it.

Sam was tall, handsome and goofy. The idea of intimacy of any kind made me cringe. But I didn't want to feel that way. I wanted to recover already, to stop making a mess out of my life. I thought if I could just convince myself it wasn't such a big deal, that I was being overly sensitive then maybe I could getting my bearings again. I borrowed a condom from one of my new housemates, I took Sam upstairs to my room, and had sex with him. I hated the whole thing. A few days later I packed what I had in my room into the back of my car and left.

I had been reading about a university up north that integrated meditation into the curriculum. I had been thinking about it for some time and realized now that I just had to go *then*. So I went. I drove through the night. The campus was snowy and hilly. I got there at five in the morning and parked in the admissions parking lot. I turned off the engine and got my blankets from the back seat, and my coat, and buried myself under everything the best I could.

Wired from all the driving I just laid there staring out into the darkness until the sun started peeking up over the hills. Most of my sunrises have happened after I'd been up all night partying. This one was different, in that it came at the end of a night spent alone in the dark. This one was particularly beautiful.

Chapter 20

ANOTHER FRESH START

For the first few months in Iowa I had nightmares every night. About the assault and jail and my mother and all the people I had upset over the last year. I couldn't remember actually having any dreams over the past year. It was like my mind had been wound up so tight that it was now frantically unravelling. Letting go of the stress. But I had no idea how or where to start dealing with it.

I had these unexpected pops of irritability; I had these moments of being completely irrational, even for me. Everyone at the university was extremely patient and called it "de-stressing". Which is a perfect name even if they couldn't imagine the crazy stuff that I was really letting out. They said I was in a state of transition, leaving the fast-paced world behind for this calmer, more coherent way of life. I was hopeful that this was true. I was very ready to let go of my past.

Sadly, by this point, regardless of whether or not I could recover, evidence of my pain could now be seen all over my body. I had been putting on weight ever since the assault. Food had been one of my escapes, a self-indulgence and a punishment all in one. But now my monthly cycle had stopped and I was starting to feel tired all the time, both of which I attributed to my dramatic weight gain. On top of that, I still had a court case waiting for me back in Texas. In many ways it seemed that the damage was done. It was too late to try and feel better now.

I had been given a new dorm room and a meal card. It felt a little surreal to go from such boundlessness to such containment, but this was the thing that steadied the ground for me. Over the weeks my nightmares went away and for a time I had nice dreams.

I had precognitive dreams, often about small things, but also about big things. I dreamt of crossing an ocean and finding myself on European shores and being blissful happy there as I met my soul mate and laughed and played with him. Then, as the weeks passed, I started struggling to get to sleep. I'd lie awake feeling like I had adrenaline searing through my veins. Sometimes I got these muscle spasms in my stomach, which I thought was an odd place to be getting muscle spasms.

One night, as I lay in my dark, quiet dorm room contemplating the oddness of it, getting muscle spasms in my stomach, I began to think about the nausea that was being triggered by the smells in the cafeteria, my new need to urinate every hour, and the woman who had taken my pulse in my Vedic Medicine class saying I was pregnant. I mean obviously that wasn't possible. Sam was the only person I had had sex with in the last year and we'd used a condom and it had already been four months. I would know by now if I was pregnant. I mean I couldn't ... "We used a condom!" I said out loud in the darkness. I needed to get a pregnancy test. Right away. I got up and swapped my yoga pants for blue jeans. I got in my car and I drove across town to the all-night grocery store.

Roughly twenty minutes later I was in the dorm's communal bathroom staring at the pink cross and thinking over and over again, *but we used a condom*. My grades were good. Life was calming down. The turnaround I had

had in the last three months had been a miracle. I did not want this. I didn't even have to think about it. I *knew* I didn’t want this. Some people were sentimental about the idea of babies. I was not one of them. People, girls sometimes thought I was cold because I didn't care. I thought children were okay, I didn't *dis*like them, but I didn't have a particular affection for them just because they were shorter than everyone else.

The next day I found a website that had information about couples wanting to adopt. Every couple had their own online profile with tons of information to read. I would read a few profiles a day in between classes, and started to fantasize about the life this child could have. At first my fantasies were beautiful and full of sunshine: a smiling toddler playing with blocks on a beige Berber carpet in a spacious, immaculately clean house. Books were everywhere, there was a piano in the corner, both the parents were intellectuals with lithe bodies, a result of all the yoga they were doing. Then gradually a cloud went in front of the sun, dimming the picture in my mind.

I started to wonder if I was bringing someone into the world who would struggle with life the way that I had. What if he ended up with parents who only pretended to be everything I'd want for my child? What if they were the type of people who might even punish him in the ways I had been punished as a child?

To ease my anxiety I started a binder of instructions for the future parents. I decided that if I was giving this child to someone, they had to abide by certain rules. The first one was, of course, that corporal punishment was not allowed. And when I wasn't in class or reading about potential parents or writing in my binder, I was in town shopping for baby clothes and toys – I didn't want to send him off empty-handed. I was already building a small library for him, starting with all the Maurice Sendak I could find. I firmly believe that every child needs to know *Where the Wild Things Are*.

My day had taken on this new routine of:

8 a.m. - Morning meditation
9 a.m. - Breakfast
10 a.m. - Class
12 p.m. - Pre-lunch meditation
1 p.m. - Quick lunch followed by shopping for baby things

2 p.m. - Class
4 p.m. - Afternoon meditation
5 p.m. - Reading adoption files
6 p.m. - Dinner
7 p.m. - Work on binder
8 p.m. - *Stress over unrealistic-ness of binder*
9 p.m. - Imagine the parents hurting the child and cry until I lost consciousness

Eventually I seemed to run out of tears. My heart started to feel heavy and numb, as if I had been given a shot before surgery. I didn't care about babies. I wasn't attached to the one inside me. I wasn't. I wasn't. I didn't want to be. But somehow I started to have this sense that after it was over I was going to wake up with some part of me missing and a pain I couldn't bear. Then one morning I woke up. Half my room was occupied with stacks of baby things. The sun was shining on them. As if to say, "What about this? Have you ever considered this?"

I looked at my bedside table, at how thick the binder was. I won't go into everything I put in there because it was ridiculously detailed. And many of the details *were* ridiculous. It had grown from just containing parenting ethos and political and educational requirements to something quite impossible for any couple to live up to. And so I replied (in response to the sun's question): *"But I'm only twenty-four. I'll be twenty-five when he's born. I'm too young."*

"Some people become parents at twenty-five," said the sun. And then I thought, *What if?* ... And in that moment I stopped being scared. I would have thought I'd be terrified. I would have thought that considering such a thing would have filled me with instant trepidation, like when I almost hit a car and my mind keeps imaging it happening and I feel sick over it. I would have thought imagining being a mother would be like that. I didn't even have anywhere to live. But instead of making me scared, it was the only thought that had really given me any comfort since I'd found out I was pregnant. Regardless of how I might look to the rest of the world, this decision gave me relief because I knew, from the core of my being, that *I* wouldn't fail at this.

In the summer, before I had my child, I returned to Texas to stay with my father and his new wife. I had been out on bail when I ran away to my university in Iowa; now I needed to go back to prison and get processed again before going to court. I had been told, by certain people in the know, that pregnant women got processed incredibly fast in prison. Evidently the state doesn't want to be responsible for the cost or potential complications of childbirth. So, with less than a month till my due date, I turned myself in.

My blonde hair was thicker than ever, my skin was glowing, and so, despite my massive weight gain (both food and pregnancy related), I managed to take a decent mug shot. I spent just under an hour in a cell with seven other women. One of the women stood up and offered me her seat.

Gratefully I accepted and looked around the room. The room was 4 x 3 meters and was filled with twelve women. At the far end of the room there was toilet with no seat and no privacy, and no way block the sounds or smells that came from it, which I realized as it was currently being used by one of the residents.

As I took in my surroundings some of the women made conversation with me. They wanted to know when I was due, what I was having and did I need anything. A former classmate from Latin class had become a police officer. When he heard I was in custody he came by to visit, bringing with him his new wife –

also a police officer – and we three stood at the door chatting casually - me on one side, them on the other - for a few minutes. It was an odd mix of normalcy and kindness in an otherwise surreal situation. Forty-five minutes after my arrival I was released again.

A week later I went to court. Before court I got half an hour with a state-appointed attorney who, within ten minutes of meeting me, told me that he and his wife adopted children, and (without me having brought this up in any way, shape or form) suggested that they would like to provide a lovely home for the one I was carrying.

His words, when he said them, hurt me in a way people might not understand, since adoption had been my own first thought. By this point I had completely embraced the idea that I would become a mother. I believed that despite the recent turmoil my life had been in, caring for a child was one thing I could do well, and I would move heaven and earth to give this child a good life. His offer made me want to cry with shame, but considering the circumstances of our meeting (those circumstances being that: 1) I *was* about to be a convicted felon; 2) I needed his help; and 3) I wanted to get all of this over with before I *had* my child rather than prolonging everything by filing a grievance about my lawyer), I felt unable to say anything other than, “No thank you.”

Before the proceedings began the judge asked if I had been coerced or bribed in anyway. Technically I had not been, so I said no and pleaded guilty to the felony charge of credit fraud. I got probation with community service.

On August 20th 2002 at 8:31, in a little hospital in south Texas, I gave birth to a healthy baby boy. Michael came quickly, with no complications. The nurses cleared his mouth and then offered me his slimy body with the cord still attached. I stayed awake for the whole seventy-two hours we were in the hospital. They kept trying to take Michael away so that I could sleep. There was a room they put the babies in, but I wouldn't let them take him. I didn't want him to feel alone or scared.

After the first twenty-four hours, staying awake became more difficult, but Aspergian-powered stamina was hard at work. My body took small naps, against my will, while Michael slept in his cot next to me. As soon as I'd realize I was sleeping I would wake up and stare at him some more. I knew I would love him this much for the rest of my life, and in that moment I also knew there was so much I wouldn't be able to protect him from. That one day, if I did my job well, he would grow up and leave me. This was our destiny.

My heart broke knowing that one day he would grow up, and it healed in knowing that in a way I was completely safe now. I knew if everything else in my life went wrong I still got to be a mother. I hadn't known I would want this so much, I hadn't known about *this* love: this love was a cloak protecting me from all the other bad things in the world because now there was nothing else on earth that could ever hurt me so much. As long as he was okay, I would be okay too. "I'll never let anything happen to you. I'll guard you with my life," I whispered. And then my body betrayed me again, and I slept.

Over the next few months Michael filled out; he had olive skin, rosebud lips and a natural blush on his cheeks. His eyes were like pools of ink showing almost nothing of the whites; they made him look impossibly beautiful, the way few boys can. But they were more than just striking; there was something very deep and soulful about them. His brows furrowed with a look of concern as he sucked on the corner of an orange wedge. He could equally have been described as an Adonis or a poster child for a Third World children's charity. Anyone would have devoted themselves to taking care of this child, but the privilege was mine.

I met with Sam to discus the practicalities of the child we had made together. I remember my own childhood and how on some occasions I would be left with my father if he hadn't paid child support, or I wouldn't be allowed to go with him, depending on which my mother felt was more of a punishment. The feeling of being a punishment for someone was horrible and my top priority for Michael was that only people who loved him and wanted him were allowed into his life. I didn't want our arrangements to be about money, my only request was that he was all in or all out.

Again a court appointed lawyer was involved. The three of us met at the court house. Sam was quiet, I suspect feeling overwhelmed at the situation and perhaps a little ashamed of not being in a better position in his life. When it comes to unplanned pregnancies the men are often seen as dead beats, especially if they don't have good jobs. The unfairness was that I also didn't have a good job. I would have been in exactly Sam's situation had I been the man. But as the mother I was seem as carrying a burden on his behalf. But that wasn't how I felt.

I didn't really wait for the lawyer to talk, as I didn't see our conversation as needing to involve him. I explained my feelings to Sam, that I would likely feel how he was feeling if our roles were reversed. I wanted as much amicability as possible. "The only thing I ask is that you commit to being in his life or not." This wasn't about how Sam felt or how I felt. Or even the law. It was about what what would be best for Michael. But the lawyer obviously felt I had over stepped my bounds in saying this.

"You can't tell him not to see his son! You have to resolve this animosity between you too." He said curtly.

I was shocked and confused. Not only had I been unaware of my animosity. I felt that both Sam and I had been making every effort to have a mature discussion about our arrangement. "I don't feel angry?" I said in confusion.

"I didn't say you felt angry!" They Lawyer barked.

I became more confuse, this time as to what the word animosity meant to him. Sam and I sat quietly as the lawyer proceeded to tell us how child custody arrangements usually worked, shaming Sam with small digs just as the arresting police officer had done to me a year earlier. Finally the lawyer left us as he went to file some paper work. There was another desk in the room, with a person working. When Sam and I were sat alone this person made a glance in our direction. I had the sense that speaking amongst ourselves was forbidden. I made a passing comment, "He seems friendly." Referring to the lawyer. The man put his eyes back down to his work. Then I spoke quickly to Sam.

"I don't want you're money. I just want you to decide what you want as a father. It has to be your choice." The truth was I didn't want Sam involved. I could see that things would likely be more difficult for Michael if he spent his childhood between two homes. Plus Sam had had his own legal troubles. I trusted myself to clean up my act, but it was hard to feel comfortable with anyone else. Still, I refused to try and influence Sam. I knew if I forced Sam into something he didn't truly chose then it would only bring more drama down the road.

After a moment Sam explained that he didn't feel he had anything to offer a child. I told him again that I would be in his situation if our roles were reversed. I told him if he wanted to change his mind later he could get in touch with me. My only priority was that there wasn't a lot of back and forth or indecision. He agreed.

The lawyer returned. Sam and I signed the papers with a silent understanding between us. We left the arbitration room. In the corridor Sam's fiancée was waiting for him and my family for me. He and I hugged and said a tearful good bye. Years later he would sign the paperwork to let my current husband become Michael's legal father.

Michael and I went back to Iowa, so that I could finish school. We took an apartment a block away from my school. I wasn't sure how I was going to make use of a bachelor's degree now that I was a felon, but I didn't know what else to do so I kept going. Michael was my top priority and school was my second, and between those two things I had little time for anything else. All my visions of motherhood were of women who were married and living in suburbia.

The idea of getting married was so far off my radar, though, that I started to wonder if it was even a possibility that could exist for me. If I would ever feel attracted to men again. And even if I did, what if it didn't happen until I was in my fifties and Michael was grown up and moved out and my chance to give him a "normal" family had passed?

Chapter 21

HOW ARE YOU? PLEASE PASS THE POTATOES

I was going through the doors at O'Hare International airport when I caught my first in-person glimpse of Trey. I stayed in the doors and revolved right back out. Outside again I took a deep breath and weighed my options: alas, I couldn't leave him in the airport waiting for someone to show up, so – nervous over what I had gotten myself into – I went back in. I decided I would treat him the way I would any foreign visitor: I would show him around, playing the guide. I loved meeting people from other places and there was no reason that things should be awkward.

We went to our hotel, I had brought Michael and Miya along. Miya had come back to the US and, was staying with me and helping with Michael while she took classes. The three of us were sharing a room and Trey was across the hall. But despite my hopes, there *was* an awkwardness between us. It had been three years since the assault and since I had dated anyone. I was nervous that Trey might have expectations that I was not prepared to meet, though this proved not to be the case; instead he had an old-fashioned chivalry about him, which offered me some comfort that I could be safely alone with him. I liked having him around.

We took Michael to the park and strolled down Michigan Avenue, and we looked like a young family on holiday. When we talked we seemed to agree on everything: ethics, politics, the best way to pack a suitcase. A week later I found myself kissing Trey in the airport before he left to go back home. Or, more correctly, I had decided that I would make this a romantic relationship and then before he went through security at the airport told him I wanted him to kiss me.

I think my request surprised him, as he had correctly concluded I was not attracted to him. What he didn't know, but I thought I did, was that I couldn't feel that way about anyone anymore. I can't explain how much it meant that I'd found a man who didn't scare me. I was sure he would not hurt me. Even if he disappeared, that would not hurt me. That made him safe and I was grateful for finding someone safe. After our first meeting the relationship graduated from emails to phone calls.

I could sit in Iowa holding Michael as he finally drifted off to sleep at 1 a.m. and be talking to Trey who had just finished his tea in England; that was the part of the relationship I fell in love with. In the summer I flew out to meet him in London, and at Thanksgiving he came out to Texas where Michael and I were with my family. Every trip was just a week here and a week there. Short enough so that I could ignore what wasn't there between us when we were together. Everyone seemed to think it was terribly romantic. The sensible British accountant and the flighty American student.

Falling in mutual love with someone has a comforting thrill to it. A feeling of rightness. But none of that was there for me. What *was* there, though, was the thrill of seeing how my family responded to him. To us. Their approval gave me a feeling of warmth that I had been longing for, for many years. So I decided that maybe I *had* found my comrade in arms. Someone who was sensitive like me, who would hold my hand as we did this dance in the world around us. While I sometimes liked excess, I always preferred too little to too much, and I was hopeful that I could find a calm contentment in the absence of romantic love. The idea of having that, of being done with the over-intensity of romance, was a comforting thrill similar to what love itself might have been.

After a year of phone conversations and a total of four, spaced-out, week-long visits, we got engaged. It was an ideal courtship for me, as it allowed me not to be physically involved with him as things progressed. A few months later I transferred to an online university and started selling or donating my belongings in preparation for moving to England. I didn't waste any more time thinking about romantic love or how I might feel some time down the road, I couldn't fathom that I would ever feel that type of love again - which was fine. I had never felt sustainably happy with romantic love. Or balanced. The unpredictability was too much for me, and it was time for me to get smart about my life. I felt a sense of resolve as I taped the last box shut.

Michael and I were going at the end of the summer after spending a few months in Texas saying goodbye to my parents; but the closer it came to the moving date the more I wondered if I was making a terrible mistake. Finally I called Trey to tell him how I was feeling. I had never told him about the sexual assault. I found myself telling him everything in one long monological explanation, leaning heavily on the assault as my excuse for why I couldn't feel attraction or love.

Then finally I said the thing which scared me the most, what I felt had a real chance of changing everything we were on the brink of, but the thing I knew he needed to hear and I needed to say. I said as clearly as I could, "I'm not in love with you. I don't think I'm capable of being *in* love. You need to know this before I come." There was silence on his end. I sat there a moment trying to steady my breathing. I had barely gotten the words out. I was scared of hurting him. I knew everything had already gone too far and I should have told him all of this a long time ago.

"Trey?"

"Wha?" He never pronounced his Ts.

"I need you to say something."

"..."

I understood his silence to be him taking it all in, so I gave him a minute and then finally asked, "Do you still want to marry me?"

"Of course I do." He said it in a reassuring way, as if I had just confessed to some horrible indiscretion and then begged him to still love me and we were at the end of some romantic movie where he takes me in his arms and tells me that of course he'll forgive me, of course he still loves me. Only that wasn't what was happening. I had told him that I hadn't been in love with him and that I *wouldn't* be in love with him, and I had left him to make his own decision about whether or not he wanted to be with me, no begging or pleading from my end. What bothers me is that years later he would claim not to recall this conversation at all. And so I have to wonder: what did he hear that day?

We spent the following Christmas and Boxing Day at Trey's aunt and uncle's house; that was the tradition for Trey's entire family. The house was small, warm and decorated with glitzy Christmas decorations. Being there felt like being in a tight and itchy Christmas sweater that I was desperate to get out of. Michael and I were both squirming and irritable within the first hour.

A few hours in I quietly suggested that I take Michael outside to get some fresh air, and Trey greeted this suggestion with shock and indignation. *No one ever leaves*. I looked out the window, longing to be swallowed up by the cool air outside, but I wasn't supposed to leave. The only thing we were expected to do was sit in one place and eat. Eating at least was a distraction.

A few minutes after being seated around the grand Christmas table, I looked to my left at Trey's aunt. "How are you?" I asked. She looked delighted to be asked, and said, "I'm doing well." Then I said, "That's great. Can you please pass the potatoes?" She looked confused, but obliged. I'm bad with knowing how much small talk I need to make before it's safe to just say what I want. When it's okay to explain why I called, or finally hang up the phone when I believe the conversation to be over, or ask someone to pass the potatoes. All I know for sure is that I've gotten these things terribly wrong in the past and so entering my thirties, to pre-empt the offences I might cause, I became humble and self-deprecating to go with my awkwardness.

I started sharing with people that I can be thoughtless and don't mean to be. In response they usually scoff in disbelief that such a thing could be true, and tell me that I’m a sweetheart and couldn't possibly offend anyone. This scares me more because I'm aware then that I've gotten myself onto a pedestal that I'll soon be falling off it. I feel like I either have to live with my antenna tuned into everyone else or risk being completely rude and selfish. They don't know that for me it's either one way or the other. That my circumference of awareness isn't big enough for the both of us. My house-of-cards social group will collapse. Suddenly everyone will hate me. I've spent years being anxious about this. And to that end I'm the nicest person everyone knows. Until, as I’ve warned them, I'm not.

On Boxing Day, just after lunch, Trey and his uncle stood up from the table to head out. I felt a wave of relief as I thought that the festivities were finally being concluded. “Oh, are we going?” I asked. The aunt looked at me kindly and said, “No, no. You'll stay right here with us, dear. They just have the game to go to.”

Trey had mentioned that he liked football. And I was quickly learning that he *never* missed a home game. “You didn't tell me,” I said, looking at Trey, as everyone else averted their attention. “I did.” he said and that was the end of that. If we had been alone I would have said more, but he wouldn't have. He was a master of short responses and simply refusing to engage in anything he considered confrontational.

After Trey and his uncle left, I sat listening to the older family members share their views about Elton John's civil partnership. To be honest I had never found sexual orientation to be as straightforward as some people do. When I loved people I loved them intensely. The euphoria I felt when in the company of someone I love is so much bigger than sexual excitement.

Although, as I grew older I could with clarity recognize I prefer a body with a larger bone structure than my own, with a hairy chest and fore arms. The features I am most physically drawn to are those of a man. Nevertheless. I'll never forget my stint as the school lesbian, being made to feel like a predator because of what others thought my sexual orientation might be. And I felt ashamed for sitting there quietly in the living room while my soon to be in-laws freely shared their discriminations.

A few hours later it was time to eat again. At the table someone was talking about their trip to the Edinburgh Zoo and what a nice zoo it was. “The Dallas Zoo is really nice too. Michael and I went last summer,” I said. Happy that I could safely contribute something to this conversation. “Oh that's nice, dear. What did you see there?” one of the aunts asked, while my future mother-in-law smiled warmly at me.

“Well, they had everything. They had apes and giraffes and these large tortoises. In fact it was so funny. The tortoises were mating. It actually looks quite violent when they have sex. You wouldn't think tortoises could have such rough sex. Or make those noises,” I said in wonder, picturing the event as I spoke.

When I re-emerged from the memory, I looked around to see my elderly future in-laws holding their cutlery mid-air, with frozen expressions on their faces. They looked like a bunch of shocked still lifes. It was one of those moments when I realized that I had said the wrong thing again. I was doing it much less frequently, but I was still getting it terribly wrong sometimes.

After having Michael, I had started

trying to be clever about how to direct the course of my life. I believed I was fundamentally flawed, so I decided that if my desire was to turn left I must actually need to go right. I thought I could outwit my personal design and future prospects for failure if I was willing to use my intellect and accept the basic truth that everything else about me could not be trusted. It was this line of thought that led me to marry a man I didn't love.

I rationalized that romantic love wasn't so important. That the lucky ones build a friendship with the person they fell in love with; they accept each other and create a home where they feel understood and valued. I could skip over the love and work on that with Trey, except Trey was rarely home. He was gone before Michael or I got up in the morning and came home at around seven and fell asleep in front of the TV while I read bedtime stories upstairs.

Trey went out of town once or twice a month for a few nights each time. On the weekends we were at his mother's. The understood routine was that we would have lunch, then an outing, then dinner. After dinner Trey would nap in the living room while his mother and I did the washing up. I hated this ritual, but I could see that he was living out his life's script. He was satisfied and happy, and it was having Michael and I that made him happy. I kept quiet for a while, then slowly I started to complain.

Gradually I started to ask Trey to work less; I even suggested we move closer to his work to reduce the commute; but nothing came of either suggestion. I asked him to stop going to every home game, but he had season tickets and he went with his uncle, who had been like a father to him since his own had passed. I asked if we could skip his mother's house some weekends, but he couldn't do that because she'd be alone, and he had promised his father that he'd look after her, which meant that we all would, every weekend, no exceptions.

I began to see that Trey had secured himself a wife and someone to look after his mother. I felt unentitled to complain, Trey had accepted the fact that I didn't love him, in a way this was simply my end of the deal. But I hadn't understood what this arrangement would be like when I entered into it. I had truly imagined we'd be partners, that there would be a growing connection between us. This was more like a business arrangement.

We didn't talk. Or, rather, he didn't talk to me. And to that end there were no fights, which was worse than fighting would have been. It finally came, a year into our co-habitation, that one weekend I told him I would not go to his mother's. I had already been telling him throughout the week, as I had many times before, but Saturday morning he woke up and prepared for us to go.

I reminded him that I was not going. He told me I was destroying the family, that I was hurting Michael, that his mother was expecting us. All the things that in the past had gotten me into the car. This time I sat on the bed, not moving. Then he cried. I had such extreme guilt, but I can't say how many weekends I'd gotten into the car only to wonder how I had given up once again. This weekend I had promised myself I wouldn't budge. And I didn't. He finally left and drove off. The moment he was gone I felt elated and triumphant. I sat there just breathing in my freedom. Feeling the air in my lungs. Then, ten minutes later he came back and asked, “Are you ready yet?”

I went.

I knew I hadn't loved him, but the longer we were together the more I realized how little I liked him or understood him. During a chat with our neighbours, Trey jokingly called a young adolescent girl, who lived down the road from us, the "neighbourhood bicycle." Everyone laughed. They all got it and agreed; I didn't understand what it meant so I asked and he leaned over and whispered, "everyone's had a ride." I don't know if he was saying it to be funny, or if he thought this way. Either way, he was a forty-year-old man, who had led a more stable and sheltered life than what I could imagine and at the other end of the road there was a fifteen-year-old girl who was the punchline of this joke.

I didn't like the man I was married to, but I had known, before I married him that I didn't love him. Marrying him had been my choice. Technically I could say it was his choice too, but I believe he loved me (Even though I was also the "neighbourhood bicycle")

I allowed myself to appreciate having the house to just Michael and myself while he continued to work long hours. I rearranged the furniture. I gave Trey's dining table a darker finish. Then, eventually, I started to feel uneasy when I heard his car pull into the drive. I felt trapped when I was with him. And guilty for *feeling* trapped. I had sent myself to a prison that I had managed to avoid in literal terms. But in doing this I had committed another great wrong. I had turned this innocent person *into* my prison. It was a role he never sought and he didn't deserve.

Over the next year I grew more miserable in my marriage. I had mostly grown out of being the tantrum-prone young girl I had once been, but my thoughtless, mistake-filled youth left me terrified of saying what I honestly wanted for myself now. It made me terrified of leaving my prison, like I couldn't be trusted in the free world. I knew that leaving Trey wouldn't mean that I would necessarily find happiness. But staying would mean Trey could hold onto the romantic love he seemed to feel for me. It was the one thing I could secure, and in that sense what he would get out of keeping me seemed to weigh more than what I might get out of leaving.

I had always felt like my own mother had given me everything she had to give until all she had left was misery for herself and all I had was guilt for the burden I had been. I couldn't say which was right. Being selfish or trying to be a martyr. Leaving or staying. There was no right answer. Just a million different opinions and voices moving around my head, arguing with each other. And beyond all the many different arguments for staying and going was simply the fact that I wanted very much to go.

I've noticed that people start to become politicians when they want out of a relationship. They start spinning the facts as they tell them to others or retell them to themselves. And I can understand this: the world judges harshly the person who initiates the end of a marriage with someone who isn't an out right monster. Just wanting to get out, having made a mistake in the first place, can't be enough. People want to shame them. To make sure the ending isn't being taken too lightly. It's as if they are concerned the sense of embarrassment, failure and exhaustion when a ending a marriage can't be trusted to come on it's own, society must be tasked with the delivery of these feelings, to ensure that the individual has truly paid for their right to exit the marriage. For many the choice is either to endure the opinions of others or to campaign, appeal for sympathy, by telling their tails of woe to anyone listening.

Now I wanted out. And beside the usual pressure not to want this, there was the additional sense that after all my years of bad choices and promiscuity that I should be nothing other than grateful to have a man like Trey. Trey wasn't perfect, but he also wasn't evil. He wasn't deserving of end-of-the-relationship-mudslinging that so many couples do to each other. People who I had considered my friends, who even encouraged me to leave my marriage suddenly disowned me when I took steps to go. It's was the social house of cards falling again. I was heart broken but didn't feel entitled to comfort when I was causing someone else pain.

The marriage itself had been an unfortunate symptom of how I saw my place in the world. I had spent my life trying to be normal and fit in - to give others what I believed I owed them - more than anything else, and finally I couldn't do it any more. What I knew to be true was that I had not been in love with him ever. That was the problem that caused or made worse all the other problems. I should never have married him. Naïvely, I had made my commitment based on the idea that I could be loyal to anyone if I was determined enough. And now I wished I had been a little less naïve for his sake. That was the truth. The mistake was mine.

Adulthood

"I know who I WAS when I got up this morning, but I think I must have been changed several times since then."

LEWIS CARROLL, *Alice's Adventures in Wonderland & Through the Looking-Glass*

Chapter 22

TO EXIST WITHOUT HAVING ANYONE TO APPEASE

After telling Trey I wanted a divorce, a month off turning thirty, I understood something I never had before. That despite my anxieties around attachment and loss, I'd *rather* be alone than be with the wrong person. Had I learned this sooner in life I would have saved many innocent people from suffering at my hands, including me. All I can say is that I didn't know this sooner, because stability was so fleeting in my childhood I never had the chance to internalize it. I simply grabbed at every outside offer of security without considering if the person offering it was good or right for me.

People judged me for wanting out of my marriage so quickly. For identifying it as being wrong for me when I did. I wanted so desperately to have a time and place in my life where I could just be in my own space and not worry what anyone else would think I was entitled to, where I could get my head around choosing to make myself happy and let go of the guilt of being me. I just wanted to exist and breathe without having anyone to appease. With or without a partner, this is what I was after.

Michael's school was in an upper-class neighbourhood full of older homes, most of which had been occupied by state officials and wealthy businessmen men in the 1800s. The age of these homes meant the area was peacefully surrounded by mature oak trees. One day, when I wasn't quite ready to return to Trey's house yet, I took a wander around one of the streets. It was then that I discovered a large brick wall that ran almost a quarter of the length of the road. I assumed it surrounded someone's very large garden, but as I walked beside it I came to an opening. If someone stood in just the right spot they could see right in, and if they didn't they would never know what was there at all. Which made this exactly the sort of place I longed to be.

Through the opening I saw a set of old

terraced houses. Most seemed to be occupied, but one had a sign that said it was for rent – I would later find out that the owners of that house were away for a few years in Australia and thus needed a tenant. The house came furnished, and the back garden had a pergola. Summer was coming.

I loved the British summer. The temperatures were just right for spending hours outside and, to me, there was a noticeable absence of mosquitoes. I had immediate fantasies about sitting out with a glass of Vouvray in the evenings. I had started working for a supply teaching firm by then. I had never held a job for more than three months in my life, and now, at twenty-nine, had over twenty jobs under my belt. It seemed like the answer was supply work. In temporary work there is no getting fired. There is only the next job.

I picked our moving date to coincide with Michael's last month at school. I was very aware that my son was highly sensitive, and while I couldn't spare him the pain of this experience I was at least going to try and provide us with a cushion to fall apart on. I wanted to be able to move while he was in school, for practical reasons, but also to be able to take him out early if he needed that for emotional reasons.

At that time I was working in a school for high-functioning Autistic children. I loved it. The students were often very bright, but their abilities varied greatly. One student, for example, who had taught himself to transliterate kanji so that he could read his Japanese comics, was only capable of very remedial math. I was constantly amazed and humbled by their talents and perseverance. Most of all I felt an easy sense of competence and belonging in this role, two things I had never felt in a job before. And the school I was working for kept requesting me from the agency.

Fortunately, my German friend Günther's job afforded him some flexibility and he had taken to arranging his schedule so that he could collect and watch Michael while I finished my work day. Unfortunately, though, my fantasy of having wine in the back garden that summer went down the gutter along with ungodly amounts of rain. It was the summer of 2006 and Brittan was experiencing a constant, country-wide monsoon.

One wet evening I came in from work to find my house smelling lovely and full of spices. I made my way into the kitchen and there was Günther standing over the hob sautéing pork chops. My heart sank. “I don't like pork,” I said, not even considering that this might not be the best thing to say when someone is standing over a hot stove cooking exactly that for dinner. Luckily Günther took my oblivious bluntness in his stride.

“You'll like this.” he said, handing me a plate. He drizzled on a blackberry Fitou sauce he had concocted.

“Oh my god. This is amazing,” I said with food still in my mouth.

“Of course. I'm a chemist.”

“What does that have to do with cooking?”

He laughed. “What do you think cooking is? You choose the temperature and the ingredients. Cooking *is* chemistry.”

I guess he had a point. I went to sit at the table as he brought me another pork chop and a glass of wine. “I really miss cooking,” I said.

“I thought you hated cooking.”

“No ... Well ... I *used* to love it. Maybe I miss enjoying it. It's not so fun when someone expects dinner to be ready every night at the same time. When I was younger I would have loved to go to Paris and take a course at the Cordon Blue.”

“Bleu,” he corrected.

“Blue.” I tried again.

“No. Watch my mouth. *Bleu*.”

“Bloo?”

“Bleuuuu.”

“Okay. Bleoooo,” I said, trying to get the right sound from the back of my throat. I sounded like Yoda. But we kept trying until I think it was undeniable that my mouth didn't work like that.

Over dinner I talked about work and the pending divorce. Günther told me about his ex-girlfriend – whom he had been with for eight years – and how her family owned a vineyard just off the Rhine. I started to feel very aware of how different we were. Günther had not come from a middle-class background, his family had been poor, but he had lived in one house until he was eighteen and left for university.

He had grown up in a four-room flat where his mother still lived, his two brothers had shared a room, his grandmother had had a room to herself, and Günther had shared a room with his parents. The fourth room was the dining/living room, and it was small, not like a normal room with two partitioned spaces. There was simply a table, and whether they were eating or talking this is where everyone spent their time when they were awake.

They did not own a TV or a phone. Making a phone call was a special event. Someone would leave the flat and go across the road to the payphone to make the call. They carried with them the sentiments of the entire family and returned with important messages to relay back. Günther told me about the time, when he was eight, he was entrusted with the task of phoning his aunt.

Günther's big challenge within the family, although he wouldn't say he had any challenges, was that he was the youngest of the six people he lived with and he often went unheard. He was told things more than he got to tell them. But upon his return from the phone call, everyone stopped talking and listened to him as he recounted the conversation. He doesn't see this as a big deal, but he's told me this particular story three times. Today he's a university lecturer with a regular audience of eager students soaking up his valuable words.

I anticipated Günther's stories with the same eagerness with which I looked forward to the next instalment of my favourite show. Even with tales of cramped space, of being the youngest, and of darning socks, I was envious of his childhood. I had somehow gotten past his PhD in chemistry and the fact that he spoke three languages while my attempts at French made me sound like a Zen space alien, but now I found myself feeling self-conscious because my family had never been as close as his or owned a vineyard like his ex-girlfriend's family had. When he knew my life story, what would he think of me? So, I told him everything in one monological rush.

I told him about my trouble with school and jobs and friends. How intensely I love the people I love. My sexual history. My criminal background. About pulling the lever on the train a few months back. How I was afraid I was crazy. He never seemed judgemental. He told me that I didn't owe anyone an explanation about anything. That people had to earn my trust first. Then he told me about *his* criminal past! (Although his was way more honourable than mine.) He had been arrested at an anti-war demonstration and was given jail time for refusing to enlist in the military.

A PhD, culinary skills and a criminal record. Günther was, hands down, the coolest guy I had ever met. I ate the meal he cooked me, and Michael played with his cars while Günther cleaned up. I watched him as he moved around my kitchen with a tea-towel slung over his shoulder, putting the spices he'd brought over away in my cupboards and then some leftover pepper into my fridge and ...

"Oh my god what's that smell? It's disgusting!"

"It's cheese."

"Cheese should not smell like that."

"It's French. It's lovely."

"Dude, get your stinky French cheese out of my fridge. This is *not* okay." He laughed and then I laughed.

I was blissfully relaxed, and somehow this was ... normal. It was in this friendship through which I had started to understand what was usually missing with others. I always felt that if I was ever brought into the inner circle it was a gift I had not earned, or could not sustain. That I was on a guest pass that would be quickly withdrawn if I said the wrong thing, if I tried to banter and got it wrong, or if I was completely honest about what I was thinking; or if I just fell apart.

Even at the best of times I was always the "narc", the "drama queen", the "weirdo", the "bitch", the one who just didn't get it somehow. It was the benevolence of others that meant I was allowed in, and not my desirability as a friend. But here in my kitchen, with Günther, I felt totally at ease. I felt desirable, and confident that this feeling was mine to own and keep.

A month later Günther and I went to London to sort out my visa. I went to the embassy and, because only the relevant person could gain entry into the embassy and Günther was not the relevant person, he went to a museum. My task took all day, and like every other day that summer, it rained the whole time. Once I was done at the embassy, and had "indefinite leave to remain" visas stamped in both Michael's and my passports, I went to find Günther at the fountains in Trafalgar Square.

Sitting on the edge of a fountain, Günther handed me a small rectangular box, an *Indefinite Leave to Remain* gift. Judging by the shape, I imagined it was a necklace or possibly a bracelet. Inside was a pen. It was brushed nickel, and engraved, "To Kate with Love." Thinking of Günther always made me smile. Involuntarily. Like my brain was flooded with dopamine and I had no choice but to smile when he popped into my head. Now I knew, not only did he make me smile but, he was the first man to ever really get it. I love to write, and he gave me a pen.

It was dusk now. The rain had stopped. The sky was cobalt blue with charcoal clouds departing in the distance. The street lamps were reflected on the wet pavement. It was a perfect moment. Then, like a built-in automatic response to happiness, it occurred to me that this might not last. We were at the beginning of something. But often these things didn't last. Panic. Dread. Uncertainty. I just couldn't know where all this would go. I wanted to believe that whatever was meant to happen would, and to just hang onto that. To, just once, not let all the good stuff get weighed down by my extreme fears of getting hurt.

So, overriding my built-in reaction, at least for this moment, I decided that was what I would do. I enjoyed the moment of calm and dry stillness. For once it wasn't coming down, and it was beautiful just like that.

Later, in my living room, after Michael was asleep, we danced. We swayed gently back and forth as Van Morrison rocked our gypsy souls. We kissed. There were no words or permission; it seemed to be understood that we had both just been waiting to do this all along. We stopped for a moment and I gave him my most sultry come-hither look. It was so completely cheesy that we both busted out laughing. Embarrassed, I hid my face in his chest. For some reason, my usual act of confidence couldn't be performed for him. With Günther everything was real. And I was terrified.

He slid his hand behind my neck, under my hair. Then, tilting my face up, he closed the gap between us again. I was kissing my best friend. It was an intimacy I had never experienced with anyone. Every nerve in my body came alive as his hands forced their way between us and started unbuttoning my dress. Suddenly panic gripped me and I froze.

It had been eight years since I had been with someone I cared about. I had put on a lot of weight after the assault and I had never taken it back off. I had had a baby. There was more at risk than there ever had been with anyone, and I was further from my ideal self than I ever had been. What if I showed him everything and he thought I was ugly?

"What's wrong?" he said, instantly backing off.

"I'm worried you won't think I'm pretty."

My words carried more truth than I meant them to. And he understood their meaning. I had made my confession about my body, but the truth was so much deeper. I was afraid of letting go with someone I actually loved. And with my confession I had just done that. I had just handed him all the power in our relationship. I stood there a moment feeling sick. And caught. Then he gave the power back.

“I'm not perfect either, you know. I've put on around twenty kilos since university. These eyes that love to look at you need stronger glasses every year, and when I'm in my seventies they'll likely be full of glaucoma. This heart, which is completely yours, has been suffering palpitations since my father passed away. It's so bad that I worry I'll have to start taking medication.” He stopped for a moment to make sure I was listening. He bent down, putting his face right in front of mine, and said, “I'm not perfect but I think you're beautiful. Can I please kiss everything that scares you?”

Then. Together. We let go.

I worried in the early months that our wonderful sex life would suddenly switch off like it had with Adrian. That all at once I wouldn't want him to touch me. What I couldn't know in those early days was that none of that would happen. We had a little difficulty in the beginning. I liked sex, and he was good at it, so I soon began asking whenever I was in the mood.

"Do you want to have sex?" I would say. "You could be more subtle," he'd say. I'd bat my eye lashes like I'd seen it done in old movies. He'd laugh. Then I'd sulk. "I don't want to have sex with you anymore." I had always been told men were only interested in one thing, which meant that this shouldn't be such hard work. Eventually he got more specific about what he wanted.

"Sorry. You're right. Maybe just touch me, put your hand on my arm or touch my feet with your feet when we're in bed. Just let it happen." Okay. Fine. That sounds simple. A few nights later I couldn't sleep, Günther had been snoring for hours and I was bored, so I gently caressed his calve with my big toe. Nothing happened. I applied a little more pressure, to which he responded with a stifled snore. A little more pressure, a little more. It was getting ridiculous, so I gave him one swift, *gentle*, kick to the calf. He woke up.

"WHAT THE HELL ARE YOU TRYING TO DO TO ME?" I batted my eye lashes at him.

He let out an exasperated sigh and rolled over to his bedside table and handed me a sleeping pill. Eventually we learned how to communicate with each other and as months turned to years we continued to enjoy each other. Sometimes, years into the relationship, with total familiarity between us, it would still be as amazing as that first time. But I couldn't know all that yet. I'd have to wait for that.

In most of my previous romantic relationships I had felt lacking, childish or impetuous. My difficulty with basic life skills such as: punctuality, a sense of direction, balancing a bank book, amongst other things, made me seem ditzy. My partners would usually assume the adult role in our relationship which highlighted how I already felt about myself. I was no good at commanding respect if it wasn't readily given. Even if it was given, I wouldn't immediately accept that I deserved it. This is where Günther was different.

From the beginning he gave me everything without hesitation. Everything from his time to his love, and most of all his patience. Patience for me to sort through all my anxiety. If I pulled away (to pre-empt my instincts to lean on him), he stayed. Still. Waiting for me to come back. If I leaned and clung, he stayed.

Still. Waiting for me to realise he wasn't going anywhere. And even after all he gave me (and all that I desperately took) he never looked down on me. He never regarded me as broken. Or crazy. Or naïve. Even as I dropped my guard and openly voice my feelings and anxieties he continued to see me as an adult deserving of respect. He treated me as an equal and continued to do so regardless of how it sat with me.

He consulted with me on all important matters in his life. He wanted my opinion on everything from bills to selling his house. He immediately assumed that what was his was mine and that my thoughts and opinions were valid. To that end he also thought my desire to do a postgraduate programme was valid. There was no sense of him having an if-you-haven't-done-it-by-now attitude. He told me how long it had taken him to finish his PhD. That he had been in his mid-thirties by the time he finished – and I was only just entering my thirties. Also he was published and assumed that one day I would be too. In his world these things weren't impossible.

Günther made me want to grow up. My goal, although I didn't know how long it would take to get there, was to contribute something to our household. I wanted to get a real job and to be an adult. I feel like that statement could have gone without saying, but my life had been so hugely unstable that I worried I wasn't capable of more. That I would never grow up. I was thirty-one, running late, stuck in traffic and still miles away from where I needed to be. But for the first time in many years I was starting to believe in myself again. I started to feel worthy and entitled to pursue my own goals.

We planned our future together, we looked for a house and sat down with a mortgage adviser to get a realistic idea of what we could afford. Günther told the man where we saw ourselves in five years, and that we needed to anticipate expenses related to me going back to school. That in ten years we could expect a second income. Günther had complete certainty that I would be a part of his life and that my goals would factor in. Some people in my family voiced the opinion that it was a bad move for Günther to trust a woman who had walked out on her first husband. Günther said they were stupid and didn't know me.

Over the next year the three of us became a family, and then our family grew when I got pregnant again. Neither Günther nor I had any nearby family to lean on. Taylor had married her high-school sweetheart, moved to Panama and gotten pregnant with her first child just a month earlier. Miya, who had married a couple years earlier, had found out she was pregnant a month after I did. I used the internet to keep up with my two friends; at night I would lie in bed almost cuddling my laptop as I poured my heart out to the both of them.

I was scared: before I met Michael I couldn't have imagined loving someone so much. Having both him and Günther was bliss, but now we were having a baby. I had never been in the inner circle of a family before. This was a reality that other people experienced. Not me. I did not believe this could be sustainable for me. I had never loved multiple people this much before, and I couldn't imagine that my heart could produce yet *another* large quantity of love with the birth of my second child. How could it be emotionally possible?

Mrs. R.S. said, "It's not division. It's multiplication. Your love will multiply. Just wait." As I tried to fathom this idea I became more anxious. If she was right that I would love both children the same, then how would I cope with holding the intensity of the love and worry that came with having a family?

Chapter 23

WHEN I'M THIS WRONG IT HURTS

Even with Günther next to me and Taylor and Miya a phone call away, I was still feeling very much alone. I've never had a large social circle, but there are some times in my life when I'm more aware of how few people I actually know. Being a lonely Aspergian wasn't something new, but being lonely, hormonal, and anxious about all the changes created more stress and insecurity than I had ever had at one time before.

My emotions were all over the place, and I started having the same ugly meltdown I had had as a teenager and young adult. I had actually gone a long time without seeing this person, but here she was again. Günther and I began arguing. And we argued often. It was usually ridiculously trivial stuff that I would get hung up on, like once he ate all my strawberries. It sounds silly but the smallest thing could set me off and then he might apologize, but soon he'd tell me I was over-reacting, or, worse, he might lose his temper too and tell me I was "crazy".

Sometimes it was so bad that we would stay home while Michael was at school and have these marathon yelling matches. Michael would get home and we'd be quiet, but the house would be thick with tension. I told Günther that we needed to end this; that he should just leave, I didn't want to drag it out any longer. He would say that he loved me and didn't want to leave.

We had this conversation more than once, but no matter how much he protested, I felt like he just couldn't see the real me yet. He couldn't feel the weight of me needing him. He was missing all my ugly and my crazy. And one day he'd get it and he'd finally cut the rope, leaving me to fall as I had so many times before.

As a young child my peers could see that I was awkward. I was badly bullied into my teens. Around the ages of thirteen and fourteen I started to develop skills for fitting in better, *acting* like others. Studying them so that I could know what they'd want from me. But, like all my endeavours, this was approached with a sense of obsession and anxiety. When I started to make a social effort I also started to agonize over being accepted.

I had a history of struggling and being lost (literally and figuratively) more than expected, so part of learning to act like everyone else was learning to not let on that I was confused. Which lead to me having problems that could have been avoided if I had felt safe enough to just ask questions, or recognize that I had them in the first place.

By my late twenties I had learned both to cope with and camouflage many of my autistic traits, but my residual social anxiety continued to complicate my life. It is this area that good early care can really change for a person.

Well into my adulthood I would examine, in forensic detail, every aspect of even the most minute social transaction. Worrying about the small stuff lead to being angry about the small stuff, the little socials rules that I had learned that seemed to be broken by others. Like it's important to say, "thank you." so I might struggle to forgive someone for not saying that.

Or I might struggle to recognize the difference between banter and insults.

Some external confirmation (An NT to AS translator perhaps) would have gone a long way towards helping me regulate my mood and self sooth. But I got little external support and so only those closest to me would get a gimps of how neurotic I truly was, and because I only opened up with them they would get my frustration and insecurities in concentrated doses.

I exhausted many people I loved. I got left a lot. Being left by people I loved hurt worse than being bullied by people I didn't. By my early to mid twenties, with great fear of abandonment, I started trying to keep those I loved the most, at arms length. When I felt myself starting to care for someone I pushed them away. My first reaction to endearment was mistrust.

We take what we believe we know about ourselves and convey it to the world through our demeanour and behaviour. We say, “I expect you to love me because I know I am loveable.” or “I won't even bother because I know I'm disgusting.” or “I'll try really hard not to burden you or show you who I am because, really, I'm scary”.

If our core message is a negative one then we often beg the world not to see our flawed self. We express shame, sending a message that we are hiding something, which punctuates our imperfections when they are seen. Sometimes, instead of hiding, we become the things we believe are most wrong with us, out of spite. If we're afraid we're scary, we become scary. It's an act of emotional self-defence for a person to hide behind the monster within.

Sadly, I didn't need to hide any more. I could have acknowledged my needs and my flaws with humility, it had become safe to do so. As I'd gotten older I'd gotten better at many things. I had gotten much better at considering other people’s feelings, and better at apologizing when I messed up, and better at being less rigid and judgemental about our differing beliefs. Had I understood my needs, been able to communicate those to others, not been so insecure about getting on everyone's nerves I might have been much less exhausting and intense by the time I reached my thirties; but I still lived with echoes of a past I couldn't fully understand. And without an explanation for the past I had no reason to believe my future could be better.

I didn't understand why I felt hugely

inferior to everyone else. I was only sure that one day Günther was going to recognise that I was. One day he would realise that he'd gotten into a relationship with a sub-par woman who was going to suck the life out of him. One day he'd run. We were only prolonging the inevitable, the moment he would realise that he could leave. He wasn't the one having a baby. Only he, ever so perfectly, disagreed with this logic.

He insisted he was having a baby too and that he wasn't leaving either of us. I understood that he might not know he was going to leave, but obviously he would. And we were running out of time for him to figure that out, so if he couldn't see it yet I'd show him. I'd make it impossible to miss. One day, then, I decided I could wait no longer; I had to conclude this before Michael got too attached to Günther, and before the baby came. I had to shake loose whatever wasn't going to hang on so that she could be spared the devastation of that loss. So she could be spared the dropping. I started again with trying to get rid of him.

“I don't want you here. Get out of my house!” I demanded.

He looked lost for words. I was like a ghost saying boo to someone who didn't realise ghosts were scary.

Sigh. Try again. “Why would you want this?” I said, motioning to myself. “You can leave. You have that option. I'm a monster and *that* won't change.”

“You're not a monster. But you do get on my nerves now.”

We went back and forth for a while. His temper escalating slowly, mine quickly. I became my ugliest, most grotesque self. But no matter what I said he wasn't budging. *God. He wasn't getting it. Why wasn't he getting it?* I stood on the balls of my feet and screamed in his face. “It's over! You have to Leave!!!!”

Then he got really mad. “You're a stubborn fucking bitch!” I felt a drop of saliva hit my cheek. “But I'm more stubborn than anyone you'll ever meet and I'm not going anywhere!” It was sheer fury, and it shot deep into me, hitting something cold and numb. It wasn't beautiful or nice, it was completely ugly, the way it is when couples argue; but it was what I needed to hear and he *made* me hear it. If he had been another man, I would have kept pushing. Knowing that we were not there yet, at that place where the red rage turns white. Where the scream becomes a menacing whisper.

But everything in Günther's voice and expression told me that there was no place like that with him. This was the extent of his rage. Beyond this point was not him leaving or lashing out, but him breaking.

Suddenly I understood what I had with him, and, by default, what I had to lose if I did push him away. I understood that I could force him out of my life. I had a say in whether or not this relationship worked. And if I let him, if I accepted that it was a partnership, he would stay. The thing that had always made love scary was that for me every moment existed separate from every other. I was so scared of the unpredictability of life that I was trying to control the only thing I could. The moment when I lost everything. Again.

But whether I controlled that moment or not, the loss was there. Controlling when it happened didn't keep me from experiencing it. I *could* break things off. I could do it now. I could do it years from now. But if I wanted to be with him, to have this, I would have to choose to trust him, over and over again every day. And I would have to trust that he would choose to love me, over and over again every day. And I had to be prepared to live like that. One moment to the next, trusting that we would choose each other over all the things that might go wrong.

Then I got it. The little girl I was trying to protect was me. I was convinced my problems made me too difficult to love. But Günther had already chosen me over and over again despite everything. I had a flash of how our relationship had unfolded so far: all the unconditional help he gave me to get moved into my new place; the moment I truly noticed his eyes; the moment at his birthday party when he was forcing food onto a skinny female guest; the things he said the first time we made love; when he gave me a pen in London; when we found out I was pregnant; and now, here, in my kitchen, screaming in my face that I couldn't get rid of him. These were all times I had fallen in love with him. Getting deeper and deeper into love, like exploring new depths of an underground cavern that was both beautiful and scary, I had to pause in awe as I discovered a new chamber. *I've never been here before.*

I don't mind apologising when I'm a little bit wrong, but when I'm *this* wrong it hurts. So it came out like a whisper. "I'm sorry." And as soon as the words were out the tension dissipated. He grabbed me and held me and kissed my head. "I would rather be miserable with you than happy with anyone else, you know." The words broke in his throat as he said them. Perhaps more dysfunctional words had never been uttered, but I loved that he said them, that someone was willing to come to hell to be with me.

Some part of my heart that I hadn't been aware of started to thaw. Tears started coming down my face. Suddenly I got it. Here stood the person who *wasn't* going to leave, who wasn't going to cut the rope. Who could take the weight of my needs. "Okay," I said softly. "You can stay." I returned his embrace. We cried and spent the day consoling each other. He was my home. Even if the place I lived in was rented and I hadn't yet adjusted to England, *he* was my home.

Chapter 24
A PROMISE

I gave birth to Grace at 7 a.m. on March 28th, 2008. My mother came over to stay with us for a few weeks; her being there meant that we were able to leave Michael asleep and just wake her up to tell her we were going to the hospital. Grace came out plump and pink and *hungry*. I put her face close to my breast and she snorted as she nuzzled around for a better grip. Günther and I laughed adoringly: Mrs. R.S. had been right about the multiplication. After giving birth I called Michael's school to see how he was doing, and the secretary sounded shocked to hear my voice and asked where I was calling from. “I'm at the hospital. I gave birth an hour ago but I'm done now and I just thought I'd check that my mother got Michael to school okay ... Hello?”

As soon as I could, I started begging the doctor for a speedy release. I kept explaining that I had another child I needed to get home to. Everyone seemed to find that amusing, and said that it was all the more reason to rest in the hospital for a few days. It was one of those times when I was aware of how different I was from everyone else. I went out to the hall to where the nurses were, and asked again to be released. At four in the afternoon I was signed out.

When I got home Michael wouldn't look at or speak to me – or anyone; he was completely inside himself. He was upset that I had left in the middle of the night without waking him, and that his morning routine had been changed. I didn't need him to explain this, I understood and had already been worrying about it. I hadn't thought about it before we left for the hospital, or at any time in the months leading up to it. I planned as much as I could for every possibility, but I completely failed to consider Michael's emotional reaction if I had to leave in the middle of the night.

While I feel that I share a special bond with both my children, I'm sometimes oblivious to their emotional needs until it's too late, and in this case I had only gotten the sinking feeling that I'd done things wrong after I was in the hospital. It was right after Grace came that I felt this overwhelming worry for Michael, that he must have been very upset to wake up and find I wasn't there and then be made to sit in a room with thirty other kids.

Everyone enjoyed seeing Grace, though, and, despite his issue with me, Michael looked at her adoringly. I was happy to see him re-emerging from himself, but heartbroken too: for a moment she had his love and I didn't. That night I put Grace in her cot and took Michael to my room to cuddle with him. "I did it wrong. I'm sorry," I whispered.

"I didn't know where you were." He finally spoke, but still wouldn't look at me. I could feel his hurt. "I know, baby. I'm sorry. I'll always come back to you and I'll never leave you like that again." I meant it too. I was resolved that even in the face of some terrible emergency I wouldn't leave without first making sure he knew I would be going. He finally looked at me, and we both cried and I held him tight. "I love you," I said, stroking his hair and kissing his face.

The next day Günther started paternity leave for a month and our life as a family officially began. Günther called us the "Atlantic Rowers", one working while the other slept. And while I slept I started having morbid dreams that I would die and not be able to *tell* Michael before I left. I would break my promise. I would never choose to do that to him, but suddenly I was dreaming of all the ways in which that choice might be taken away from me.

From a young age I had started to anticipate loss, and throughout my life when I started to trust that someone would stay it was usually the case that they left. Often suddenly. Which made having three people I loved more than I could ever have imagined loving anyone terrifying for me. It violated my most core beliefs about what was possible in my life. If my children were going to stay and my partner couldn't be pushed away, then what? How was I going to lose all of this? I became *convinced* that something tragically bad was about to happen to me. That one way or another I would die soon. It was the only possibility, and I was more certain of it than I would have been if a doctor had sat me down, test results in hand, and told me I only had a few weeks left to live.

This certainty delayed my bonding with Grace. I would look at my gorgeous new baby, whom I loved more than I could bear to feel, believing with all my heart that I would soon be saying goodbye. Except that weeks went by and it didn't happen. As the weeks turned into months, I couldn't help but start to fall into that deep irresistible love with her. There was just no way to avoid it, she was enchanting. She had big blue cow eyes and a beautiful gummy smile. But loving her hurt, because with every ounce of love I felt I was aware of how much more I stood to lose when my inevitable demise finally came.

I had been put on a waiting list for post-natal counselling in April after the birth, but it was now August and I was *still* waiting. I felt so guilty for letting Michael see me like this. The pain he must have felt for me – it wasn't fair. Günther would come home as early as he could and take us all out to the beach for fish and chips, and Grace would sit happily in her pram while Michael played in the sand. I would stare out at the sky in its vastness, and for a fleeting moment I'd feel peace; then I would cry because the beautiful sky was one more thing I was going to be missing soon.

I started going to my doctor every week with a new issue. It occurred to me that I probably complained more than a patient who *knew* they had a terminal illness. The thing was I couldn't make my peace with whatever I had because I didn't know what *it* was. I felt a pain in my side so I thought I had kidney cancer. Then I felt a headache = brain cancer. Then I got diarrhoea = bowel cancer. Heart palpitation = heart arrhythmia. Muscle spasms = neurological problems. I Googled everything, and everything equalled *death*. But I couldn't stop investigating because what if I stopped trying to save my life when I still could have made a difference? Then I'd break my promise to Michael because I hadn't tried hard enough to live.

One day I was sitting on the bus, coming back from the doctor's, I heard a ringing in my ears.

It's a tumour.

Stop it! You thought the last three things that were wrong were something serious, and the doctors say I'm fine.

But what if it is something and you ignore it?

Just stop. Look at the people around you. Everyone looks normal and fine. You are normal and fine too.

Just then I realized I was staring at the woman across the aisle and that she was now looking back. Feeling a bit awkward, I smiled sheepishly and looked away. I could feel the muscles in my face twitching again. My whole body seemed to be malfunctioning.

It could be neurological. It could be a brain tumour.

"Stop it!" I screamed at myself. I hadn't realized until it was too late that the words had come out of my mouth. Everyone on the bus was looking at me.

They think you're crazy.

It doesn't matter, they're strangers.

You're losing your mind ...

What finally started to help me was making a list of my symptoms and putting everything *together* and cross-referencing them with each other. This led to only *one* possibility that caused everything my body was experiencing: stress. Stress caused muscle tension, especially in the back and neck. That caused headaches. Stress caused irritable bowel syndrome. Which in turn could cause a loss of magnesium. Which caused muscle twitching. Stress caused heart palpitations. Heart palpitations caused ringing in the ears.

After reading as much as I needed to read to settle my anxieties and no more, I printed out my results. I wanted to have something concrete that I could reread whenever I needed to feel better, without having to go back on the internet and do more dangerous research. After that I turned off the computer and grounded myself from it.

I sat quietly and thought about where my panic was coming from. I thought about all the love I had lost in my life, how I was afraid to trust anyone, and that if the person I loved was *undeniably* trustworthy, then it was the situation itself that I had to believe was going to end in tragedy. I just couldn't fathom being happy. Thinking logically about it I knew that most relationships didn't last, but by that same logic most people do at some point marry, most people do find that one relationship that is supposed to last. Even if half of those marriages end in divorce that still means the other half doesn't. Statistically speaking, at some point, I could have love and happiness. But my problem wasn't statistics.

Even if I could get my head around the idea that happiness was possible I still, then, needed to accept that I deserved it. And I wasn't sure I did anymore. Maybe at one point all of my challenges had meant I was due some happiness, but I hadn't waited for that to happen naturally. When I had had too much I became a thief. When I made a mess of my life in one country I left for another. I married a man, who for better or worse, had loved me, and I left him, the same way I had been left so many times. I had hurt people. That wasn't what I really wanted for my suffering, but that was what I had taken.

The only way to accept the love I had before me was to look at it differently. To believe that there was no earning love, there was only surrendering to it and appreciating it. To recognise love isn't only for the worthy, it's for everyone. Our entitlement to be loved is innate. Which meant everyone who had hurt me was entitled to be loved, and I was entitled to be loved, and everyone whom I had hurt was entitled to be loved.

So I could accept love, but I wanted something else with it. I wanted peace. Maybe the thing that meant I was allowed to have my happiness wasn't all the pain I had felt in life, like some penance that I needed to do first, but my finding a way to forgive it all, because, if I gave my forgiveness, I could be forgiven too. If I could let go of the past, and grant others the thing I most wished to have, grace, then I could give that to myself too. Pain wasn't the payment for happiness. Forgiveness was. I had been hurt and I had hurt back and now the only thing standing between myself and my happily-ever-after was whether I could forgive myself and the world.

My big act of heroism and rescue wasn't in fight, but in forgiving and letting go. And so I did. At three in the morning in our quiet living room, out loud, I forgave the past. I cried in release as I felt the weight lifting off my shoulders. And finally, for the first time in weeks, I felt tired.

I went upstairs to where Günther was sleeping. I could see the past few months on him, the line between his brows still furrowed even as he slept. My dear partner had been doing everything in his power to take care of all of us and to rescue me from my disrepair at the same time, but that had never been within his power. It wasn't in his, or anyone's, power to make me the person I wanted to be. In the end, the only one who could save me, was me. I lay down next to him, our arms touching, I slid my fingers between his and went to sleep.

Chapter 25

UNTI, AT LAST, SHE WENT HOME

Driving down the autobahn on our way back to the Chunnel, I stared out the window at endless rows of bare birch trees sitting in a snowy earth. When I was twenty I flew to Holland to look at Van Gogh's sunflowers. During that holiday I took a day trip to Antwerp, and as it turned out Günther was in Antwerp for a lecture on the same day. Of course we didn't know each other back then. What really gets me, though, is that exactly one year later Günther took his only trip to America, so far. Most people when they go to America go to New York or Las Vegas or Orlando, but not Günther. Günther went to San Antonio. He was there exactly when I was there at my first university, and still, we didn't know each other.

As the birch trees sped by in a hypnotic rhythm I could imagine us in these slightly random cities – not the main tourist attractions of America or Europe – walking right past each other. Now here we were, those two once-strangers, sitting side by side with their children nestled in the back between piles of coats and soft toys. "Will you marry me?" I asked almost thoughtlessly, but with complete clarity about what I wanted.

He said nothing, the stared to slow until he pulled over. He looked at me, elated. "Yes!" Then he wrapped his arms around me and buried my face in kisses. At the end of the following summer Günther and I were married on a sunny day at Alnwick Gardens in the North East of England. We had *limoncello* cupcakes my mother and I had made. There were sunflowers and BBQ and balloons and rock and roll.

The week after Günther put his house up for sale we woke up to images across our TV of people queuing to get into their banks and get their money out. The market had crashed. In the two years that followed we had a total of three viewers for the house. An older couple who seemed to like the garden but not the fitted furniture. A young professional just starting out who liked the fitted furniture but not the garden. And a couple who seemed to like everything but never called back.

Finally after months of silence a single mum came by. And made an offer. We accepted and suddenly our big focus was on finding a home for us to move into. We found a slightly older (slightly larger) mid-terrace house with a front and back garden. There were four bedrooms and a huge loft. It was a great house. We put in an offer which, after brief negotiations, was accepted. This would be my first ever house. I had lived with people who owned their own houses, like my parents and my first husband, but I had never lived anywhere where I was allowed to paint the walls or remove the carpets or hang a swing from the support beams in the living room.

Knowing I was about to get my first home did something to me; it was like I was finally allowed to grow up and take charge. And so I did. Packing and moving to-do lists materialized like ever-expanding fractals all over the place; I bought six different colours of packing tape (which was meant to help organize the boxes according to room); I called a moving company and sorted everything out.

We were a week away from our move date when things started going wrong. The woman who had agreed to buy Günther's house was still going through her divorce and there was an issue over whether or not she was going to get the money off of her future ex-husband. Evidently they had come to an understanding, but nothing was legally binding until the divorce was over, and I knew that wasn't a quick process.

I was getting daily calls from the estate agent relaying threats from the people whose house we had agreed to buy, saying that they were going to sell to someone else who wasn't taking so long. Every afternoon was a new drama. For me it felt like that same old tortuous experience of someone else having a decision to make about my life and me waiting to find out what would happen next. Again I was in a state of desperation and anxiety.

At the start of November it seemed that things had been sorted with the buyer, so we set up another move date, finished packing, and I re-booked the moving company. Then, three days before *that* move date, everything was called off again, as this woman's mortgage *still* hadn't come through. Finally we told the people whose house we were supposed to buy that we would understand if they sold to someone else. Our agreement to purchase dissolved and we watched as they put the house back on the market. I cried and tried to let go of my plans to live in the house I thought would be mine.

Everything we owned was boxed up, and we didn't even know if we should unpack. Anyone would have found this stressful, but I was almost inconsolable. Another two weeks later our buyer's mortgage *finally* came through and miraculously the house we wanted was still available and we got another move date. With four days to go I booked another moving company, or at least I thought I had.

At 9:30 a.m. on the moving day, they still hadn't shown up. I called and spoke to the same woman I had before. She told me I hadn't said I wanted to "book" them. Evidently that was the key word I needed to have said. Instead I had gotten the quote and had simply said, "Okay, thanks," and she had said, "No problem," and we had hung up. And now they were all booked up for the day. I went into a momentary trance, my mouth hanging open, as I processed what I was hearing. I *hate* the phone.

Günther's family was in Germany and mine were in America and neither of us had made many friends since moving to England. The only thing we had going for us was time, and not much of that. Michael was at school and then after-school club. Grace was at nursery. We would have eight hours to figure out how – with no van or help – to move a houseful of furniture and boxes. The clock was officially ticking. So it wasn't helpful that this was the point at which I started hyperventilating.

Normally a meltdown would last hours. If not the whole day. If not whole days. But I didn't have the time for that. The plan for the day was to move house. And ... I'm a little obsessive about completion. We woke up planning to move house. We were going to move house. That was all. I took command of my emotions. I stopped my heaving breaths. I stood up, the way I would have done when I was six and someone had knocked over my dominoes, and I started trying to reconstruct my design.

I called every moving company in the phone book , one after the other. No one was available at such short notice. Then I called every company that hired out vans – I mean, obviously we were two capable adults and we could just do this ourselves. But there were no vans available either. Finally some guy I talked to said he knew another group of guys with a van and they would do what they could. “They're cowboys,” the guy on the phone warned. It's a term that, in the UK, means unprofessional and unreliable, and I suppose I should have been offended, being from Texas, but honestly I just didn't care. I called them immediately.

My lists and colour-coded packing tape might as well never have existed; things got thrown in to the van and then thrown back out. Our new foyer doubled as a mud slide for this process. Did I mention that it was raining? It was raining. Both carpets in both houses got destroyed. The van was small, as was my guestimation of how many boxes we had. (It was about double what I'd thought.) How either one of us had managed to accumulate so much stuff in our short time in England, I cannot explain.

The cowboys went back and forth between our two houses, moving the biggest things first, until in the late afternoon when they had to leave us to get *their* kids, which reminded us that we were now on after-school-club time with our own. We had two hours of child-free moving left. We thanked them dearly, and even paid more than we had agreed out of gratitude for their hard work. After that, Günther called one of his post-doctorate students to see if he could help. The call went like this:

"Paul, I'm going to ask you something and if you can't do it just say so, but we're in big trouble. Can you stop whatever you're doing, get in a cab and come straight here?" A few hours later we had to collect our kids. I plugged in the TV so that they could be entertained as I readied the house for the next shipment the two men would be making. They kept going back and forth, shoving as much into, and on top of, our little yellow Fiat as they possibly could until, after one o'clock in the morning, the last of our stuff was finally in our new home.

Günther drove Paul home and came back; I was waiting in the living room and the kids were asleep in their new rooms. Günther and I looked at each other with something like elation and triumph. This was the moment when, if the movers had actually shown up, we would have hugged each other and twirled around our new living room. This was the house that would make the four of us a family; that would make England my home; there was some amount of knowing that this was a proper beginning for us. Then, because the movers had *not* shown up, we collapsed exhausted on the sofa. Zombie-like and shoulder to shoulder, we stared at Spongebob Squarepants and ate cold pizza from the box.

Weeks before Grace turned two, I had the pleasure of calling my family to tell them we had gotten moved into our new house. It was then that Mrs. R.S. finally told me something that she had been waiting to tell me for a while. She was sick. I had to think back to all those years ago, at the start of Latin class, when she told everyone she couldn't yell. She had pulmonary fibrosis. I had known about this, but I hadn't realised how serious it was; it hadn't occurred to me to wonder, because she paid it so little attention. I knew right away, though, that her telling me now meant she no longer had a choice.

Günther and I immediately planned our trip to America. As we got to the terminal with our two children, I looked at him. "I don't know if I can do this," I mouthed. My two fears were colliding: I was getting on a plane and I was losing someone I loved. "It will be all right," he said, taking my hand. I did not want to get on that plane. I could feel coldness running down the backs of my shoulders and an aching in my stomach. I was terrified of flying. And this time it was worse. Tears ran down my face.

I had always had shame over being a person whose anxieties were bigger than her love for others. I thought of all the times I clang to Adrian, the time I wanted the church group to leave the firework display. Shame wasn't bigger than fear. When I was afraid it completely hijacked my brain. No sense of moral obligation could dictate my choice when I was afraid. My brain was revolting. The rest of my body agreed with my brain.

So I ignored everything and told my feet to walk.

Günther lifted a blue-lipped Grace out of my mother's pool. My daughter was already exhibiting many of the same idiosyncratic behaviours I had had as a child. Her intense focus on whatever she wanted. Her independence. Her will. Traits that all children have, but with us it was always on another level, unfortunately because these traits are common amongst children, outsiders will assume the child is simply spoiled, that the parents are lazy or the child is just "bad".

She can be difficult to tolerate, like my son, like me. I get it. When she screams she shrieks. It's blood curdling. When she looses her temper she lashes out, she hits, she kicks, she throws things. I can't go up to anyone and tell them they need to look beyond all that. Why should they? But as her mother I can see those meltdowns that come and go. I can see *how* they come and go. The triggers that upset her that no one else notices. The rigidity and circular thinking that really hurts her head. I can see how much pain she is in when she's behaving badly and making everyone else miserable.

She doesn't like having her brain work like this either. I've seen how she goes from rigid screaming to crawling into my arms looking for a way to leave the pain behind. I can not tell anyone to tolerate someone who acts like she does. But I know that people who don't tolerate such behaviour also don't know what she's going though. They don't have to know. It is hard to be a self assured parent, while fully aware of the ignorance of others. I thought about the mother's I used to watch at the import store I once worked at. I knew how I wanted to be, but it was Günther who truly taught me the art of loving someone without apology.

Günther handed me a tightly towel wrapped Grace. She sat on my lap, resting her cheek on my chest as I rubbed her head with my towel. She smelled like a summer from my childhood. Like sun-block, cut grass and Kool-Aid. I watched as a layer of pale blonde down covering her back dried in the wind, and goose-bumps appeared on her shoulders. Soon her breathing took on the rhythm of a child sleeping.

They say that ignorance is bliss. This is not the truth. Ignorance is the weed that grows when wisdom isn't cultivated. The innate knowledge that we are perfect and worthy as is, *is* bliss. And it is wisdom. And we are born with this beautiful blissful wisdom about ourselves. And often this is lost as we grow older. Sometimes it is taken from us by people desperately trying to relocate their own lost wisdom. Other times those people put on a false wisdom we call confidence. And often this is seen as beautiful. But to find true beauty one needs only to look at children.

Wisdom cannot be replaced by taking someone else's. But in recognising my daughter's, her simple understanding that she was entitled to be safe, held, loved and protected and that she was *so* entitled to this that she would just fall asleep as all her needs were being met, I was able to remember my own perfect beauty. And suddenly, like that, I found what I had lost. As I stared at Grace, sleeping, unaware of the world outside my arms, I knew it was my solemn duty to protect this amazing girl.

Günther watched the children while I went to lunches with Mrs. R.S.. She looked smaller than I remembered, and was carting around an oxygen tank covered with a cosy her daughter had knitted. I made visits to her house and told her I loved her, that she had saved my life, that she had taught me how to love, while I gently hugged her. But no matter what I said and did, I always walked away feeling incomplete. Now that I had travelled all this way, I was suddenly aware that I didn't have the nerve to say what I had come to say: I couldn't say goodbye. I felt like a complete coward while she held my hand and said it was okay. She had given me gifts I could never repay.

Before we left Texas I drove Günther around showing him where I had gone to school, the café where I drank my first coffee, the pizza parlour were I used to hang out with Zoe and Adrian, playing cards. Then I drove us to the little town where I had lived when I suffered the worst of my bullying and felt the ugliest. As we drove to the outskirts of the town the road turned to dirt and dust. I was curious to see the little shack with no air-conditioning that I had been made to move out of so abruptly, and which I had been sure I would never see again. I didn't know what to expect from seeing it now – maybe just to show it to Günther so he could know it was real, that such a place had existed.

To my utter disbelief, when we got to where the house had been, it was gone. I couldn't accept what I seeing. I got out of the car and stared, as if something might materialize out of the overgrowth. As if somehow it was hiding between the tall blades of grass. I kept looking, but there was nothing. No structures of any kind. No barn. No chicken coop. No house. It had all disappeared.

I had once lived there, in that place that didn't like me. I used to hide in the chicken coop, staring out between the slats of wood towards the old dirt road, the place I now stood, like a caterpillar planning my transformation, planning the ways I would conform and wash away my ugliness, imagining who I might one day be. And here I was. My adult self, standing out in the open, staring at where the place had once been, where now there was nothing but wilderness. And a field of sunflowers. A breeze pushed against us and we stood there for a moment looking.

"I'm ready to go home."

Days before Mrs. R.S. died, I started to feel her presence. At first when this happened I wondered if she had just passed, but I kept getting updates from her husband about how she was doing. There seems to be a transcendent sort of connectedness I share with certain people, as if we are connected beyond our individual selves, and so I wondered if that connectedness simply became clearer and more pronou-
nced as my friend neared the end of her physical life. I worried for her. For how she was feeling. I wanted to give back to her all that she had given to me, and I couldn't think how to do that. The one thing she needed, more time, was not within my gift.

My heart ached with sadness and frustration, and my grief came in unexpected waves. One morning I was brushing Grace's hair when the pain came, this time hitting me in the stomach so that I couldn't breathe. All I had to do was look at Günther and he nodded, excusing me; he took over with the kids while I went into our room to be by myself. A few minutes later a dressed and brushed Michael came up to find his jumper. After locating it in his room, he wandered into mine and got on the bed behind me and stroked my hair.

"Mummy. I'm sorry your friend is dying."

I grabbed his hand and gave it a squeeze. "I know you are, baby. You haven't got to worry about me. We're allowed to be sad when someone dies. I won't be this sad forever," I said, still having some guilt over my low mood after Grace.

"I feel for you, Mummy."

Günther called up. "Michael! Have you got your jumper yet?"

"I'm sorry. I have to go." He kissed me on the temple and hopped up.

"Michael." I stopped him before he left the room. "I love you." I could hear her voice coming through me as I said the words. "*And I'm so proud of you.*" Then he ran down the stairs and left for school.

Perhaps it was a bit cheesy, but the fact that she had always said that to me had had an effect, and parents should remember to say this to their children. Frequently. It should be one of the unconditional things that every child knows. That their parents love them and are proud of them. And I was going to remember that because it was the most important thing she had taught me.

Mrs. R.S. spent her final days in her music room. It was a lovely room with a piano and a towering, twenty-year-old *ficus* tree in the window. She listened to Mozart records and live music being played by her children until, at last, she went home.

A Diagnosis

"I'm not strange, weird, off, nor crazy;
my reality is just different from yours."

LEWIS CARROLL, *Alice's Adventures in Wonderland & Through the Looking-Glass*

Chapter 26
"I THINK IT MIGHT BE ASPERGER'S"

One of my early parental insecurities was Michael's sleep issues. The issue being that he didn't do much of it. At first he would take brief naps during the day, but at three months old he stopped doing that. He wouldn't nap or sleep alone. He was hyper-aware of me leaving him. He would scream if I put him down. My mother and father told me I had been exactly the same at his age and I just had to let him cry himself to sleep, that eventually he would learn to "self-soothe". I tried this for a few weeks. Every night I would feed him, put him down and then let him cry (scream) for as long as I could take it.

My heart would break every night. Being in the next room listening was not an act of ignoring: I could hear and feel every moment of his torture. Without knowing anything about attachment theory or autism or what to me is an obvious link between the two – and amid a culture of people who insisted that I needed to leave my son to adapt and *self-soothe* – I decided I didn't have it in me to let him scream. With great guilt, then, I went against the common opinion of my culture and thus began our routine of me holding him until he fell asleep.

I would turn everything off at 7 p.m., close the blinds and try to pretend we were *both* going to sleep. I would lie there holding him, thinking, *If this works I can get up and do some dishes, homework, read for pleasure, oh wouldn't that be nice, oooh I could have a hot bath, or maybe ...* But Michael was there next to me. Calm and quiet and wide awake. I wonder what he was thinking about. Maybe he was thinking, *When she turns the lights back on I can organize all my stuffed animals again.*

A neighbour warned me that Michael would get used to falling asleep in my arms and would never sleep on his own. But he wasn't sleeping on his own anyway. At what point was I allowed to give up on my child's future nocturnal independence so that I could get my own sleep in the present? I listened to a TV psychologist tell a single mother, who was letting her child sleep in her bed at night, that she was trying to make up for the lack of an adult relationship. That she was messing with her child's development so that she could have this void filled in her own life.

Cuddling with Michael, my human hot water bottle, was such a pleasure that I had to wonder if this was true of me. Would I have more stamina for letting him scream at night if I had a man in my bed? In the same show this doctor told a couple that if they continued to let their young son sleep in their bed, then one day, when he was a young man, he'd walk in, toss the car keys on the dresser and crawl into bed with them. It was actually this flippant comment that gave me reassurance. I was so certain that, regardless of how Michael was raised, *no* teenager would do such a thing. I just couldn't fathom that such a reality could come to pass, and at that moment I became certain that letting Michael sleep with me was safe. At the very least he'd want his own space once he hit puberty. (*Incidentally, Michael was comfortable sleeping in his own room from around the age of seven.*)

I cannot imagine a job that brings more

insecurity, guilt and worry than motherhood. I give talks to parents of children on the autistic spectrum. These are often people who regularly have the experience of attending meetings with "the professionals" (a situation that can leave a regular parent, without official qualifications in child development, feeling inadequate). I take great joy in telling these parents that when they are in those meetings they need to remember that *they* are the experts. If their child is three they have done a BA in learning about that child. If their child is four they have their master's. If their child is six, congratulations! ... they have done their doctorate. Everything a parent says to a "professional" is valuable information because *the parents* are the real experts on their child.

Psychological theory will continue to evolve and change for as long as humans are around, but it's always going to be just that. Theory. Doctors do studies, often gathering statistical data, and then they write out conclusions about what it all means. It is usually these conclusions (opinion stated as fact) which seep into the mainstream. To be repeated first by clinicians to parents and educators, and then parents and educators talking among themselves.

They feel enlightened by new information, and share theories as if they were gold. Then years, often decades, later, new information comes to light and younger clinicians will take a *now*-we-know-better attitude. All *anyone* can do is look at the data and make their best guess.

Opinions coming from someone with a PhD are still opinions. Sometimes they are presented with confidence because the person concerned wants to make complicated idea more easily understood. Other times it is because they do not believe they could be wrong, or are scared to admit that they could be. But *anyone* with a working brain is free to think for themselves, and shame on those who uses a suit, tie and degree to make someone else feel inadequate about their own experience and observations.

Another issue I didn't know how to handle was that Michael screamed when I left him at nursery. Most parents who have had to leave their children at nursery have experienced this. Because it was so common, the nursery workers would smile casually and say that it would get better as soon as I left. So I would kiss him and say goodbye over the screaming and walk out as quickly as I could so that he could have his promised peace. I would then never stop thinking about him throughout class.

At lunchtime I would be on the phone to the nursery, and I would hear the hesitation in their voice as they didn't want to tell me that no, actually, he hadn't stopped screaming. This was separation anxiety (or an extremely insecure attachment style emerging), which many young children on the autistic spectrum exhibit. And the best way to combat it is to answer the screaming as much as possible, let the infant have a sense of control over their world. Which, for an infant, means a sense of control over the parents, because parents *are* an infant's world.

A competing message I was hearing was that this was a necessary stage of development he needed to go through. But development will happen no matter what. Infants and children will either develop into people who trust the world around them to meet their needs, or they will develop into people who don't feel entitled to cry out when they are distressed. The only question is, which message does the parent send?

I was living off school loans had a very unhappy baby who had decided he did not like public child care, and I had no idea what to do about it. I had no experience in these things – but there was no way that screaming eight hours a day was normal, and even if it was, then that still didn't make it acceptable.

Miya stayed with us for a while looking after Michael at our home. When Michael was two and we were in England, I tried taking him to a playgroup twice a week. At this playgroup all the other mums left their children and went to get a coffee or do some shopping; I tried to leave too, but this was just a repeat of how nursery had been in Iowa. So instead I stayed outside and listened to him scream.

The staff told me to stay out of sight, thinking this would make it easier for him. I did. But it didn't. My instinct was to stop trying to push this on him, but the following autumn he would be expected to go to public nursery for three hours a day. I wasn't sure how Michael would ever learn to cope with being left if we didn't actually get through this. So twice a week for six weeks, thirty-six hours of screaming, this is what we did. Him crying in one room. Me crying in the other.

In September I took him to nursery, and

predictably things did not go well. He would cry hysterically from the time I left him until the time I returned for him three hours later. I worried that this was because I hadn't held out longer during his first stint at nursery, or that I hadn't held out at night-time, or that I hadn't let them put him in that room with the other babies when he was first born. I worried that all the people who claimed that holding him too much would damage him were right, and that, all this time, I had selfishly been indulging myself to his detriment.

Again the nursery teacher assured me this would soon subside and I kept leaving him there, but the next week they told me that it was *not* getting better and they hadn't had a child cry this much before. At that point they asked me to stay with them for the duration of the nursery day. I was relieved that they asked me to do this, and happy to oblige. I would sit, often in a quiet corner off to the side, while Michael stayed with his class. He could see me, but I tried to make myself look as unengaging as possible so he'd want to explore the room and play with the other children. This worked. He stopped screaming.

The following spring, Michael was finally

able to be left at nursery. I would drop him off and return to work in the garden for two hours before heading back to collect him. At the end of the year, there was a parent–teacher conference. Michael sat colouring at a table while the nursery nurse and I stood talking a few feet away. She mentioned that she was concerned about Michael's speech development. “Okay,” I said, taking her words in. “He's my first child so I'm not sure what's normal.” She was nodding and smiling as if she understood this, but wasn't offering anything more. *I hate it when they do that.* “Can you tell me why you're worried?”

“Because he doesn't talk?” she said slowly and with an implied question mark, as if she was questioning why she had to explain this to me.

“I don't understand.”

She said nothing. She just looked at me with her fixed smile, waiting for me to get it. And I stood there waiting for her to start making sense.

“I mean obviously he talks.”

“Um, no. Not that *I've* ever heard.”

Okay, let's clear this up right now. “Michael.” I said raising my voice, but watching *her* face. "What did you do at school today?"

"I played with the blue car," he responded.

Her smile crystallized before it disappeared altogether. And that's when I got it, the thing she had been expecting me to get. She had *never* heard my child speak. Not once. And she had never said anything about this until now. What kind of teacher doesn't bring this up sooner? I was ready to lose my temper right then and there. But then I understood: the kind of teacher who thinks I should know because I spent most of the year in class *with* them. I hadn't noticed that Michael wasn't talking in school because I myself (being in a room with thirty young kids) was on *serious* sensory overload.

I had assumed that he had always been screaming at nursery and playgroup for the same reason that he screamed at night. Then, right in front of my eyes, one issue became two. I remember my feelings of hysteria in the crowds. The scream I almost let out the museum. It hadn't even occurred to me that Michael was over-stimulated by crowds. Which explained why I could leave him with Miya but not at a nursery or playgroup.

I had always felt like I was under pressure to do the same things everyone else could do, and now, without stopping to even question it, I was putting that same expectations on my son. He was quiet when I started staying in nursery. My presence must have soothed him, but only so much. All I had noticed was him screaming if I tried to leave. His total silence, while I was there with him, had gone unnoticed.

The next year was full of changes. In the autumn there was a new problem with Michael's behaviour. At least once a day he would hit someone or destroy someone's artwork. At home Michael was docile and sweet to the point of being almost withdrawn. I had never even seen him have a tantrum, which I thought all kids were supposed to do. I almost couldn't believe what I was hearing from the school staff – but of course I did believe it. But I also assumed Michael had his reasons for his behaviour. I held onto this belief even though my son struggled to explain his reasons to me.

Michael could communicate simple things like, “I played with the blue car,” or “Smoking will kill you.” But if I asked, “Why did you hit Oliver at school today?” he seemed lost. There was something difficult about expressing internal emotions, and the reasons behind his behaviours were too abstract to verbalize. I remembered being a child, being told to explain myself to the adults. To just *be* better. I wanted to support my son even when he couldn't defend or explain himself. I wanted to believe there was a deeper reason, rather than just malice, for his behaviour, and that this reason needed teasing out rather than punishment. Looking back, I feel certain that this was him responding poorly to sensory overload; but this was all still pre-Asperger's awareness for us.

Michael's teachers would tell me about an incident and I would go initiate a chat with the relevant parent. Despite my own history of being bullied and my fear of how others looked at me I made the conscious decision that I would, apologise for my son's behaviour, but not offer up any shame for my son. Children have a way of knowing when people are ashamed of them, and that stays with them far longer than their behaviours, which are typically just passing phases at such a young age. So I always approached parents only with the aim of letting them know I was aware of what was going on and trying to deal with it. Surprisingly some people seemed genuinely kind and understanding and we actually got a few play dates out of it. After lots of talking with Michael, but without any real explanation, the hitting and destroying seemed to go away.

The headmistress had sat me down and expressed concern over Michael's ability to take things in at school. “He always seems to be in a daze.”

“Last week he was telling me your mother just got remarried.” I remarked. Perhaps this was not exactly the thing she had meant for him to take in.

Her mouth dropped open. “How could he know that?” I remembered hearing teachers who thought they were speaking quietly in the hallway when I was little.

“So it's true?”

“Yes. I can't believe he was listening.”

“I think he's listening more than you know. He just doesn't always respond or perform on command.”

Some of the school staff seemed to get the idea that there *was* something going on in his head. A few weeks later they discovered an unknown car in the school parking lot. Everyone started trying to figure out whose car it was. One of the receptionists had a light bulb moment and went to Michael. She told him the make, model, and license plate number of the car and in return he told her that it belonged to the football coach who came in on Tuesdays.

When Christmas came, Michael was an angel in the school play. It was amazing to see him up there; he was darling. After the play ended, the headmistress announced that the children could be collected in the courtyard as usual. I ran into to the cloakroom to tell Michael how great he had been. I thought this would be okay since I wasn't trying to collect him.

"Parents can pick their children up in the courtyard," his teacher said as soon as I appeared in the room.

"Yeah. I heard. Thanks." Then I spotted Michael and went over to him. "You were brilliant!" I said.

"The children will be sent out just as soon as they're changed," the teacher said curtly as she appeared at our side.

"Okay, thanks. I was so proud of you," I said, turning back to Michael.

"There's tea and biscuits in the main hall." The teacher had interrupted *again*, in a voice that hinted she meant something else.

"Oh, sorry," I said. "Would you like me to

go get you a biscuit?" I asked Michael. "Would you like something?" I offered to the teacher.

She let out a sigh and walked off. *Odd.* I gave Michael a cuddle and went back to Günther. Over a cup of tea I replayed the conversation verbatim and asked why the teacher had kept interrupting me when I was trying to talk to Michael.

"She wanted you to leave while the kids were getting changed."

Oh. "Why didn't she just say *that*?" The embarrassment of not getting this stung. Then came the anger that she had left me to be a fool rather than saying what she meant. "It's dishonest when people don't use their words."

"It's not dishonest. You know I don't like it when you say that."

Well, it's not fair at least. And it feels dishonest. Why should I have to be the idiot because people don't say what they mean?

I could smell the tinned vegetables left over from school dinner. Just then a woman with a pram scooted past, making me flinch as she brushed my bump carrying the unborn Grace. Suddenly I was very aware of how loud the hall was and how many people were between us and the exit. My throat ached and I could feel tears behind my eyes.

"I want to leave," I whispered.

"Come on," Günther said, taking our teacups and setting them down on a random table. I could never do that sort of thing. Even on the verge of a meltdown I would feel compelled to walk the length of a store just to put an item back exactly where I'd gotten it from. But I was glad of him doing it. Then he put his arm around my large waist and escorted me out.

The next spring, at the town baths I ran into a mum from school. Michael and I were just getting into the water as she approached.

"Hi, I'm Vicky," she said when she got to us. "I work with Michael in class sometimes. Michael's a *lovely* boy."

"Thank you."

"You know, I don't want to offend you ..." Of course at that moment my mind starts going crazy with anxiety about what's coming next. "... but my older son has been diagnosed with Asperger's and Michael just reminds me so much of him. I was wondering if anyone's suggested that he might have it."

Asperger's? Is that what they're calling us these days? "Michael and I are both very sensitive. I think it just runs in the family."

"Okay ... Well, I thought I would just mention it. I know I would want someone to tell me."

"Of course. It's always better to tell people what you think. People are so scared of offending each other that no one is communicating these days."

By "communicating", I meant *my* desired form. Literal and straightforward. At least this woman had done that, even if she was wrong. Occasionally I was wrong about things too. To me Asperger's was just one more label. I had had labels all my life and had long since decided they were all rubbish.

Chapter 27

OBVIOUSLY IT'S TODAY BECAUSE HERE I AM

A couple of years later, on a wet summer's day, Günther and I took the kids to a bookshop. Günther and Grace were looking at picture books, Michael was in his section near Horrid Henry and I just sat down to relax for a moment on a bench. Then I noticed right in front of where I sat was a single row on Autism and Asperger's. I remembered that woman from the swimming pool, a couple of years ago now. Sitting, staring at this row of books just on this one topic, and with nothing else to do for a few minutes, I became curious. I went through every book they had, picking nine I would like to read, then I narrowed it down to three I would actually buy. I read the first book, *The ASD*

Answer Book, by William Stillman, in one sitting. *Every single word in that book described us.*

Decades ago I had started copying neurotypicals to fit in. I had spent so much time copying others, looking to others for a guide of what I was supposed to feel and think and do that I had stopped acknowledging my own experiences and desires. I stopped being able to articulate these things for myself and for others. I dismissed myself as crazy or bitchy when what I needed didn't fit in with what others expected of me. On a level too deep to acknowledge I had always felt at fault for these differences. I wished I could have known so I could have explained or defended myself and my rights or asked for help. Mostly, I wished I could have known so I could have accepted myself.

I immediately started looking back over my life remembering this time and that and replaying each moment. I remembered the psychologist who thought I was on drugs. I remembered the locker in my hallway in middle school. The dominoes when I was seven. I remembered jaws dropping open every time I did or said the wrong thing. All the friendships I'd lost. All the bridges I'd burned. It all came flooding back in one big rush, but I had another thing to worry about now. I had to make sure my son's childhood was nothing like my own. I went to our GP and asked for a referral to get Michael assessed for Asperger's.

Michael had become more independent in his play lately. He could be trusted not to run off or into anyone's house and I could sit in the living room with Grace while he played outside. It was a welcome reprieve for me. One day though he dropped a little matchbox car in the gutter outside our house. He came in noticeably upset. As if he could have cried, but he didn't.

All he said, quite cryptically, was, "It was my fault."

"What was your fault?" A dark segment from *Of Mice and Men* flashed in my head. I don't know what it is about that book.

He just took my hand and led me outside to the gutter and I looked down. There, three meters down, was the unmistakable metallic red of his favourite car. I quickly went through all my Matlock like ideas of how I might get the car back. Things involving bubble gum and a stick. Or maybe a magnet. But nothing seemed feasible.

"Oh baby I'm so sorry. I don't think we

can get it back." I just looked at him feeling helpless. I understood why he said it was his fault. It was his way of trying to take responsibility, to sooth the frustration that came when something unfair happened. A skill I had learned at a much older age and one that sometimes meant I didn't allow myself to feel the grief I should. I rubbed his head. "It's okay to cry, you know." But he didn't.

It was mid-October when we finally got in to see someone about the assessment. The doctor doing the assessment was a beautiful *young* woman named Dr. Evans. I kept staring at her, wondering when she had graduated from University and asking when we would get to see the *real* doctor. She was nice, but finally held up her ID badge and said, "I am a *real* doctor. See?" Michael loved ID badges so that started him on wanting to play with hers. I was quiet about my concerns of her age after that.

Later that afternoon Michael and I went to a small shop to pick up a few bits and pieces. I gave Michael a pound and told him he could choose something. He came back with a long stick with a net on the end for 99p. It was the sort of thing you chase butterflies with or take to a rock pool. I assumed the net was not what interested him.

"If all you want is a long stick I'm sure we can find one in the woods. Why don't you spend your pound on a packet of Buttons or some new play dough?"

"You said *I* could pick it out."

"You're right. Okay. We'll get the stick."

When we got home he wanted to play with it right away. I told him to be very careful and not to hit anyone or anything with it. A moment later Michael came in, half the stick brown with muck and in the net was his little red car. This is the genius of Asperger's single-minded focus. We may have our struggles but if there's something we want we usually get it.

Months later Michael was offered a diagnosis of Autistic Spectrum Disorder. It was my prerogative to either take it or leave it. I took it of course. Then I learned of another issue, which was that, because of our house move the year before, we were now no longer in their catchment area. I found this particularly distressing as there had been so much upheaval recently. I couldn't begin to explain how much stress the idea of being moved to another practice gave me. I gave Dr. Evans my whole life story in one quick monological rush, including that I felt I too was on the spectrum and I wanted my son not to have to struggle the way I had. “When will my son ever start getting help if we have to move to another practice?”

When I finally came up for air she said “If you think you are on the spectrum then you should tell your GP you want to get assessed.”

“I'm a grown-up. I have a house and a partner with a job. I just assumed...”

“You might be right. They may not consider it a *need*. Hmmm. Okay. Leave this with me. I'll talk to Erin about the catchment area issue.”

“Erin?”

“Dr. Erin Harris is the doctor that heads the department and would be the one treating your son if a diagnosis is made.”

I don't know why but I immediately got this image of a red-headed woman in a pant suit and black high heels. I was convinced Erin would not care about us. It could be said that I am prone to snap judgements about people. I tried to prepare myself for the disappointment of being made to move and wait for this process to start all over.

It was both a surprise and relief when Dr.

Evans contacted me a week later to let me know that Dr. Harris had said we could stay. I felt utterly grateful to this person who I did not know, and who did not know me, for sparing me what, to her, must have seemed like a routine and minor stress. Suddenly my image of her changed. I decided she was an older woman with kind eyes and greying hair. I was sure I would adore her as soon as I met her.

I had a follow up appointment with Dr. Evans scheduled for early December. I was notorious for showing up late so I was feeling proud for managing to get there on time this particular day. I went to the man at the front desk to say I was there. "Dr. Evans isn't here today." He said apologetically. I'd never even seen a man at this clinic before. He, looked slightly too administrative to be a receptionist. I decided he was confused about Dr. Evans not being in.

"Well, we have an appointment for four." I said indignantly.

The man looked genuinely concerned and started flicking through the appointment log. "How do you spell your last name?"

I let out a loud sigh and started spelling.

"Oh, here it is," he said, looking up.

"Yes?" I said expectantly.

"It's tomorrow."

What? I'm sure it was today. Obviously it's today because here I am. "Well I made time for it *today*. I scheduled it in for today. I didn't write it down for tomorrow. I *won't* come back tomorrow." I threatened. This isn't a huge threat when you live in a country with socialised medicine.

"I'm sorry. We have it down for tomorrow," his voice was soothing, his eyes were warm and soft. He reminded me of Kaa, the snake from the Jungle Book.

"I won't come back." I said indignantly. I knew full well there was nothing else I could really say and that we needed them more than they needed us, and that surely this man knew that as well, that's why he could be kind. He had all the power. Hanging on tightly to my indignation, feeling ridiculous, I left. I was consoled by the idea that I had never seen this man before so I would likely never have to see him again.

Except, when I showed up the next day, he was still there, at the front desk. *Doesn't he ever leave?* Dr. Evans came out to get me. It was just a follow-up appointment to let me know that now that Michael could start seeing Dr.

Harris, to discuss medication. I was looking forward to meeting the doctor and thanking her for letting us stay.

"When do we get to meet Dr. Harris?" I asked as we walked towards the corridor.

"I think you met him yesterday."

I glanced towards the desk, where I could see Dr. Aaron Harris – the "stand in receptionist" watching us. *Oh.*

I didn't know at the time what a huge support Dr. Harris would provide to our family. He was very genuine and kind, helping anyone who happened his way. The longer I knew him the more he grew to remind me of Mrs. R.S.. There isn't a higher complement I can give a person.

Chapter 28

REFERRAL. DENIAL. APPEAL. REPEAT.

Part of what I went through after I lost Ms. R.S. was an examination of why I loved her, what she had brought to my life, and how I could pay that forward into the world. My life had been challenging and hard, but it had also been full of blessings and breaks and second chances. I had been gifted enough chances and good people to help me figure out how to start getting things right, and I needed to do something good with that.

I had thought I could go into teaching; I had loved my previous supply work, but equally I knew it wasn't my real bliss. I didn't actually like the teaching part of teaching. I liked the emotional part. I liked calming a person who was on the edge of a meltdown. I liked empowering the parents when they doubted themselves. Whether with children or adults, I liked working one-to-one the best.

I started thinking I might like to be a therapist rather than a teacher. It would mean I could work for myself, I could control my environment. However, this path would definitely require more training. Thinking about my past school experiences, I knew I would want to get the right support in place before I went forward. And to give myself the best possible chance of success I would need an official diagnosis of Asperger's.

I started making a list of all my Asperger's traits, and once I had completed my list I made an appointment with my GP. On my visit, the GP went through everything with me.

"You don't strike me as having Asperger's." She glanced at my list. "These issues could be caused by a combination of an anxiety disorder, depression and possible OCD.

"All three?"

"Yes. It doesn't have to be Asperger's."

"You know, Asperger's isn't diagnosed by ruling out everything else. It's not like it's the least likely possibility. I think it's more unlikely that I would have three disorders rather than just one."

"You speak very well."

"Thanks. And you."

"You have a house and are a mother to two children."

"My husband and my uterous both work."

"I mean I don't see the point for you getting a diagnosis."

"Because I have a house?"

"Why do you feel you need a diagnosis?"

"I'd like to be able to work on a career for myself rather than just be married to someone who has one. I want to go back to school. I struggled a lot the first time around. It took me eight years to get my bachelor's degree. I want to go back to school and be able to ask for the support I need this time."

"I'm sorry," she said, glancing again at my list. "Look ..." Sigh. "I'll refer you to the adult diagnostic team. They can say for sure. The waiting list is long though, and my guess is you won't warrant a diagnosis."

The truth is that I had withheld my real reasons for wanting an assessment done. Going back to school had been my motivation for going to the GP when I did – it had been the thing I could explain to others so they would see a valid reason for needing this done – but it wasn't my real reason. The truth was that I wanted something tangible I could hold in my hand as permission to stop hiding who I was. Something I could use to draw a line between the past and the present and finally start to feel brave with myself again.

Over the years I had grown out of some difficulties and learned to hide others, but my biggest act of hiding had come from simply hiding the real me. Because where there was once a girl who was always saying the wrong things, there was now a woman who was scared to speak. As I was finally starting to understand my past, what I desperately wanted was to have my original quirks back instead of this fear I had taken in their place. I wanted a diagnosis because I wanted proof that I had made a bad trade all those years ago.

Two years after my request for an assessment had been filed, the paperwork was declared officially lost. People had seen it. My name sounded familiar. But no one knew what had happened to the request. (On a side note, I know three other women in the North East of England who asked their GPs for a referral to get assessed for Asperger's, and *all three of them* then had their paper work “lost” too.)

I had to go back to the GP, repeat the first conversation and get my request re-filed. The second time I was queried about whether or not I enjoyed sex with my husband. I think a sheepish smile appeared on my face. Evidently, like having a house, good sex was another reason I probably did not have Asperger's.

After my "lost" paperwork was re-filed, it was then denied. They weren't saying I didn't have Asperger's, they were simply refusing to assess me at all, saying I had no "clinical need" (which is a term that doesn't have a standard definition within the NHS. They can use it to deny a service but they can't, when asked, explain what "clinical need" is).

I then went back to my GP a third time to very specifically tell her what I wanted the appeal letter to say. I had to be specific because she didn't want to write it at all. She informed me that some people had cancer. As in, some people had *real* problems. Today I'm part of a team that gives ASD training to general practitioners, giving advice about what common needs might be and what not to say to a person with autism.

After the appeal was filed I started calling the regional office a few times a week to check the status of my appeal and to make sure they hadn't "lost" it again. Three months later funding was approved and a date was finally set for an assessment in a further three months' time. I wondered then, as I do now, what happens to people who do not harass their GPs and the regional offices.

Between all the GP appointments and the waiting, I started taking a course for parents of children with Autistic Spectrum Disorder. The class mainly sought to give a view of what it was like to live with ASD so that we could better relate to our children; it didn't take long for me to tell everyone that I was sure I had Asperger's myself, how I saw the world, and how I would like to have been helped as a young child. I clarified, for my own conscience, that I might never get a diagnosis; but many of the parents seemed to feel that my life experiences mirrored those of their children. At the end of the course I was asked if I would give a small, more formal, talk about my educational experience. I ended up speaking for about forty-five minutes. I monologued my way through, mostly in a random stream of consciousness.

Coming back to myself as I concluded my talk, I felt exposed and embarrassed. I tried to tie it all together, worried that everything I had said had been wrong or inappropriate or didn't make sense. I worried that I had talked too long and that everyone was bored. But when I looked around I could see that no one was looking bored or uncomfortable or trying to be polite: one woman was crying, and when I stopped talking everyone clapped. Afterwards there was a small queue of people wanting to talk to me and ask more personal or specific questions.

The next day I got an email from the course leader to say that other instructors had expressed interest in having me visit their class and give the same talk – which would mean that I would have to think back and figure out what I had actually said. The applause and the compliments always made me anxious, but I loved being told that something I said was meaningful to a person. I loved validating and bearing witness to their experiences. *This* was what I wanted of a career.

Chapter 29

KEEP CALM AND CARRY ON

"So I thought for today I might want to talk about Ugg boots..."

"Ugg boots?"

"Yea but then I thought do I really want to spend my therapy session talking about Ugg boots so maybe we should talk about personality adaptations or my husband or the fact that I think I might have a terminal illness again."

"I'm curious about the Ugg boots?"

"Well ... Okay; for starters it's 2014!"

"I own a pair, but they have gotten to be a bit chav recently." She says laughing.

"Yea! But were they ever cool? I mean really? Secondly, it's spring and thirdly ..." I say, getting my index finger ready for a lecture. "Even in the winter these are not practical shoes. They don't look like they have any grip. They don't look like they were made to get wet. Who spends money on these shoes?"

"Well, you know, they are comfortable."

Suddenly it dawns on me that my words might be hurtful for someone who owns and likes Ugg boots. "Are they? They look like they would be." I sit quietly for a moment looking around the room.

"Do you know what else drives me crazy? All this 'Keep Calm and Carry On' crap."

Nervous, I put on my typical confident demeanour and sat down across from Bob, the mental health nurse who looked like the hot guy from university only in his fifties and with a pot belly. Next to him was a pale and *very* young psychologist. I guessed his being there meant that they could say a psychologist had been present. And finally, at the far end of the table, was a female nurse. I guessed she was present so that they could say a woman had been in the room.

It was mostly Bob who did the talking. Everyone seemed to regard him as being the authority in the room. He asked me about my interest. I told him I liked literature; what I meant was that I liked writing. Then he started quoting someone, a poet from the Romantic Movement, if I had to guess. I didn't know who he was quoting or why. I guessed his expectation was that I would identify the references or start spewing off facts about whoever it was he was quoting. But if this was the test for Asperger's, I was going to fail. I felt stupid and stayed quiet. Bob looked at me for a minute, then wrote something down. He moved on to ask about my family and my few relationships growing up. I told him of my sparse friendships.

Although admittedly my life had shifted in my mid–twenties, I was still bad at things. Bad with over-stimulation, bad with staying organised or multi-tasking, really bad with anxiety. But the stories from my mid-twenties and onward seemed to sound more “normal”. I had noted almost immediately during my time at the university in Iowa there seemed to be some transformation in my ability to connect with others. I started to feel more a part of the world than ever before. I had always credited the meditation, which probably did have some significant influence, but I realise now as I do more research in neurological science, that I was likely more influenced by my pregnancy.

During that time in my life my body was

producing large doses of hormones that led to development in the regions of my brain that control compassion, concern, and judgement. These changes were designed to make me a better carer and to prepare me to be the forward-thinking multi-tasker motherhood often requires women to be. During my first pregnancy this was a time of great neurological development (one of many) that created an ability to feel more connected to others.

After our *hour* for the assessment, a far cry from the thirteen months my son received – keep in mind that it's more difficult to diagnose adults than children - I left the room so that the three could talk amongst themselves. When I came back in, the female nurse wouldn't look at me. I immediately knew their conclusion. But I hoped I was wrong. Then the young doctor started to waffle endlessly about what Asperger's meant. I recognised his excessive talking as a tactic to soften the final response. I knew before they said it that I was presenting as too neurotypical for a diagnosis. I remembered the Tony Attwood quote:

> "Eventually, some pieces of the puzzle fit together in small groups of disconnected

> 'islands', and after three or four decades, a pattern is recognized and the completion of the puzzle accelerates. Some people with Asperger's syndrome are eventually able to socialize reasonably well, with typical people unaware of the mental energy, support, understanding and education that is required to achieve such success." (2010)

I was too good. In my three decades of life I had finally learned and developed enough to be missed by the clinicians sitting across from me. I wanted to snap back at them that all their time at school could not explain what it meant to live on the autistic spectrum as well as I could. I stayed quiet.

Finally Bob took over and said, "You are too empathic. I work with people with Asperger's and they would rather not have anything to do with the world around them." He said that I seemed to consider my family's needs too much for this diagnosis. I disagreed. I couldn't imagine how someone with an abundance of experience working with people with Asperger's could conclude that we didn't want to be in the world. But also I started to realise that I had been leaving out the *ugly* stories.

I had not told him that I got Michael to school only after I had written and rewritten my daily to-do list until it was perfect and *complete* every morning. My lists often evolved around my caring for the family: cleaning the house, dinner, fun activities, the schedule for our lives. I might use up twenty pieces of paper trying to get the list just right on any given day. And the Local Education Authority called me repeatedly about Michael's lateness. I told the stories about my plans. Showing that I was a good mother. I left out exactly what that meant in real life. I would never administer a physical punishment. I didn't believe in spanking. But I had shortcomings that I was ashamed of.

I hadn't told him that the week after my daughter, Grace, was born Günther and I had taken to doing puzzles in the middle of the night rather than trying to sleep. One night he and I were working on a 3D puzzle of a globe. Grace woke and I went up to her. When I came back down Günther had finished the puzzle without me. Which meant there was no way for me to be involved in its completion. My explosive temper took over and I picked the puzzle up and threw it across the room so that hours of our work were destroyed.

There was the time when Grace was three and she fell down the stairs while I was in the next room sorting out my papers. My lists. My writing. The papers were partially correlated and scattered around me. I heard Grace scream. I felt my spine stiffen. My circumference of awareness restricted to a very a fine point and all I could see were the papers in front of me. They were safe. I couldn't leave them. I couldn't run to my daughter.

Go to your daughter, you stupid bitch!

I stayed frozen on my spot as my husband ran past to see to her, demanding, “What's wrong with you!” on the way. “My lists aren’t sorted,” I whisperer feebly. The truth was I couldn't move. I felt pathetic and broken and terribly ashamed. Anyone else would have run to their child. What was wrong with me? What if Günther hadn't been there? He rescued Grace while I sobbed over my papers, selfishly indulging my own pain rather than seeing to hers.

I never told *anyone* these stories. And

here he was telling me I didn't have Asperger's because a person with Asperger's wouldn't take such good care of her family. I did love them very much, but I struggled with certain aspects of motherhood and I hid it. I had gone into that office acting the way I always acted in public. Wearing my mask. Hiding the bits I was ashamed of. Without thinking. Hiding what I understood was not normal or acceptable. Putting on the persona that, after decades of building, I now just automatically wore whenever anyone else was around.

I thought my list *explaining* my quirks in general terms, with only cute light examples, would be enough. I wasn't even sure I could choose to be my authentic self in front of someone else anymore. He couldn't see the me that I am when I've been overloaded and have no energy left for hiding. Or the me that I am when I'm completely alone and relaxed. The me that only a few very select people get to know.

I quickly tried explaining this to him. I told him the really hard-to-tell stories. I told him that when I said "friends" I might just be talking about the random stranger who spoke to me on the bus last week, or referring to a character in a book, rather than an actual person. That I had been doing that since I was a teenager. That I just liked being able to refer to “my friends” the way other people do.

I told him that my dating relationships had rarely lasted longer than six weeks. Then I desperately shared every shameful and humiliating detail of my life. My meltdowns. My obsessions. Giving him the truth that he must have needed in order to make a diagnosis.

The nurse and young doctor shifted uncomfortably as I did this. Did they not want to hear these things? How does anyone get diagnosed if these details make the clinicians uncomfortable? But I guessed that recognising their discomfort would be another contra-indicator. I was a thirty-four-year-old woman. Of course I've learned to recognise such things. I spent years making a study out of such things. And these experts would need me to pretend to still be oblivious. Pretend that I haven't led the life I have, so that they could see me fitting into the diagnosis the way they thought I should.

Bob couldn't be swayed. He wasn't listening to or considering my words; he had the resolve of a parent not wanting to reward a child for protesting. He said he'd have to type up an official report but his answer was going to be no. I was devastated. After I got home I continued to protest, sending emails and citing articles about people with Asperger's being capable of empathy. I sent Bob an article about women on the spectrum and how they hide well in social situations. One article I sent him, which I found online, read:

> "The current international diagnostic criteria do not give examples of the types of difficulties experienced by girls and women ... girls and women learn to act in social settings. Unenlightened diagnosticians perceive someone who appears able and who has reciprocal conversation and who uses appropriate affect and gestures as not fulfilling the criteria set out in the international classification systems. Therefore a diagnosis is missed." (Gould and Ashton)

Within the same article there was another quote that supported my point.

> "The fact that girls with undiagnosed autism are painstakingly copying some behaviour is not picked up and therefore any social and communication problems

they may be having are also overlooked. This sort of mimicking and repressing their autistic behaviour is **exhausting**, perhaps resulting in the high statistics of women with mental health problems."
(Dale Yaull-Smith, 2008)

The nurse responded by telling me not to believe everything I read on the internet. I felt offended that the man tasked with diagnosing me, insisting I didn't have autism, obviously didn't recognize the names of the people I was quoting. Dr Judith Gould is the director of the National Autistic Society Lorna Wing Centre for Autism. Dr Jacqui Ashton Smith was Head of Operations at the National Autistic Society. And Dale Yaull-Smith was already a well known writer in the field.

Nurse Bob's final report simply said that from his meeting with me he could see no evidence of autism in me. That up until now I had managed to take care of my family, I had made friends in my life, I had good hygiene and, despite my claimed interest in literature, I failed to show any interest when he quoted Byron.

Logically I knew that he was judging my

life with inadequate information. But illogically, I started to wonder ... *If everyone thinks they're right, then how can I truly be objective about my own opinion?* This felt like a dangerous question to ask myself, especially because I suspected that the nurse had never asked himself that same thing. But I had to consider it. Was I just crazy? Was I so desperate for attention that I would steal my son's condition? Did I have Munchausen's Syndrome? I felt attention-seeking. I felt devastated. Not by the possibility that I was wrong, but by the possibility that I was *this* pathetic.

But in my devastation I was doing something important, I was putting aside my certainty. And, as hard as it was, I was giving honest consideration to an opposing opinion. I sat, disillusioned, on my back stoop, considering that I may have made a mistake. But even after completely relinquishing my hold on the belief that I had Asperger's, it was still there. Sitting next to me. Waiting for me to look at it again.

Bob blamed my mother and my turbulent childhood for my social challenges. To him, having both a history of abuse and Asperger's was too big a coincidence. But Bob did not address my difficulties with fine-motor skills, my uneven academic achievements, my literal understanding of language, my rigid obsessiveness, or my sensory sensitivities.

I was a well-groomed, articulate woman, married to a successful man, with whom I shared a house and two children. Some people seemed almost offended that I could dare to claim I fell on the autistic spectrum when I had such things. But none of it had come easy to me, and I continued to struggle within my roles and, obnoxiously, I felt, I still wanted more *personal* achievement. Something that wasn't about being a mother or a wife. Something of my own, and I wanted the right kind of support to help myself get that.

A week later Günther told me about a talk being given at the university, by a PhD student doing a study on Asperger's in young children. Two things happened at that talk. The first is that I met many women just like myself who were on the spectrum, and they talked about how we learn to conform and how we get missed by the professionals. About how we've *always* been under-studied. That Leo Kranner, the man who introduced the "Autism" as we know it today, studied no females. And that Hans Asperger, whom Asperger's Syndrome is named after, studied very few. Then, when the student speaker casually announced that he didn't like to work with girls because they were too hard to diagnose, he got eaten alive by those lovely women.

The second thing that happened was that I recognised the name of the event's host. She was a very well respected local psychologist, Dr. Sylvia Harwell, who studied and did assessments on adults. After the talk I ran up to Dr. Harwell and introduced myself. She knew who I was because I had been copying her in on all my correspondence with Nurse Bob. This must have seemed a little odd to her, since we had never before met. She was good about not recoiling, though, when I approached in person.

I then proceeded, as fast as I could, to tell her my entire life story. (Because I have a need to complete things and a fear of being interrupted, I have learned to talk fast.) When I stopped for breath she said, “Okay. Let’s go ahead with the reassessment.” Sometimes it's that crazy ranting that gets the job done.

I had been keeping my mother updated with everything for the last couple of years. We both agreed that this was part of our shared genetic make-up. That she had it, that her father had had it, that his mother had had it, and that it had been travelling down our lineage for a while now. We bonded over this new understanding of ourselves.

I felt, for the first time, that I could honestly forgive the past. I could see that my own life had afforded me more opportunity for self-exploration and understanding than hers had; and that the time and culture I had grown up in, despite everything, had still offered more compassion and enlightenment than she had received. Knowing all that, it is hard to truly hold a grudge.

Once I had the second assessment all set up, I called my mother and asked if she would be willing to write a letter for me to describe my early childhood. That was when she dropped the bombshell. "Well, you know when you were six ... *someone said you had this*." Like I was with Michael, my mother had been offered the opportunity to take or leave the diagnosis, and she chose to leave it.

My mother rejected the diagnosis and I wasn't told about it. She honestly felt the doctor had been wrong. To be fair, back then (in the early 80s) it came under the heading of Pervasive Developmental Disorder, which sounds far less appealing than Asperger's syndrome. She wanted to spare me a label that she felt implied I was somehow intellectually challenged. Although I *was* intellectually challenged. I have always struggled with certain things. But I have also been intellectually gifted. In some ways, and on some topics, my mind moves incredibly fast. Some things I just get. I regret that I spent my life focusing on my challenges more than my gifts.

Rather than write the letter I asked for, my mother booked a plane ticket and came out to meet the doctor in person. At the first appointment, my mother and my husband went with Dr. Harwell into one room while I went into another to be interviewed by a second psychologist. My job was to be the real me this time. I found making a conscious effort to remove my persona very uncomfortable. I was thirty-four and I had been hiding – more often than not – since I was fourteen. To act like myself in public felt like acting. My mother was meant to contribute historical data, while Günther could fill in the gaps in terms of how I was on a day-to-day basis. Later that night he told me that my mother spent a large chunk of the meeting repenting for her parenting regrets.

I went in for multiple appointments over

the next few months. The doctor who interviewed me asked if I was hoping to get a free laptop after my diagnosis. There was a scheme where I lived that university students with autism could apply for laptops to be given to them. I wasn't interested in that. It bothered me that this was how some clinicians thought. It bothered me that she felt entitled to ask such an inappropriate question, that even a psychiatrist would not have a sense of obligation to treat a mental health patient with the same dignity they would treat anyone else with.

There was an additional psychologist brought in on one occasion. Despite the lack of respect from that one doctor I had no feeling that I was not getting an adequate assessment this time. I knew they were making a real effort to see me. So, as terrifying as it was, I had to make a real effort to let myself be seen. Then, after all the meetings, the doctors set aside a few weeks to compile their work and talk amongst themselves before letting me know.

The morning I finally went to get my assessment results was rushed. It was the first real autumn morning of that year. I could smell the summer's dust burning off the radiators as I made my way downstairs past a Wellington with a baguette sticking out of it, and a row of dog-food kernels perfectly spaced out in a straight line across the kitchen floor – both courtesy of Grace.

Clean laundry in my arms, I made my way back up to Grace's room. “Come on, it's time to get up,” I said, rubbing her shoulder. She turned her head away. “We're late,” I said, laying out the clothes. Still nothing. “If you don't get up and come with us you'll be all alone.” I remember an article I had read in the *Guardian* about the lies parents tell their children. Evidently, threatening to leave them if they don't willingly come along is the most common. I feel a little caught out for using this ploy, but it's usually highly effective and I really needed it to work at that moment.

I glanced at her and could see her eyes open to phoenix-like slits, as if providing entry for my words. A moment later, judging my threat as weak and unworthy, they closed again and Grace shifted her body away from me while burrowing deeper into her duvet. I bent over and pecked kisses all over the side of her face that was still exposed; her breath smelled like oatmeal from the night before, but was still the breath of a sleeping child. I steadied myself for the high-pitched screams that I knew would come once I yanked the duvet off.

Then, miraculously, as if my efforts were having a delayed-time-release effect, she started to stir. Fifteen minutes later I was dropping a dazed Grace at the front gates of school with a half-eaten banana in her hand and a patch of unbrushed hair sticking out from her head. Ten minutes after that I was clomping down the hospital corridor towards the doctor's office.

"I'm here. I'm here. I'm here," I said, racing in. Sometimes if a patient is late for their appointment, the appointment must be rescheduled. This had never happened with this particular doctor, but I was so desperate to have my results that I couldn't help but worry.

"Oh that's fine, Mrs. Uher, just have a seat. Can I get you a tea or anything? I won't be a minute."

Okay ... that means ... (take a breath) they are going to see me. This is real. This is the day I get to know one way or the other. Remember to breathe.

The fact that they had been so thorough was both reassuring and scary. Because of their great efforts I had decided to trust them, which meant I would have to accept whatever they told me. So I sat there *not* breathing as Dr. Harwell went over the results. She explained everything so slowly and in so much detail I wasn't sure what I was hearing. I thought, *Oh no, she's doing that over-elaborating thing – to soften the results.* But I wouldn't know for sure unless I listened, so I listened hard. My small circumference of awareness was only listening for the words, "Our conclusion is that you warrant a diagnosis of ASD." Or, "Our conclusion is that you do *not* warrant a diagnosis of ASD."

Every sentence she said came into my head; I then determined if it was one of those sentences, and if it wasn't I let it go. Doing this meant that I was only actually hearing every *third* sentence. I must have sat there for around twenty minutes not sure what she was saying. Finally, she took a pause and looked at me. *She's said the answer.* I could tell by her expression that she was expecting a reaction. *But what did she say?*

"You look confused. Is there something you need me to clarify?"

"Yes. I just want to know what the result is. Do I have a diagnosis or not?"

She smiled a little and then very gently

said, “See this sentence here?” She took her finger to the exact spot where it was written. So that I could both hear her words and read them for myself. “Katherine's traits meet the diagnostic criteria for an Autistic Spectrum Disorder.”

I took a deep breath and let it out.

“Can I get you anything. A cup of tea?”

“No thank you ... This is all I need,” I said, motioning to the paper.

“You've done very well for yourself.”

“I'm exhausted,” I whispered.

“I know,” she said softly.

I looked at her for a moment. I believed she did know. I thought: we are all struggling behind the scenes.

Knowing that I'm coping makes me feel a little like a fraud. A little guilty for asking for patience or tolerance. Not because I don't deserve those things, or because my Asperger's isn't a valid explanation for my quirks. I do deserve those things (as we all do), and it is a valid explanation. My guilt comes from knowing that there are many, many people in the world who go undiagnosed, who will live their life never being able to fully understand themselves, offer an explanation for themselves, or ask for the compassion and support they need.

Also, in my life, perhaps *because* of my intellect and because old wounds have healed, I have learned how to do some social tap-dancing. I have learned how to play the jester, both laughing at and apologising for myself in a way that others seem to find acceptable. And so compassion, finally, is mine. But there are others who are less high-functioning, or simply less socially inclined, who have not learned to tap-dance, and they are often not afforded the tolerance I find myself getting. And it's an injustice.

Who knows what other explanations there are for all the different behaviours we encounter in humanity? It won't always be Asperger's. It may not always have a name. All we can do is accept that we will always be, on some level, ignorant of what someone else is going through, and give them our compassion and tolerance without needing an explanation for their behaviours. Trust that they're doing their best. That their reasons, whatever they are, are real. And only offer help from a place of equality and acceptance.

At my first university, I twisted my ankle on a running track. I was given a splint to wear and told to keep my leg elevated whenever I could. One day I was in a computer lab with my leg propped up on a chair. It was obvious that my leg was resting on the chair, but because my foot was under the desk it was not obvious that I was wearing a splint. It must have looked like I was just making myself comfortable. A young woman approached and without saying anything abruptly grabbed the chair my foot was resting on and yanked it out from beneath me. My foot hit the floor and a sharp pain shot through my ankle. As soon as she saw the splint she apologised and said, "I didn't know." Of course she didn't know. But nor had she asked or made any effort to investigate. She had assumed that my foot being propped up was an act of selfishness rather than one of need.

Behaviours can look much the same, and also have a hidden reason. Nowadays, when I tell people I have Asperger's, I get most of the understanding I wish I had had all my life. I imagine that some of the people who judged me as I grew up would apologise and say they didn't know. I wonder, in thirty years from now, who *I* will owe an apology to. Who did I misjudge with inadequate information? The only thing we can really know is that we don't know.

Chapter 30

A NEW BEGINNING

Following my diagnosis I bought nurse Bob a copy of Aspergirls, by Rudy Simone, a brilliant book about women with Asperger's Syndrome. He later came to my house and offered an apology for not diagnosing me. He said that he and the team suspected that the difficulty in my case was with seeing the autism despite how I presented culturally, as I am an American living in England.

I understand the difficulties this can cause: One, the cultural differences are a type of social gap, which are where my quirks often manage to hide. Good for friendships. Bad when I want a diagnosis of Asperger's Syndrome. Two, while many women on the spectrum learn to conform to their culture, for Americans that means something else.

America is an outgoing country which puts great value on personal expression. As individuals many of us, “brand” ourselves as part of finding and asserting our own unique identity. If one is disorganized, quirky or awkward we learn to work with that, to be charmingly irrelevant, or self deprecating in a witty way, so that our quirks seem cute. Many of these learned behaviours actually seem to be the height of social skill, but learning to do this doesn't rid one of autism. The exhaustion is still there underneath the mask. And worse, I find I have developed an approachability that I can't maintain.

My persona says, *come talk to me, I'm nice.* (what I'm really trying to say is, *Don't hate me. I'm scared of being hated.*) But then I burn out, at some point I disappear on the people I've lured in. I run out of fuel and just stop going, leaving them to feel whatever they will about me: that I'm flaky or in a bad mood, when often I'm just out of energy for preforming. The answer to sorting this out is to stop preforming. To be comfortable just being me, let people see that person from the start. I can be selfish without realizing it, I can say inappropriate things, not ask questions when I should, not understand unspoken communication and I will occasionally just bugger off without much warning.

My diagnosis was a weight off my shoulders and I was ready for another sabbatical. But this time I understood what I was going into. That there was nothing to fix or complete. I was already complete in my own way. This time I was going to figure out how to live the rest of my life with more balance. To not live in survival mode any more, pushing myself beyond my own healthy limits.

All my life, everything I've achieved I've done while fighting hurdles I couldn't properly see. And I have come quite far and done quite well despite it all. But now I could see them, I could name them and I could deal with them. I was going inside myself to re-evaluate my priorities. When I returned, I would only put effort where I felt it was important. Only give the world as much of myself as I was comfortable with.

While I could prop myself up on adrenaline and cortisol and junk food temporarily, I could not keep going indefinitely like that. After creating my retreat, I notified the rest of the family that from now on, whatever else was going on, I would be going into my room at exactly eight o'clock, and everyone else would have to figure out how to survive without me. Whoever wanted a story had fair warning at seven. Going into my room and shutting out the world became a regular, and permanent, part of my evening regimen. It was a drastic change at first, but one that quickly started paying off.

First, mornings were better. Then my mood in general was better. After a few weeks of digging in my heels about having "me time", it was recognised throughout the house as a sacred and necessary thing. Once my door was shut in the evening I would lie or sit on my bed and relax in the serenity of my space. I finally understood that creating a space in which I could thoroughly relax wasn't a luxury. It wasn't something I would do *when* I could. I needed this every day for the rest of my life the way people need sleep and food and air. I needed sensory recovery time. Without it I might not sleep. I wouldn't eat well and I wouldn't be emotionally well.

I started experimenting with different music to see how it affected me. I fell particularly in love with Frederick Delius's *In a Summer Garden*. It was a sensory experience that left me tasting dry, dusty earth and smelling gardenia bushes. Certain music could do that sort of thing.

As a single person, I had done stints of self-work which involved intensive journaling and meditation. I had found during these times that I could live a calm and balanced life, but because I could not maintain the intensity of those regimes I would lose my footing when I re-entered the world. I wanted this time to be different. I wanted to be *in* the world.

People on the autistic spectrum can have an uneven release of dopamine. Sometimes not getting any, and other times getting too much. Some people we fall madly in love with and others we don't notice at all. Some topics we can't get enough of and others can't hold our attention. The lack of dopamine release can leave us feeling like we don't "get" the world around us. We don't understand the joy of making friends, or why everyone else can tolerate topics that totally bore us. Then the release of too much dopamine can result in triggering addiction-like behaviours, contributing to our famous obsessions. So we might eat only one preferred food. Watch the same movie over and over again. Talk about only one favourite topic. Make lists. Hand flap. Rock. Live in our own inner world thinking about only what we like.

The problem is that while our obsessions may be born of pleasure, our complete surrender to them often causes us other problems in life, which may lead to alienation and often sadness. I take a very low dose of a mood stabiliser and it helps me just enough to maintain balance amid the daily stresses of life and fluctuating hormones. I find that I am simply less of a slave to my compulsions, but can still experience full and satisfying pleasures of the things I have always loved. Only now I can walk away from these things in order to do other things that I also might need to do. And I find gratification in living a more balanced life.

As I came out of my fourth sabbatical, back into the world, I continued to pay close attention to my sensory intake. My adrenaline levels remained balanced, and if there was a fluctuation I was more aware of it, why it was happening, and I was often prepared for it. If I did extend myself socially, like helping someone move house or volunteering at the school fair, then I created a decompression plan for afterwards. I also consulted with Günther about what my planned activity would take out of me, and made sure he was okay with being on his own with the kids even after I was physically back at home. I have been grateful for my warm bed and my loving family. It has been a luxury to have a home like this. To go out into the world and meet people and have experiences and come back to a place where I have been safe and free to recover from life.

One evening I sat down with Gunther and Vincent to play Uno while Emma played with her blocks. I dealt out seven well used card to each of us and then flipped the top one from the deck face side up to start the game. It was a green 1.

"What an appropriate card to start the game with." I said.

"Why is this an appropriate card to start the game with?" Vincent asked.

"Well because it's a green which means go. And a 1 which is the first number."

Vincent liked watching us shuffle so the cards got shuffled a lot. What I find interesting is that despite all the shuffling we got the green 1 as our starting card three times in the first five games. The second time happened right away and I had to wonder what the odds were. Then the third time happened on the fourth game at that point I took it as a friendly nudge from an angle or friend in the room.

Weeks later I was organizing my photos from the past months. I found one from our game night with Emma standing in front of her blocks smiling and next to her face there is a small squiggle of light, like some blurry movement in the air. I remembered the three green ones from that night and had to wonder how friends or angles might be able to communicate with us and what other nudges I had gotten in my life.

There was a few years following my conviction for credit fraud that I started to notice hearts everywhere. At first it was around my house in Iowa. I was walking somewhere in town and then suddenly there would be a heart-shaped water mark on the pavement, I'd see a heart shaped pebble as I walked along the beach or a broken leaf in the shape of a heart on a walking path. Remembering as many hearts as I could I started to realize that they were always on a path as I was walking somewhere.

I started to think about symbolism. What messages were hidden in these little winks. Wondering if my heart symbols could have meant something other than romance. It never really sat right with me that it represented romantic love. It was too simplistic and commercial, angles had to be more sophisticated than that. I did a quick investigation on heart symbolism. What I learned was that the heart has historically symbolized spirituality and morality rather than romance.

I thought back to my teens and early twenties and the decisions I made when I was feeling so hurt and lost. I had many regrets about things that had happened to me and guilt about how I had dealt with those things. Looking back I could see that everything I'd gone through, whether it was suffering at the hands of someone else or struggling with frustration over my own behaviour has always lead me to developing love, empathy and enlightenment.

As a teenager my parent's turned away from me and because of that Mrs. RS came into my life. As a young adult having my heartbroken lead to a summer of great insight and growth. Then my assault and legal troubles sent me running to Iowa where I started meditating. It was after I had Vincent, even though I had still felt distant from God, that I started to see the hearts. Suddenly they made sense to me. They were my guidepost, not to romantic love, but towards something more lasting, more transcendent. I was on my own journey development.

Years later I found myself sitting with a friend and colleague, having a conversation about Carl Jung and symbolism, which had gotten started by a passage in the DSM 4, but never mind... With no awareness of my experiences relating to this story, he mentioned seeing the number 1 quite often, and stated that this was a common phenomenon experienced by many people. It reminded me of the game night with my family.

When I went home I started looking into the meaning behind the number 1 and the colour green. I hadn't been far off with what I had said to Michael. Green meant the start of something. What I didn't realize was that three ones in close proximity where also meant to represent a new beginning. It's amazing to think that's the message I was getting right after finally getting my diagnosis and right before starting school, but that wasn't to be the only new beginning.

In the two years following my diagnosis, Michael moved on from primary school to secondary; Grace received her diagnosis of ASD; and I enrolled on an undergraduate degree course in psychotherapeutic counselling. I knew this would mean going back into the world and meeting new people with the aim of starting a new career. I was ready for that, but there was still so much I didn't know. I couldn't know.

I couldn't know then that the personal therapy I was required to take as part of my course was going to be the most helpful I'd ever had. That my seventeen new classmates would each become dear to me in some way and would reopen parts of me I had shut off out of fear. That I would make a new best friend outside of school. I couldn't imagine how my speaking and writing would bring to me more and more people who had lived through similar experiences. And that with each person who listened and shared back, I would begin to feel that much more a part of the world. There was so much I hadn't anticipated. I simply sat there in my living room, my bookshelf filled with my first batch of psychology books and my growing collection of family photos. Feeling that, one more time, I was ready to try again.

If you enjoyed this book, please leave a brief review on Amazon. Thanks.

A Note from the Author About the Book...

Dear Reader,

First my disclaimer: I am trying to cover 36 years of life in a coherent way so I compress some events. (Two main areas where I have done this are: first, in the passages on my compulsory education, during which I changed schools many times. Because I am not disclosing school names and wish to avoid confusion, it made sense not to cover every change. Secondly, in my mid-twenties I experienced some legal difficulties, and here I have focused on my own behaviour and emotional process, as these are the most relevant areas for this book.) As well, I have been writing from personal perspective and memory, which are both subjective. This would no doubt be a different story if it were told from another person's point of view. It is my story alone, and therefore reflects my own truth.

The other thing I would like to say is, as I've written in this book, I struggle with literacy. I was diagnosed with dyslexia in my childhood. I'm not the first person with dyslexia to love writing or have a desire to share their story with the world. Hans Christian Anderson was also thought to be dyslexic.

Because of my attachment to this story and my desire to make it as good as it can be I've put it through 5 rounds of professional editing, (Which was as many as I could afford) the last two were copy editors meant to focus on spelling and grammar errors. Despite this I can't help but spot mistakes every time I read. This represents the extent of my struggle and not the effort of my editors who have all been lovely. I could keep all hints of my imperfections hidden away, but that is not what this story is about. I do hope, that if you've seen some of these mistakes for yourself they did not detract from your reading.

Kindest Regards,
Kate

A *note from the author's mother...*

My daughter, Katherine has overcome many challenges and continues to meet life's trials with grace and growing confidence. Her vivacious and captivating speaking ability amazes me. I am proud of her accomplishments and try to be supportive in any way she will let me. In this mother-daughter relationship, we often disagree. Both of us are impulsive and straight to the point talkers. It is not easy to think before blurting out our thoughts, but we try.

My logical side tries to put my feelings in perspective; it's an on-going struggle. In the back of my mind I thought I shouldn't have children; I wouldn't be a good enough parent. I wondered about my capacity for love. Later my life and marriage was in a good place for a child; I took the plunge and we easily conceived Kate. In preparation for motherhood I read lots of books. Logic told me this knowledge was only a resource and I wasn't wrong. Nothing teaches as well as real life experience. During my pregnancy my health and emotional state was very good, which lulled me into thinking maybe everything would be OK. Kate's delivery went well. She was a beautiful baby. My husband was over joyed and immediately took to being a father. Even though Kate was healthy, my emotional state was not. Little things kept me second guessing myself. Convinced I should have felt happy and blessed caused more guilt. The books I read didn't discuss postpartum depression. At this point I should have gotten help, but my husband convinced me not to expose our private lives in that way. Knowing now that medication would have helped in this respect, I strongly lament not getting help for myself sooner. Like many people I hesitated too long to seek help as my postpartum depression became chronic depression. Despite my growing melancholy I did everything needed to care for Kate. Finally I sought help when Kate was six years old, I wish people were more open to getting assistance when they need it. It is not a total solution, but the people you care about will know you love them enough to help yourself and the family. Raising children, especially the smart ones can drive parents and care givers to distraction.

As a newborn Kate didn't smile which is not unusual. Infants don't usually smile right away, but again there was self-doubt. Kate only slept a total of 8 hours spread over 24 hours which is unusual. Most newborns sleep, wake and eat with little time in between. Putting her sleepy head down almost always resulted in screaming fits. I had never been able to fall asleep easily. Out type of sleep problems are indicative of other neurological conditions, but at the time hyperactivity was my concern for Kate. The paediatrician told me to let her cry; that's easier said, then done. When a baby cries nonstop for 30 minutes, it wears on your nerves, which brought more self-doubt, more guilt. By the time Kate was 2, she had evolved from crying to talking and singing to herself, long into the night. I would hear her as late as 11:30 at night. This behaviour continued through her teenage years, at which time I'd find her on the phone or looking at books. Having attended university, before Kate was born, I hurried to get my degree. In my mind I felt no one should expect their child to go to college if they did not lead by example. Being a worrier and guilt-prone mother, leaving Kate with a baby sitter was difficult. In all aspects of life a certain amount of anxiety is good, but too much stress makes things worse. Still, I continued to do everything I knew to do. I took Kate on walks, read books and tried to enrich her life with lots of exposure to child centred activities. I made 2 lifelong friends during this time, other late blooming mother's like myself. We made the rounds together, gymnastics, zoo trips, sports, museum school. Our children grew up to become very creative people, which serves them well in their careers.

During my own childhood, the classroom was a good place to be as opposed to the drama going on at home. Many teachers come from these situations. From the age of 10 I wanted to be a teacher. I hoped I could help others with disabilities and unhappy home lives. School can be a welcome refuge for many children. This goal was always foremost in my mind. Not as much was known about Asperger's Syndrome, when I earned my master's in education, years ago. Strengths, weakness and different disabilities were in my realm of understanding, but autism to me involved communication difficulties and lack of a connection to the environment. I would soon observe Asperger behaviors during my last summer practicum in special education. A young boy used a wrist communication device, printing words that related to what he was thinking. I wondered how he ever learned to read and write without being in a conventional instructional setting. In my first teaching position a teenage boy with Autistic symptoms drew fantastically precise illustrations of building designs and illustrating complete pages of the TV guide. He shouted out statements at odd times that didn't relate to classroom activities. He also had his first seizure while in speech class next door. Seizures are not uncommon to people on Autism spectrum. He could read and write, although his reading sounded robotic. Again I wondered, who taught him. Today the number of children and adults being identified with AS is growing due to a greater understanding of the criteria.

As a child my parents used spanking as a punishment; it was a natural reaction for me to use this as discipline, although I felt guilt, that I was over doing it and that it made little difference to Kate's behaviour. I felt shame and regret when I lost control, yelled or struck Kate. Kate doesn't approve of this method of child rearing. We have discussed these times. She has forgiven me, but there's no forgetting. I likened my losing control to falling down stairs and not being able to stop. My "mommy dearest" nature clashed with the calm loving mother I wanted to be. No child should have to experience this dichotomy. We are all a result of our genes, environment and experiences. The traits we inherit and develop, can aid and impede us in reaching our aspirations. Within the last 10 years my daughter and grandchildren have been identified as having Asperger traits that fit in the Autism spectrum. Although I haven't been formally diagnosed, I feel certain that I am a member of this group.

Despite challenges and setbacks, we continue to meet our goals and improve ourselves. Going through life with square wheels makes a bumpy and sometimes painful ride. Most of us experience bumps and keep going, and self-knowledge may help cushion the ride. Besides therapy and medication which made my life easier, faith, family and friends make it rewarding.

Books on Autism

10 THINGS EVERY CHILD WITH AUTISM WISHES YOU KNEW, Ellen Notbohm

THE ASD ANSWER BOOK, William Stillman

AUTISM AND THE GOD CONNECTION, William Stillman

THE AUTISTIC SPECTRUM, Lorna Wing

THE COMPLETE GUIDE TO ASPERGER'S SYNDROME, Tony Attwood

NOBODY NOWHERE, Donna Williams

Articles and Studies

A Barain Link to Autism
http://news.harvard.edu/gazette/story/2015/12/a-brain-link-to-autism/

Adults with Asperger's Syndrome at Greater Risk of Suicidal Thoughts
www.cam.ac.uk/research/news/adults-with-asperger-syndrome-at-greater-risk-of-suicidal-thought

Gender and Autism
www.autism.org.uk/about/what-is/gender.aspx

Maltreatment of Children with Disabilities
http://pediatrics.aappublications.org/content/119/5/1018

Prevalence of Premenstral Syndrome in Autism
www.ncbi.nlm.nih.gov/pubmed/18380936

Other Literature

ALICE IN WONDERLAND, Lewis, Carroll

OF MICE AND MEN, John Steinbeck (You have a lot to answer for.)

NO EXIT, Jean-Paul Sartre

WHERE THE WILD THINGS ARE, Maurice Sendak

ACKNOWLEDGEMENTS

To my Mother & Father:
For doing the best you could from one moment to the next. The thing about being a parent is that it's more than just a full time job, it's life. There really isn't a pause button. We start parenting, often before we've healed from our own childhoods. We do the bast we can in the moment. I love you both. I know you both have loved me and you gave me what you had to give. And most of all you both have given me your blessing to remember my past and tell my story. Thank you.

My Husband:
In many ways I don't know if I could have written this book without you. You were next to me as I took a hard honest look at my life and myself. I was able to be both critical and compassionate and find the truth. I knew I could do that because someone I loved, who loved me back, already saw me for who I was.

My Children:
It is my solemn privilege to be your mother. In you I've seen the unfiltered parts of myself, and because you were both so obviously loveable, I could finally understand I had been loveable too. As you have grown, I have grown. We have been there for each

other, mirrored each other and we three are individuating. I can see that you are both your own people and feel honoured to have provided the secure base from which you push off. I'm excited to see where you both go.

Friends:

- Veronica, for ignoring my walls and being a second mother to my children. I needed you.
- Alicia, for telling me to pluck my eyebrows and dragging me along to the party.
- Michiko, for putting up with me no matter how lost I got us.
- Anthony, for not giving up on me and for paying the rent. A lot.
- Michelle, for being there.

To Chris Holifield. The time and effort you spent encouraging me was extremely nourishing. Every email from you brought a boost that kept me believing in myself.

For Mrs. R.S.

74542400R00263

Made in the USA
Columbia, SC
01 August 2017